HESWALL

THROUGH TIME

Jenny McRonald & Roger Lane

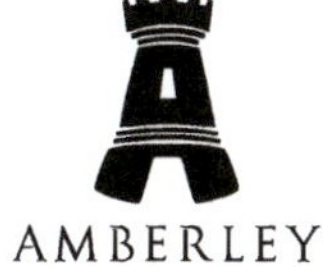

AMBERLEY

First published 2015

Amberley Publishing
The Hill, Stroud, Gloucestershire, GL5 4EP
www.amberley-books.com

ISBN 978 1 4456 3633 7 (print)
ISBN 978 1 4456 3661 0 (ebook)

British Library Cataloguing in Publication Data.
A catalogue record for this book is available from the
British Library.

Typesetting by Amberley Publishing.
Printed in Great Britain.

Introduction

The Parish of Heswall contains two townships, Gayton and Heswall cum Oldfield. The historic centres of these townships were located at the bottom of the prominent red sandstone ridge that runs down the north-west side of Wirral and provides the characteristic red sandstone features of West Kirby, Thurstaston and Caldy, in addition to those of Heswall and Gayton. To the west of this ridge at Heswall and Gayton there is a fertile plain leading to the shores of the Dee Estuary, the rich soil having been deposited by glaciers during the last Ice Age. The sandstone ridge achieves its highest point in Heswall at Poll Hill and, being also the highest point on Wirral, it was used as a site for warning beacons. It was later the natural choice for the site of the water tower and a covered reservoir. The ridge itself was a bleak, wild and rocky heath covered in heather and gorse, as can be seen preserved today on the Dales. In contrast, at the foot of the ridge on the meadow land, there was an abundance of fresh water from the many springs, a ready supply of sandstone building material, fish from the sea and plenty of fertile land to farm. It was only much later in the latter part of the nineteenth century that the ridge was used for residential purposes through the development of access roads and landscaping.

Popular legend attributes the derivation of the name Heswall to 'Hazel Spring', derived from the Old English words *Hesel* and *Wella*. This explanation is supported by the presence in Wall Rake of the Hessle Well, now filled in but still commemorated with a plaque. However, there have been dozens of spellings of the place name in historic documents and maps over the centuries and there can be no certainty regarding its true origin. The origin of Gayton is most likely to derive from *geit* and *tun*, meaning Goat Farm.

The first written record of the place names occurs in the Domesday Book in 1086 when the entries for 'Eswelle' and 'Gaitone' indicate many acres were under cultivation. In addition, there were two fisheries active in Gayton. After the Norman Conquest in 1066, the previous Anglo-Saxon landowners had been displaced and both Heswall and Gayton were granted to Robert of Rhuddlan, who was the cousin of the first Earl of Chester. After Robert's death, the Lordship of the Manor of Heswall passed through many descendants and has finally ended up shared between the Bromley Davenport and Lloyd families. The Lordship of Gayton passed through the Abbey of Vale Royal and finally in 1359 to the Baskervyle-Glegg family, who lived in Gayton Hall until the end of the eighteenth century. The current building dating from the 1660s is an enlargement of an even earlier timber-framed building dating back at least to the sixteenth century. In 1690, William III stayed in Gayton Hall as guest of William Glegg on his way from Chester to Hoylake to sail to Ireland and victory at the Battle of the Boyne.

Oldfield Hall (now divided into separate dwellings) is reputed to be shown on old maps as far back as 1295. Sir Roland Stanley of Hooton spent the last years of his life here, dying in 1614 aged ninety-six, according to his epitaph in Eastham church – the oldest knight in the land. The two halls of Gayton and Oldfield, together with Pensby Hall, built in 1668, and the tower of St Peter's church (dating back to the fourteenth century) are the oldest known buildings in the Heswall area. There was another old hall in Heswall now long vanished, but the memory lives on in the name of Farr Hall Drive where it was located ('the Far Hall').

Before the roads were developed, river transport along and across the Dee was the most effective means of transport. There are medieval reports of trade in agricultural products across the Dee with Wales. There was a very active fishing fleet in Heswall, with many of the fishermen living in the cottages in Banks Road. There was a ferry service from Gayton Cottage to Flint. Unlike the neighbouring ports of Parkgate and Dawpool, there was not sufficient depth of water to allow ships with a large draft to be moored. However there are many tales of smuggling taking place in Heswall and Gayton, involving caves and secret passages. Up to sixty years ago, Heswall beach was a popular bathing beach, which is difficult to imagine now due to the silting of the Dee estuary and the encroachment of spartina grass. For the same reason, the Heswall Sailing Club was forced to move from its premises at the end of Banks Road to a new building at Thurstaston.

The commercial and industrial growth of Liverpool had a huge impact on Heswall, which had become accessible from this booming city through horse-drawn omnibus services operating across Wirral from Woodside Ferry. Successful businessmen from Liverpool built large holiday homes on the slopes and summit of Heswall Hill, which were previously undeveloped apart from an occasional farm, small holding or quarry. The fresh air, views and sea breezes provided a welcome relief from the smoke and smog produced by the factories in Liverpool, but it was only practicable to occupy these properties in the summer due to the poor condition of the roads in winter. The Cave and Hill House are good examples of such houses that still exist; many others were demolished after the Second World War when the cost of the staff needed to run the larger properties became uneconomic. The pace of development increased when the railway to West Kirby was opened in 1886, allowing businessmen to commute on a daily basis to Liverpool and to establish Heswall as their permanent residence. In 1898 a second station, Heswall Hills, was opened, providing a link to Bidston and Chester, stimulating development to the east of the township. The railways also attracted many holidaymakers and day trippers to enjoy the views and beach at Heswall, and the Hotel Victoria opened in 1896 to cater for this trade.

The fresh air and magnificent views across the Dee Estuary that attracted the wealthy merchants also led to two large hospitals being built in Heswall – the Cleaver Hospital in 1902 and the Royal Liverpool Children's Hospital on Telegraph Road in 1909. Both of these hospitals had open-air wards, as fresh air was the only way known to tackle tuberculosis, which was so prevalent at the time. The eventual closure of these hospitals in the 1980s, which had become important landmarks, and their eventual demolition was regretted by many, but was a testament to the improvement in medicine and social conditions that enabled TB to be virtually eliminated. The fresh air of Heswall prompted the Liverpool Female Orphan Asylum to acquire The Towers, a large folly known popularly as Heswall Castle, in 1891 to use as a summer holiday retreat. This use continued until the 1930s and the property was demolished in 1935, to be replaced by Castle Buildings.

The development of the Top Village, starting in the late 1800s, created a new direct route from Neston to West Kirby, which previously ran through the Lower Village. Telegraph Road evolved from a sandy track along the top of the sandstone ridge following a line of telegraph posts to become the main thoroughfare. Churches were built along this road to serve the growing population: the Methodist church and the Mission church (later to be rebuilt as the Church of the Good Shepherd) in 1891; the Presbyterian church in 1909; Our Lady and St John

Catholic church in 1939; and the Quaker Meeting house in 1963. Telegraph Road became the main shopping centre and many private houses were converted into shops, the original front gardens explaining why so many shops and restaurants are set so far back from the pavement. The bus station was built in the 1920s after Crosville took over the bus services to Birkenhead – pioneered by John Pye. These frequent bus services further increased the popularity of Heswall as a dormitory town for people working in other parts of Wirral, and there was much housing development between the wars, during which time Pensby, Barnston, and Heswall effectively merged into a continuous conurbation. The population of Heswall and Gayton was 423 in 1801, 2,347 in 1901, and 7,747 in 1951. The 2001 census indicated the total population of Heswall, Gayton and Barnston was 16,012.

Many private schools were opened to meet the needs of the growing population, the largest of these being Moorland House in Hillside Road, St Fillan's in Riverbank Road, Murrayfield in North Drive, and Broomlands in Thurstaston Road. None of these schools still exist and their sites have all been used for housing developments. The Heswall Primary School on the Puddydale moved to larger premises in Whitfield Lane in 1976, and St Peter's Church of England School moved from its bomb-damaged site in School Hill to Thurstaston Road in 1961. The Naval Reformatory School, the Akbar, was moved to Heswall from a ship moored in the Mersey to new premises in Oldfield Drive in 1909, and remained in this location until it was closed in 1956. The Liverpool Boys' Association ran summer camps in premises in Broad Lane (previously the summer base of the Akbar when ship-based) until 1991.

Many farms, market gardens and dairies were established to meet the needs of the growing population, but with the increasing demand for building plots most of these have been redeveloped as housing. There was extensive quarrying of red sandstone in Heswall and much was exported from Heswall shore, some used for the construction of the Menai Bridge in Anglesey.

The huge growth in the population of Heswall, and its continuing popularity as a place to live, inevitably presents a potential threat to the unique character that makes it so attractive. The special features of the Lower Village and Gayton in terms of red sandstone walls, attractive architecture and gardens, open spaces and mature trees have been recognised by the establishment of two Conservation Areas covering these sites. The open spaces are now protected against development, including the Dales, which provide stunning views across the estuary and are designated a Site of Special Scientific Interest. The Heswall Society was founded in 1953 'for the public benefit to conserve the heritage of the Parish of Heswall', its formation triggered by concerns over the clearance of the last of the stone and thatched cottages in the lower village. It still plays a very active role in lobbying to protect Heswall and Gayton from developments that are detrimental to the character of these beautiful villages.

Acknowledgements

The authors would like to thank the following for providing images for this book: John Billington, Ian Boumphrey, Ann Chase, Jean and Peter Connah (for access to material collected by Harry Connah), Suzanne Cook, Jane and Fiona Lane, Mike Nickson, John Ryan, St Peter's Church Archive, Tom Stapledon and Peter Watson. We are grateful to the householders who allowed us to use close-up images of their houses. Finally, special mention and thanks must be made to current and past members and committee members of the Heswall Society for the enormous contribution the society has made to preserve the beauty and heritage of Heswall for more than sixty years.

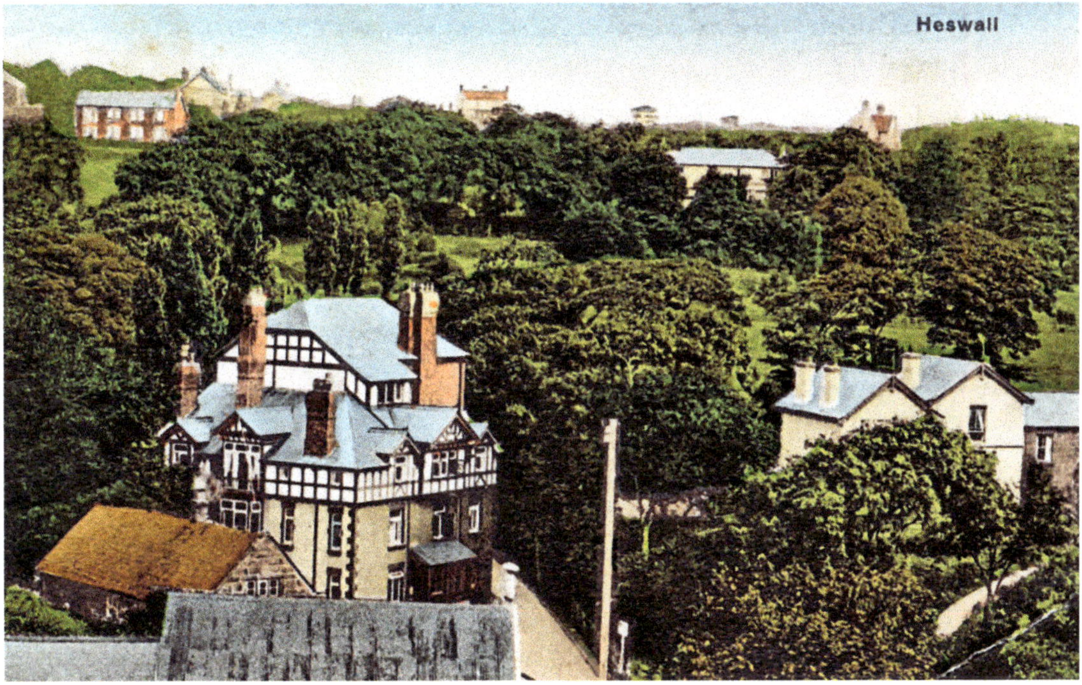

View from St Peter's Church Tower

From the left, Elder Cottage, the Black Horse, Random and Wellwood House can be seen in the foreground. The field in the centre, now St Peter's Close, was used for many years for children's sports days. The house above is Dawstone in Dawstone Road.

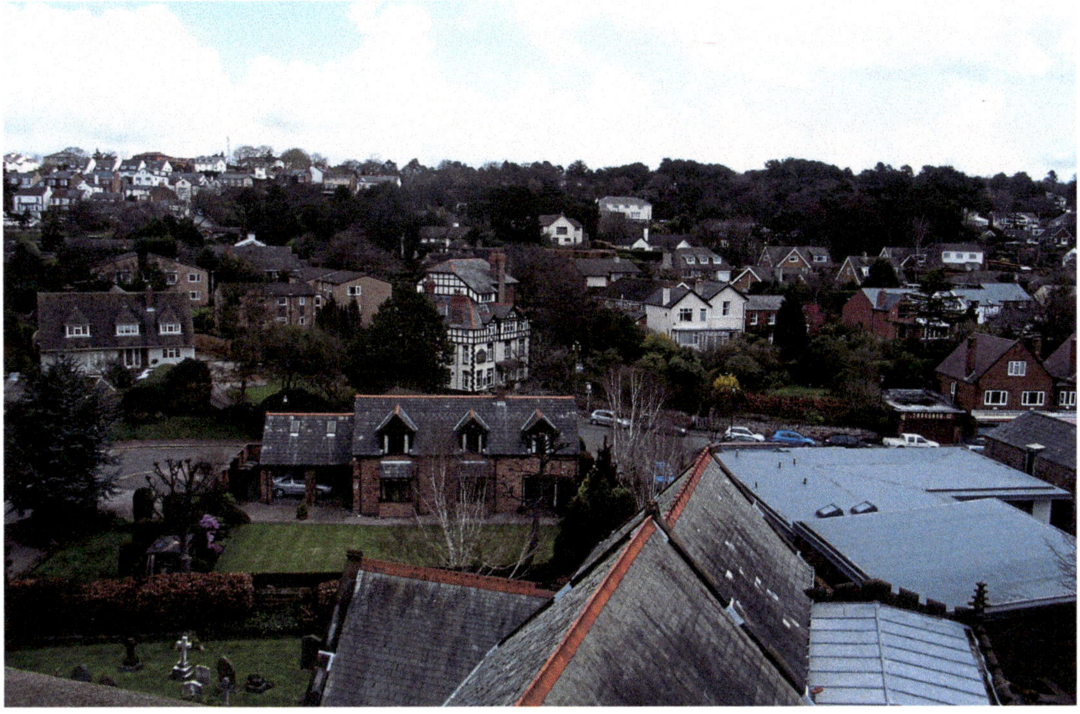

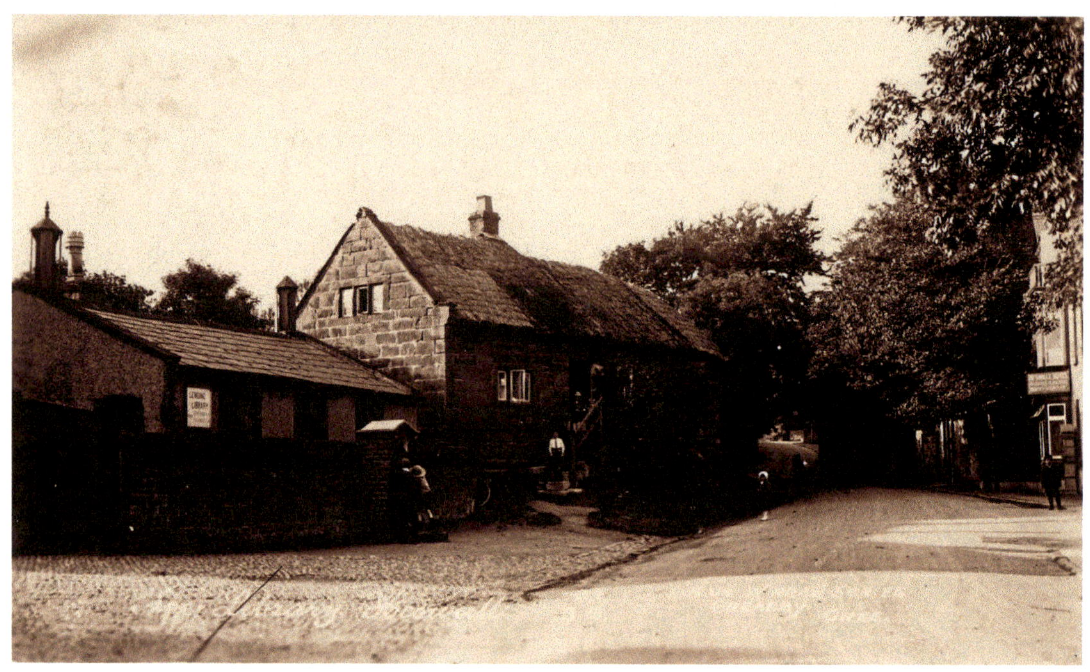

Elder Cottage

This thatched building housed the original Dame school in Heswall from 1847 when it had sixty pupils. The building probably dates back to 1686. The extension added in 1840, now privately owned, has been used as a library, children's church and parish office, and is the only remaining part of the building today. Elder Cottage remained a school until the church school opened in School Hill in 1872, and was demolished in 1954 due to widening of the road.

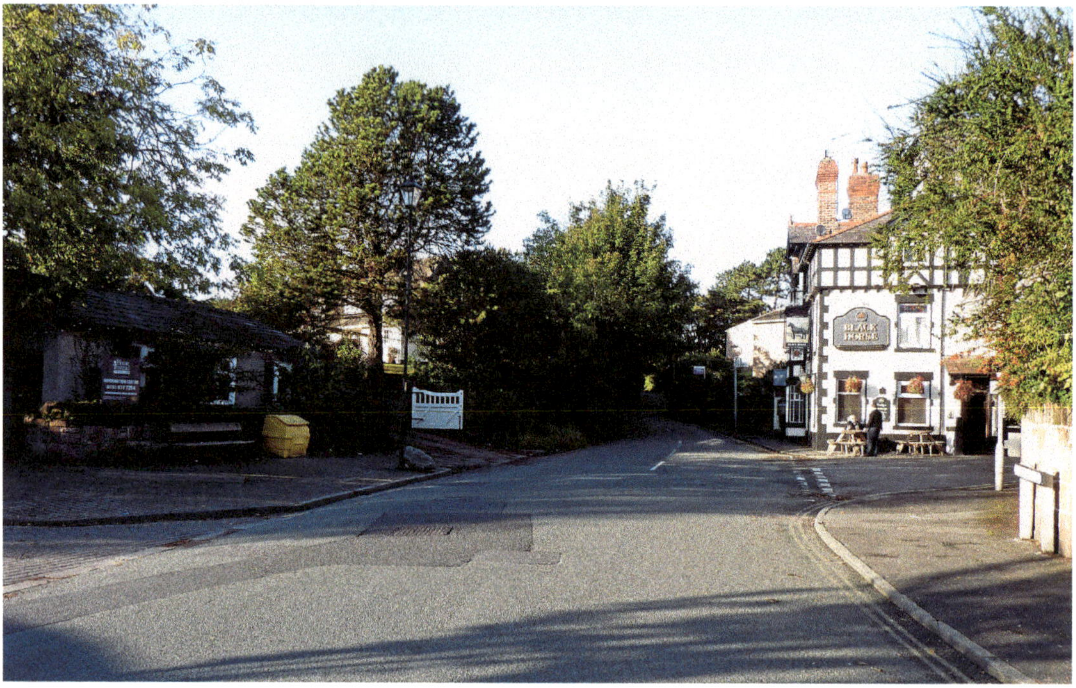

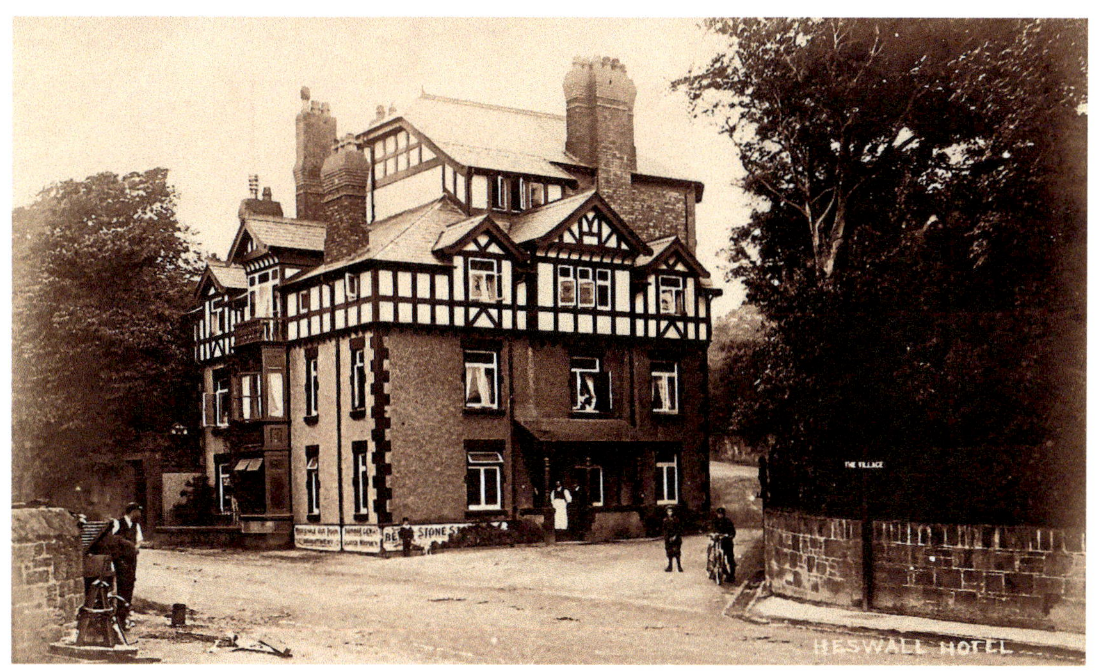

The Black Horse

Built in the 1870s as the Black Horse, it was renamed the Heswall Hotel in the 1920s by Mr Leeman, the licensee, the name reverting back to the Black Horse in the 1940s. In the early 1900s an advertisement describes it as having thirteen bedrooms, a dining and billiards room and a tea garden famous for ham teas. The village pump can be seen on the left.

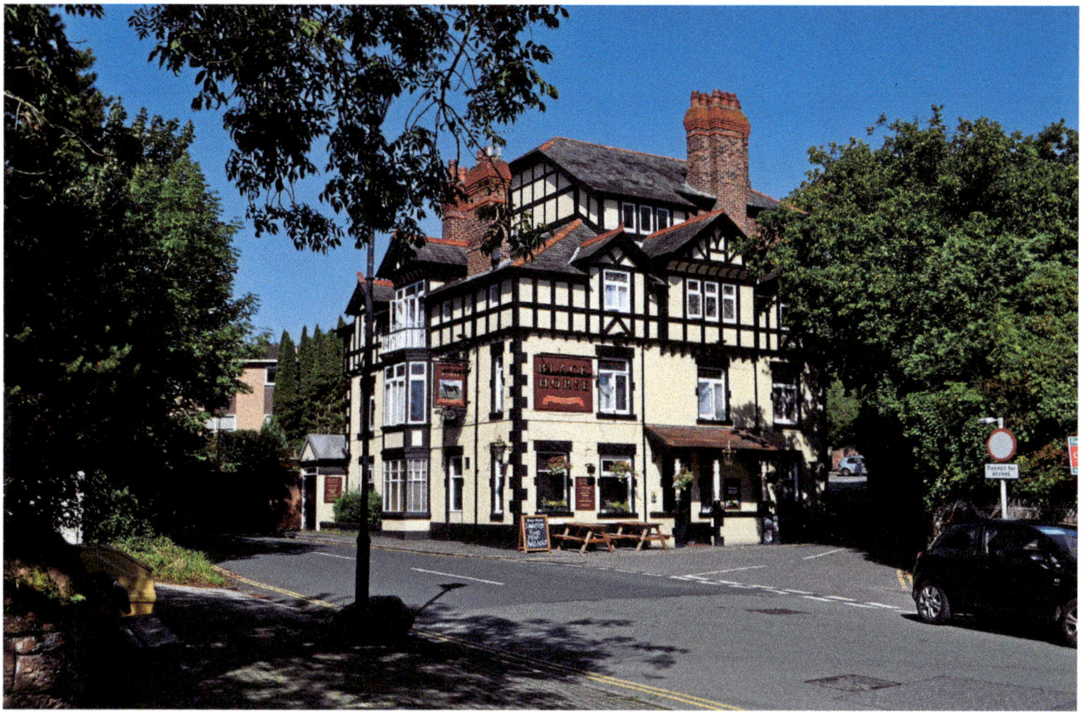

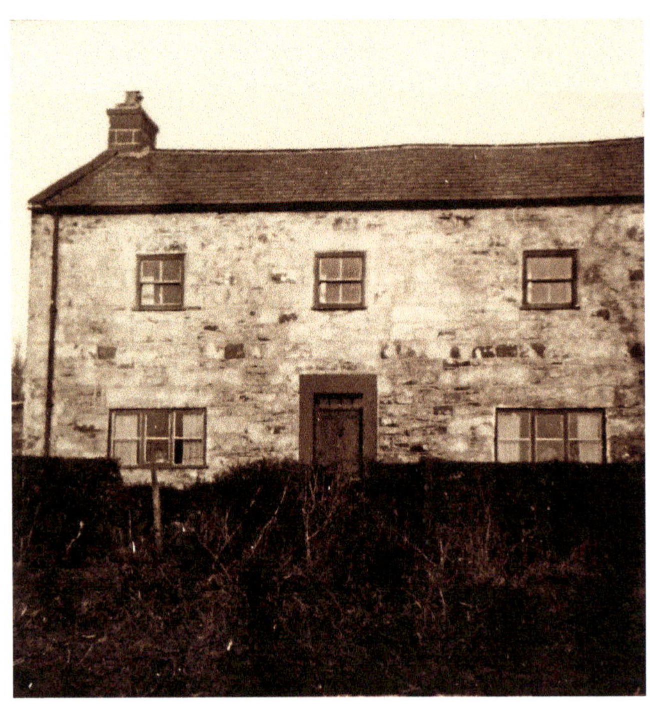

Church Farm

Occupied at one time by the Smallwood family, this farmhouse now forms part of Church Farm Court in Village Road. As well as being farmers, the Smallwood family owned a bakery and the post office. Other members of the family were the local funeral directors, blacksmith and quarry owners. Other local farming families also tenanted this farm.

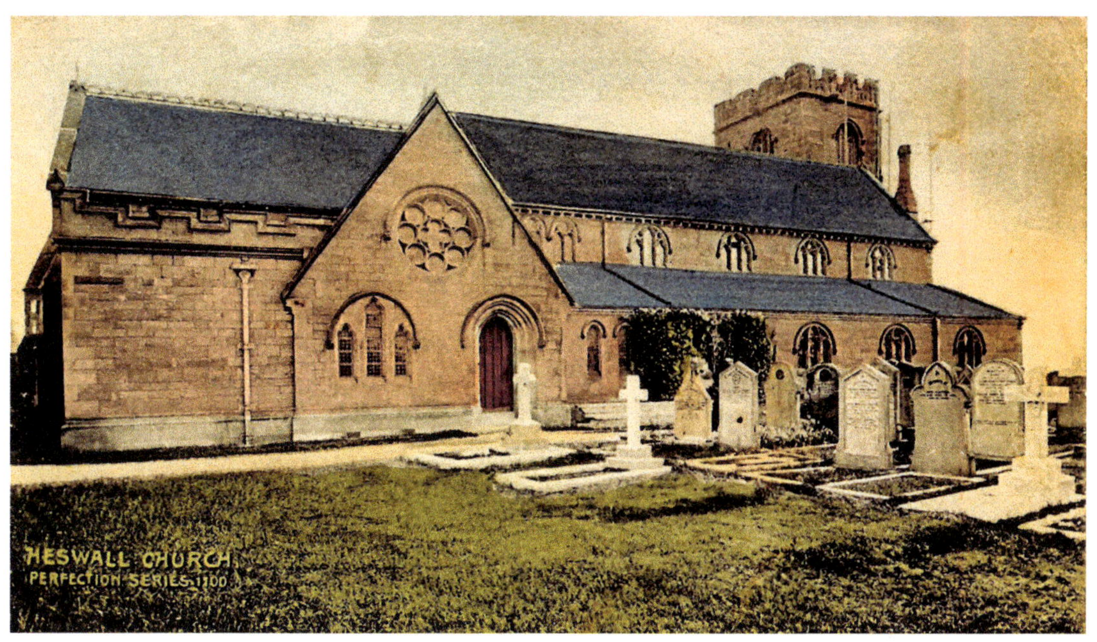

St Peter's Church

This is the third church to stand on this site and was designed by Francis Doyle, a famous architect who also designed the White Star Building in Liverpool and The Grand Hotel in Llandudno. This church was completed and consecrated to Saint Peter in 1879. The Lady chapel, also known as the Brocklebank chapel, was added in 1893. Outside the church a sundial dated 1726 and a grave with the earliest inscription of 1728 can be found.

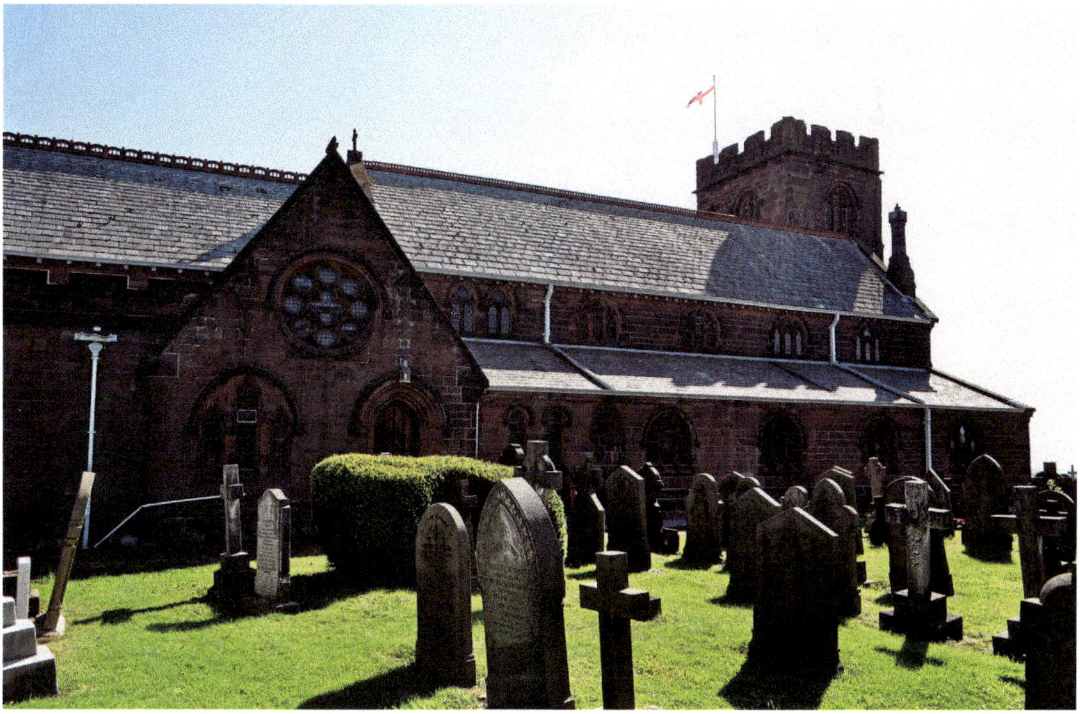

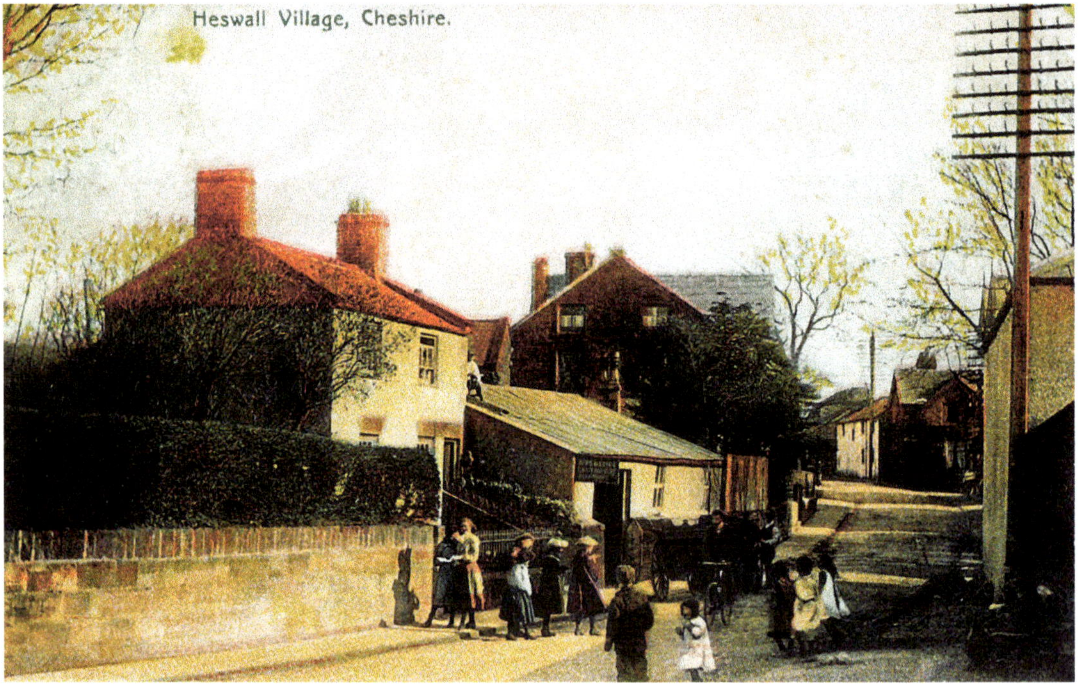

Wellwood Cottage Looking Along Village Road

This was lived in for many years by the Griffiths family, one of whom, David Griffiths, born in 1872, was sexton of St Peter's church. In the early 1900s, Mr Davies ran a cab hire business from the low building seen next to the cottage. The site is now occupied by a single-storey shop, the last of the row of shops to be built.

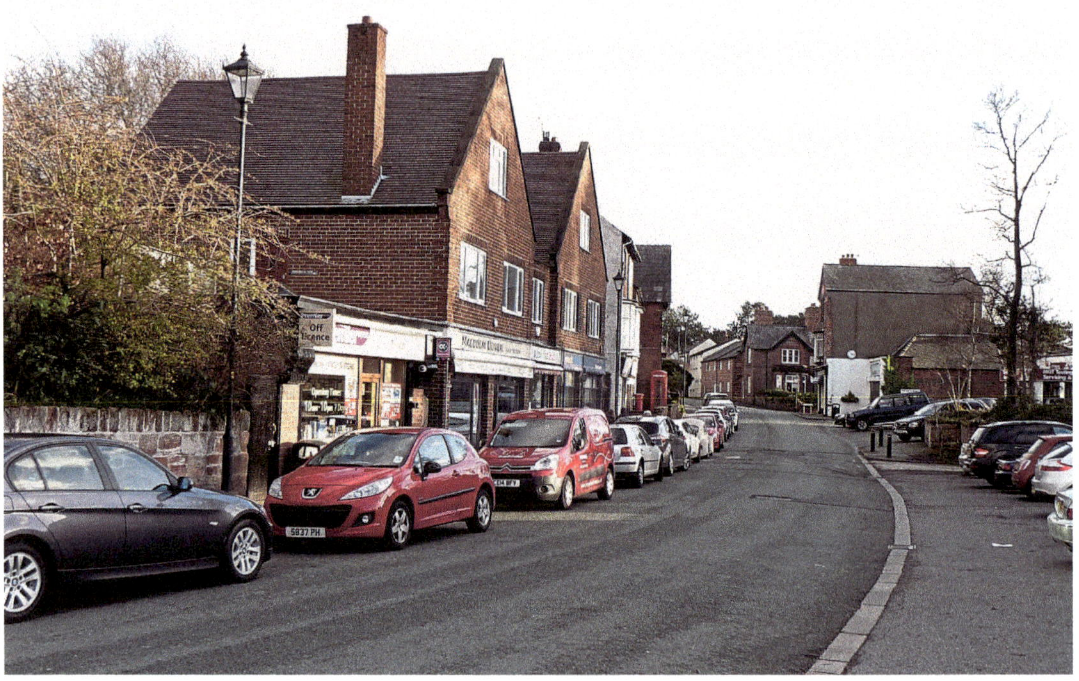

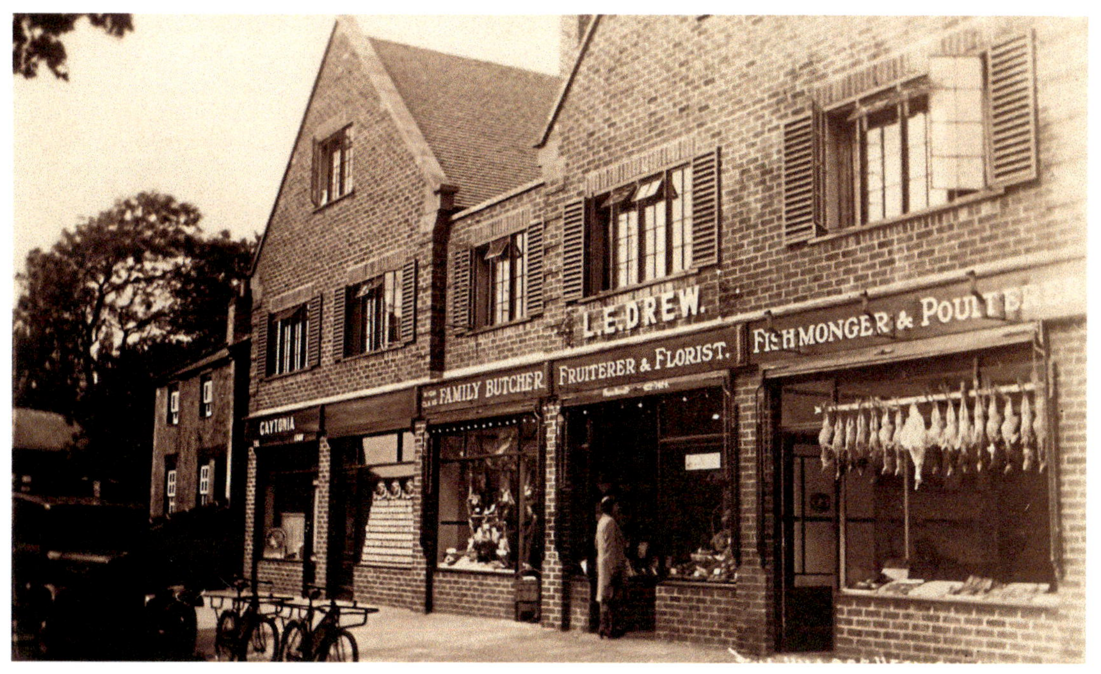

Lower Village Shops – Drew's

Until the 1920s there were only a few shops in the village. This block was built for L. E. Drew to be used as butcher's, fishmonger's and greengrocer's shops. He had expanded from a single shop next door. In the 1950s the business was owned by A. Chapman. Wellwood Cottage can be seen on the left.

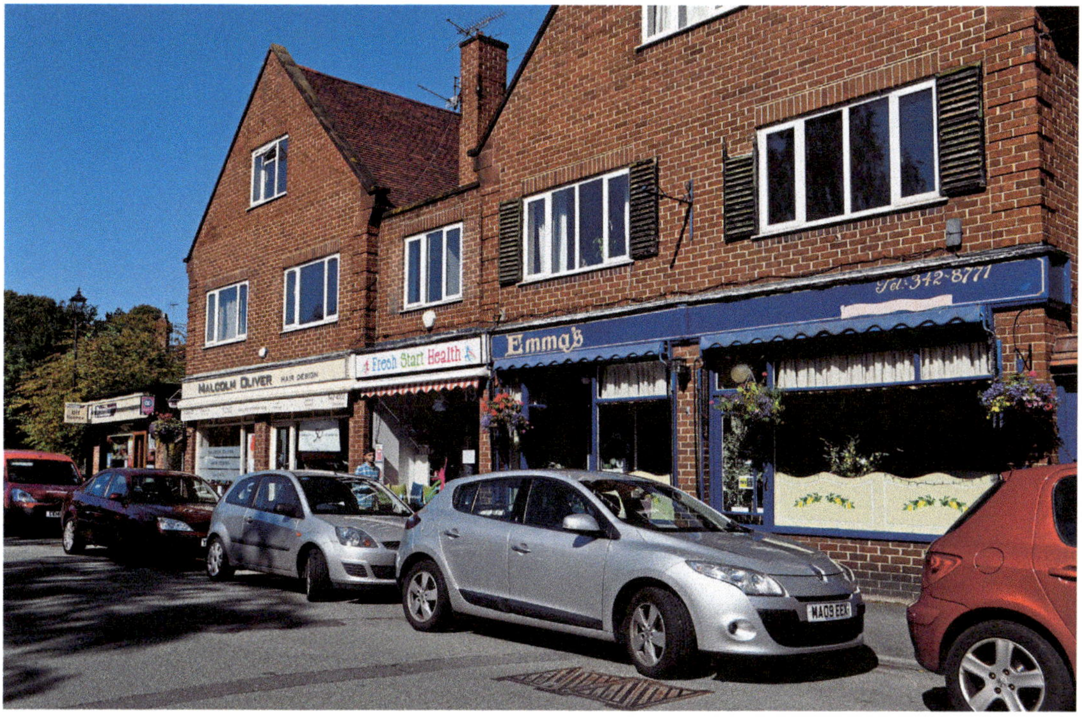

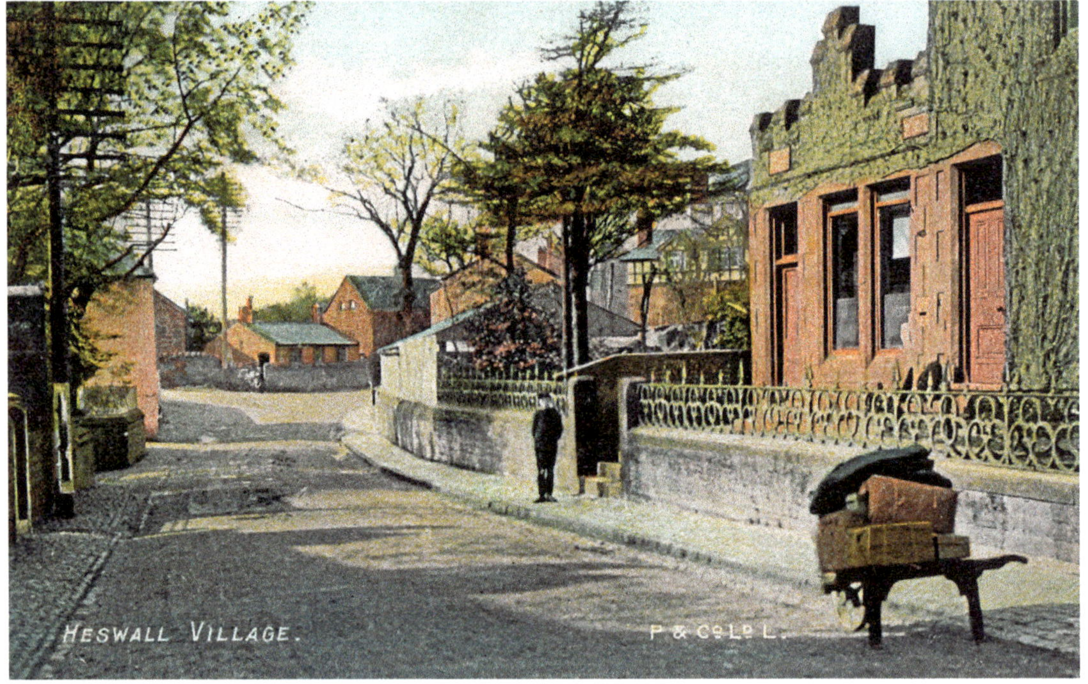

Lower Village Post Office

The post office was originally run by the Misses Smallwood in the next door bakery, in Ivy Cottage. It moved into these purpose-built premises in 1899. The tithe barn can be seen on the left, later to be reduced in size to allow a car park to be created. Elder Cottage and the Black Horse can be seen in the background.

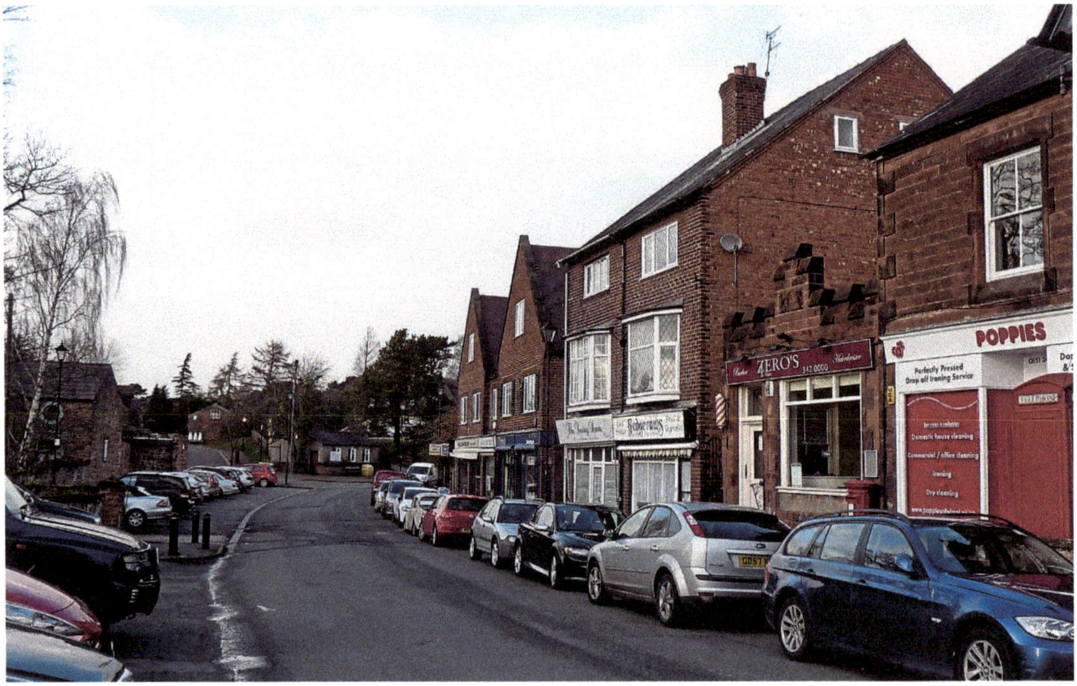

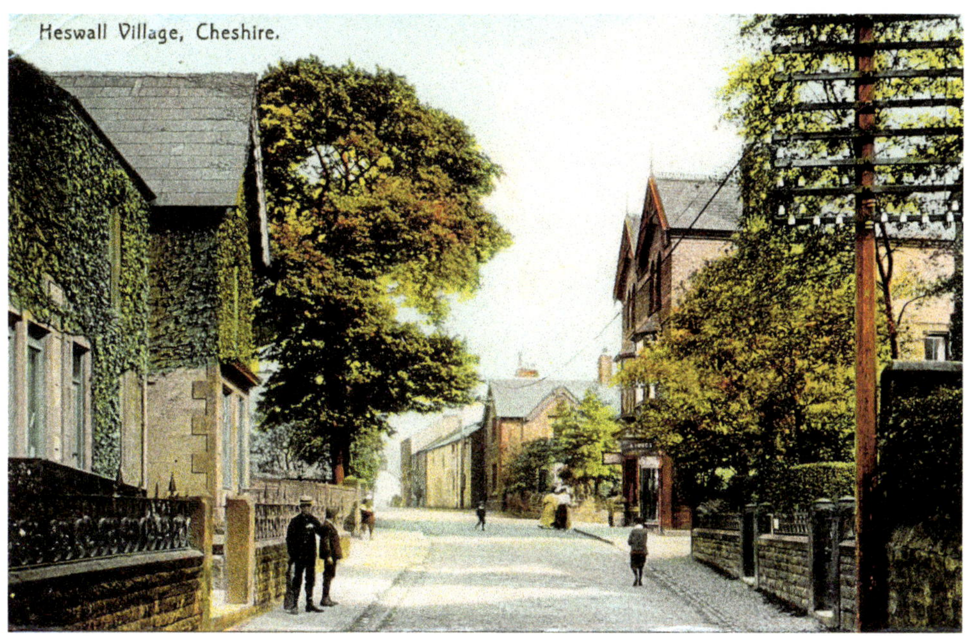

Lower Village Looking Towards Lydiate Farm

On the left is Smallwood's bakery, which later became Lloyds Bank, and today is The Village Salon. Opposite is the front garden wall of three houses, which were later destroyed in the Second World War. Lydiate Farm can be seen in the centre, beyond the two shops on the right. The first public telephone in the village was in one of its rooms. Henry Totty lived here; a facsimile of his diary from the 1870s in Heswall library makes interesting reading.

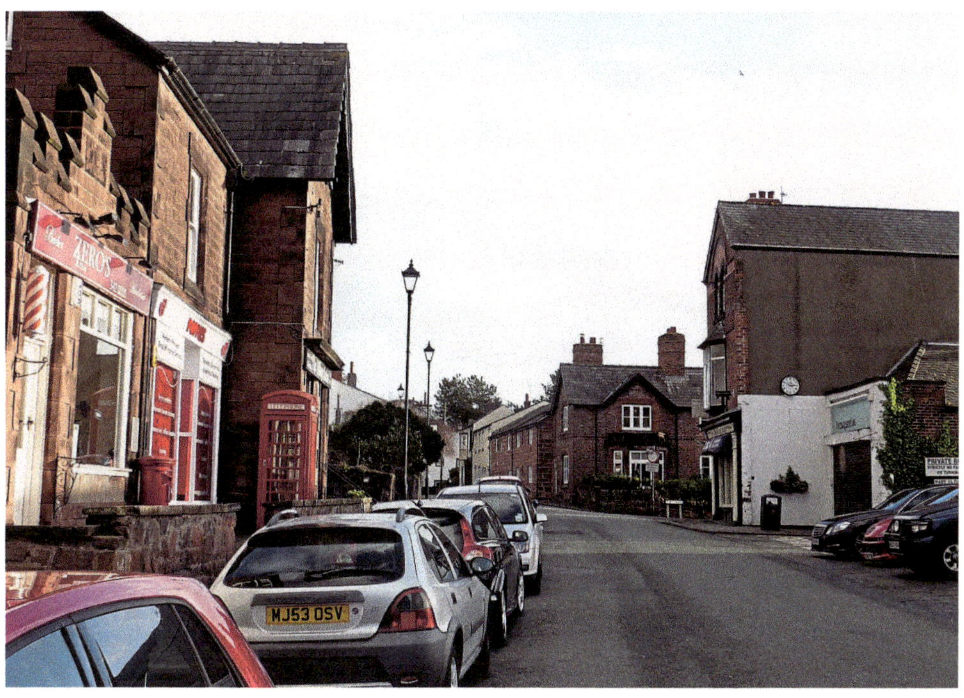

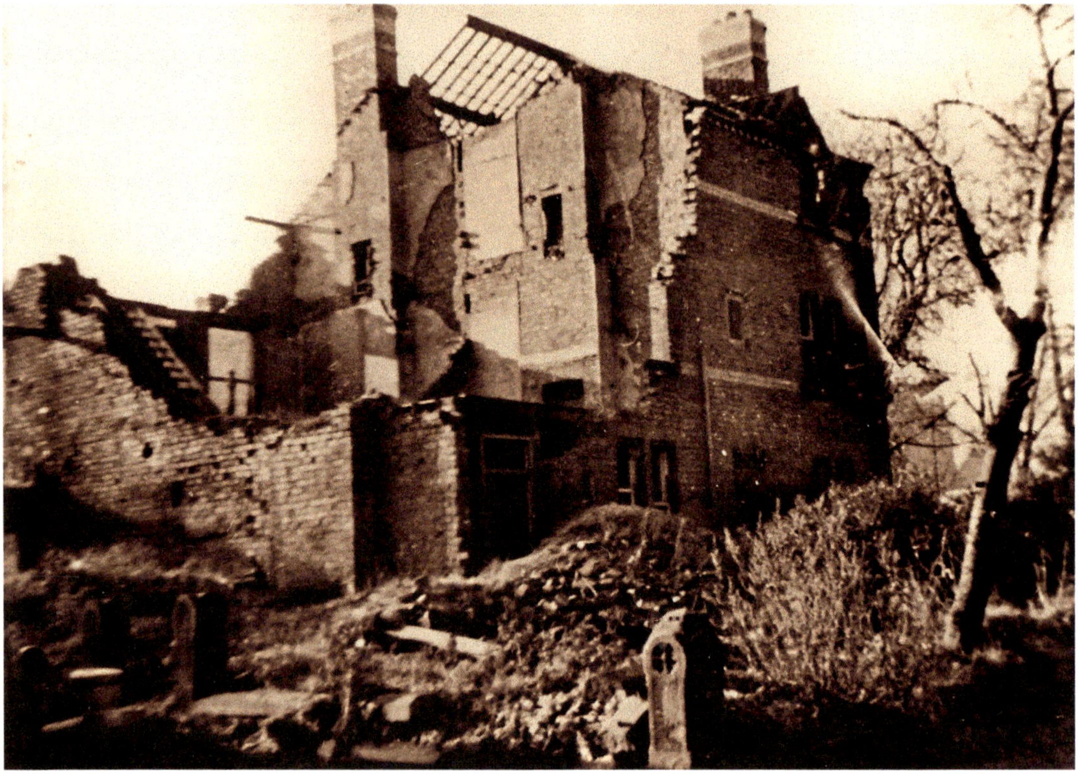

Bombed Houses, Village Road

The Lower Village Garage stands on the site of three houses that were bombed in June 1941. These were The Rookery, The Laurels, and, nearest the church, Whitby House, where the Shone family lived. Mr and Mrs Shone and their daughter Dorothy were killed in their home by the bomb. Their daughter Marjorie was rescued from the rubble.

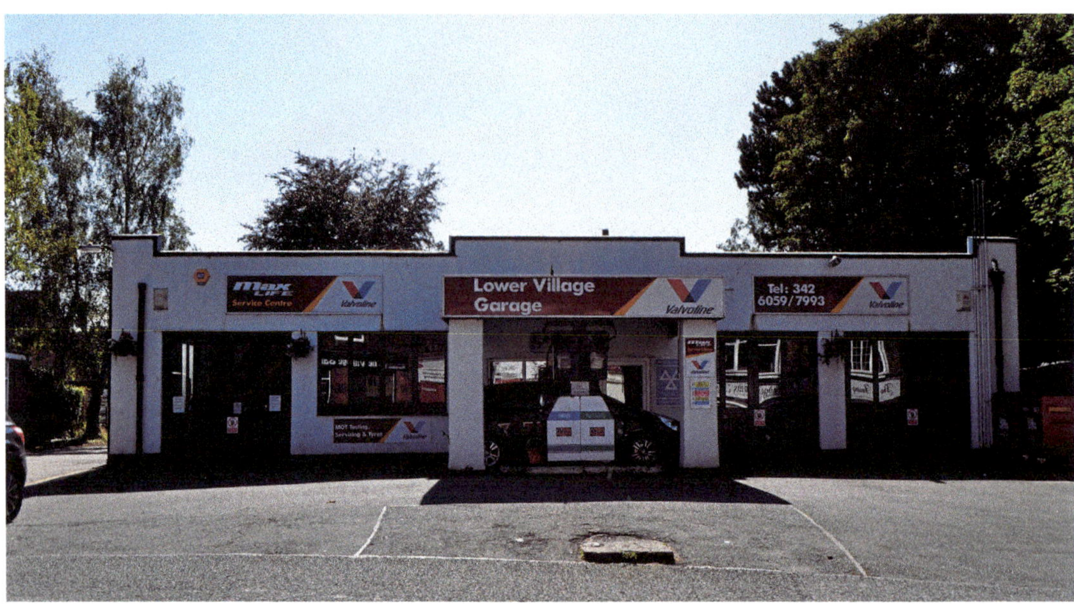

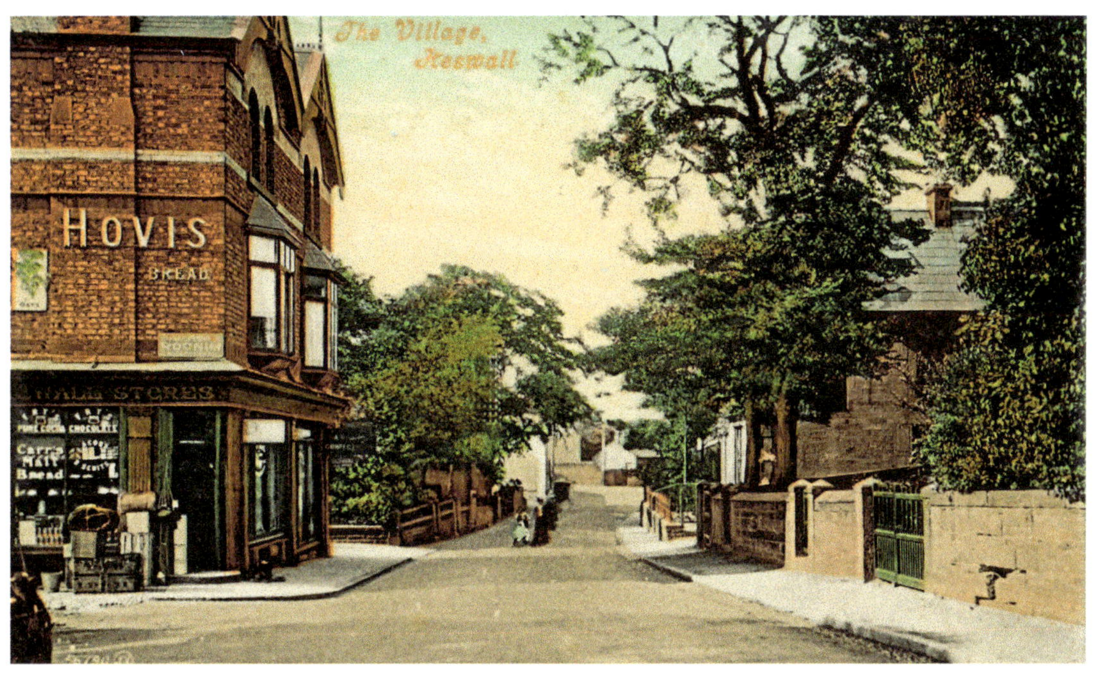

Heswall Stores

In the foreground is Mr Pennington's grocery store, now The Village Shop. The café confectioner next door was Youd's, later to become Atherton's, and was also destroyed by the bombing in June 1941. It has been replaced by a modern chemist's shop.

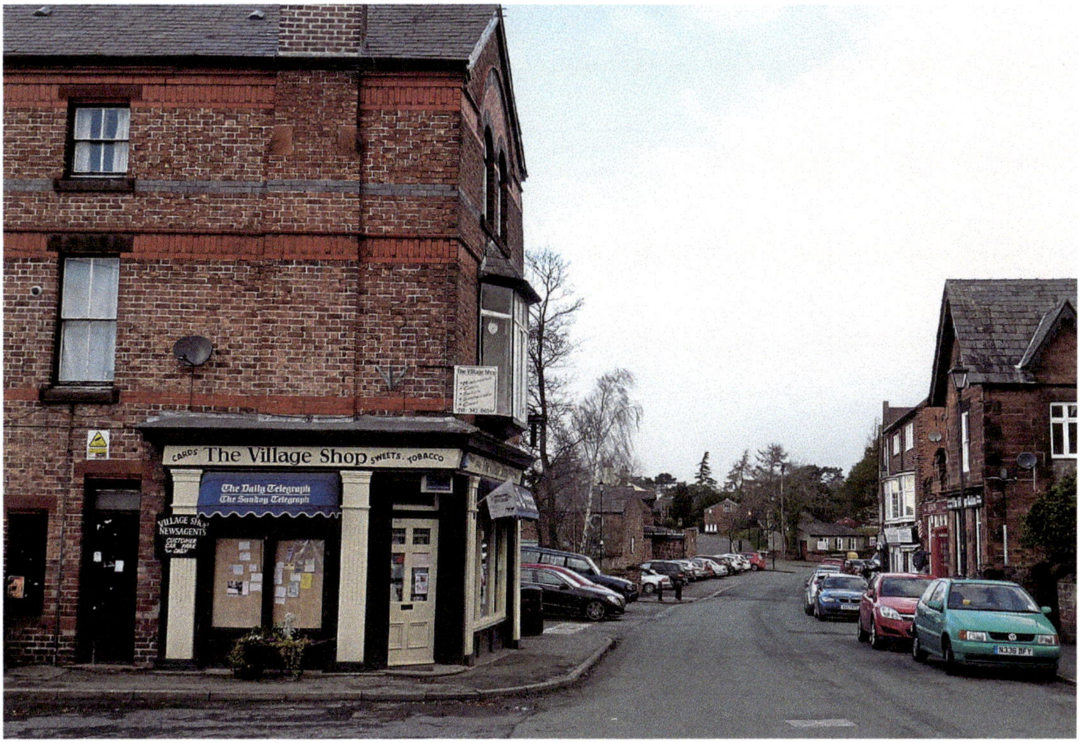

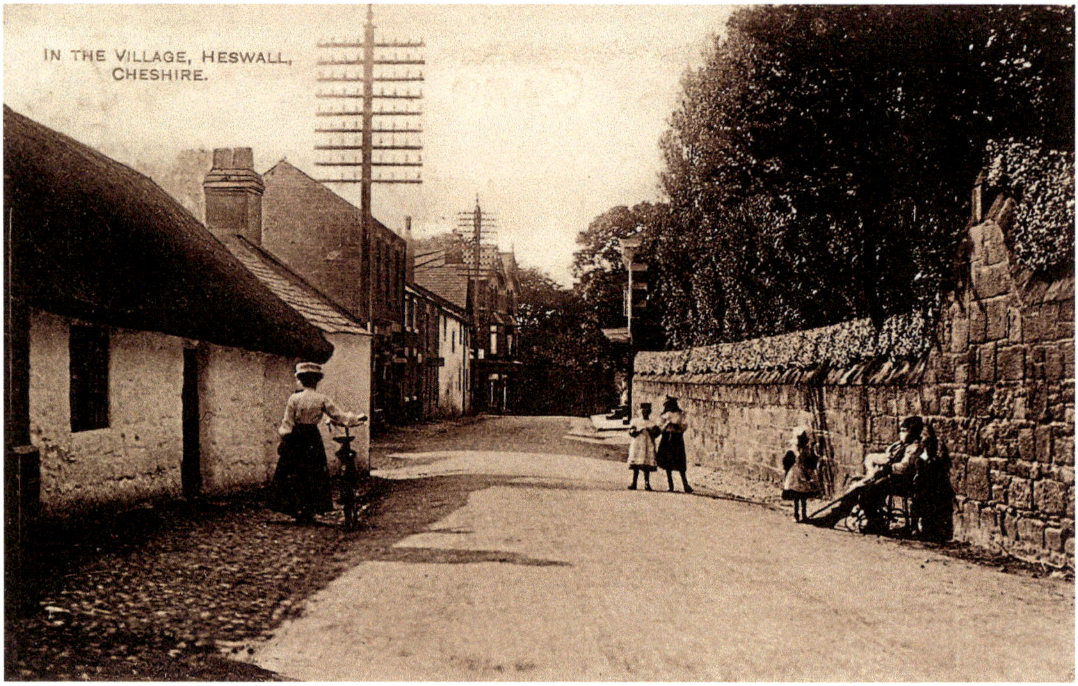

Stacey's Cottage, Village Road

The Stacey family brought up many children in this partially thatched cottage in Village Road, which was also used as the registrar's office for Heswall. The cottage was demolished between the two world wars, and has been replaced by a modern house.

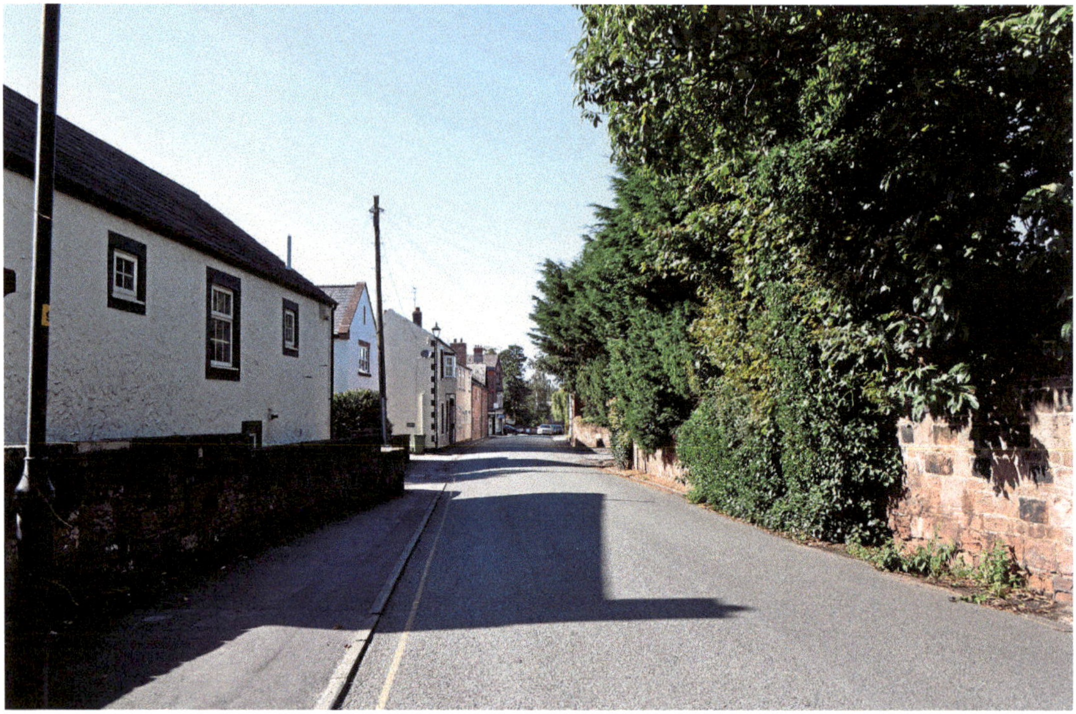

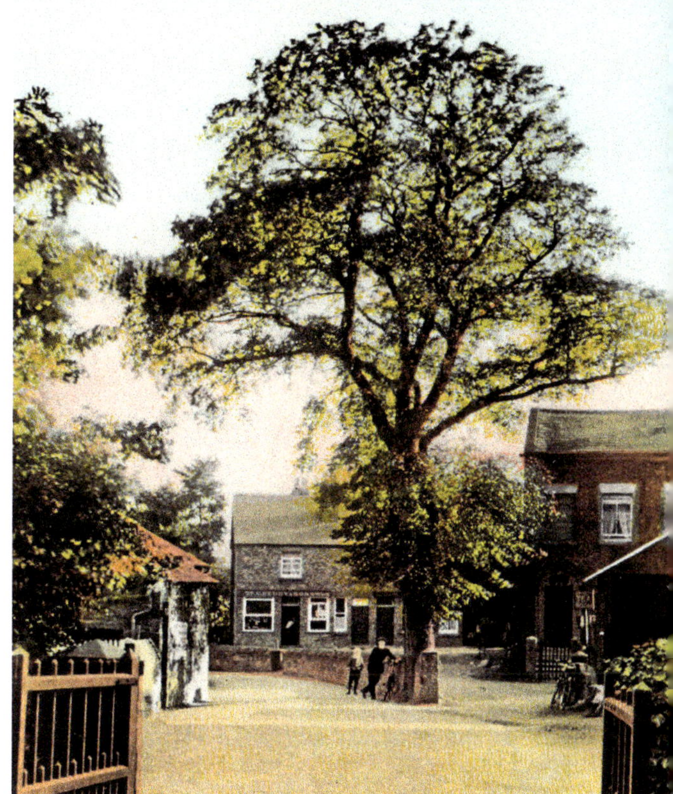

The Lydiate from Village Road

Annabel's Cottage, now a private house, can be seen in the centre. It was once a café catering for the day trippers on their way to the sandy beach or walkers in need of refreshment. Earlier it was a branch of Reddy's butchers and Shone's paint shop. The outbuildings on the left of the photograph are part of Totty's (Lydiate) Farm.

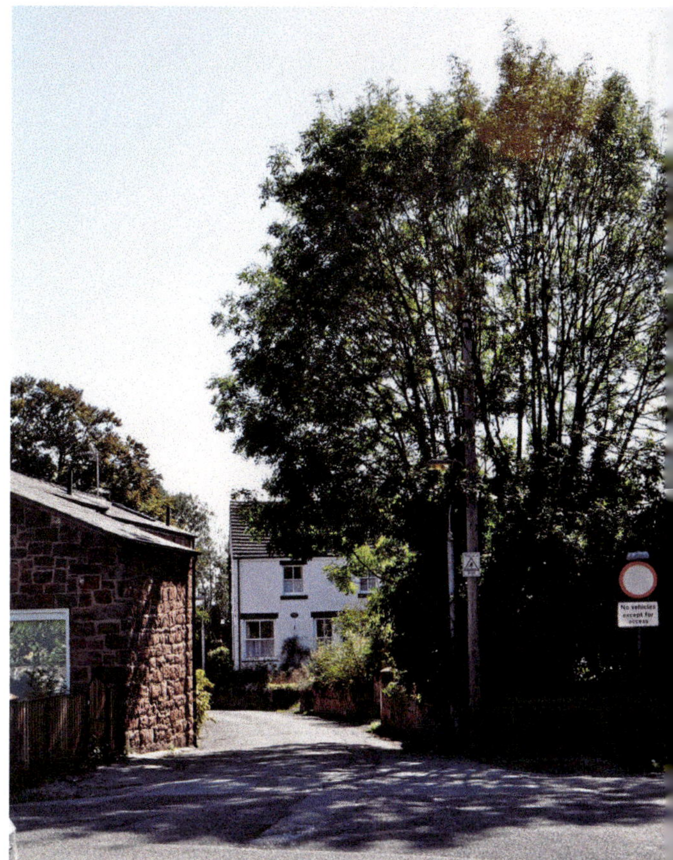

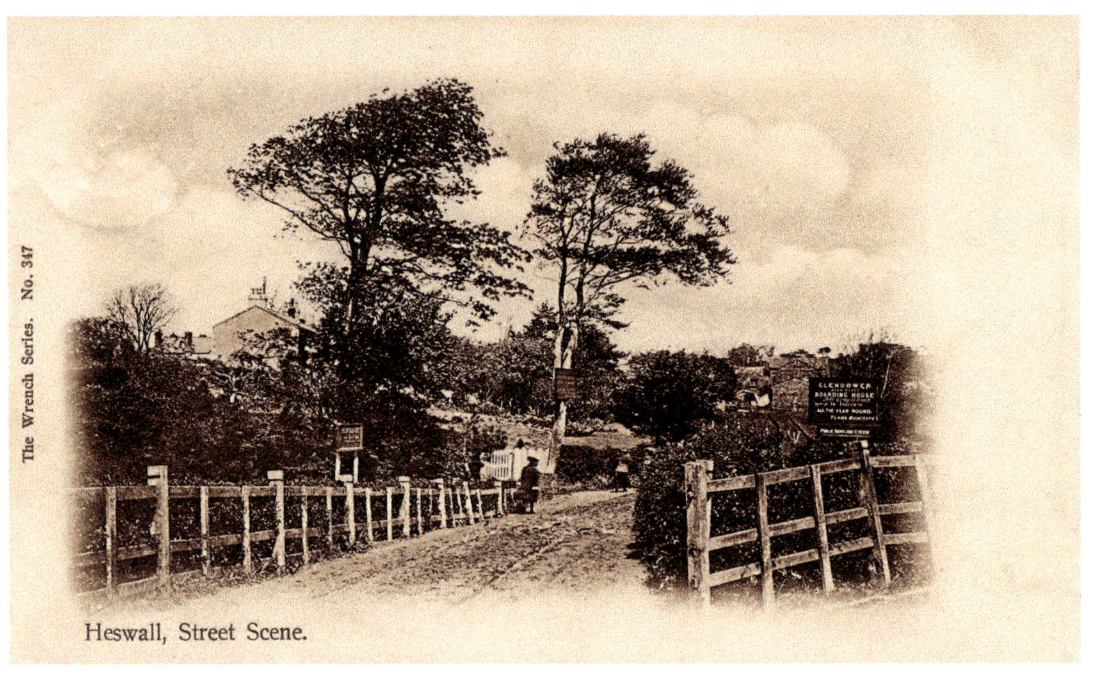

Heswall, Street Scene.

The Lydiate from Station Road

Looking up The Lydiate from Station Road, the sign on the right-hand side is advertising Glendower Boarding House, which was in Telegraph Road on the site of the current ambulance station (see page 58). This was a good place for an advertisement as it was the main thoroughfare from the station to the village.

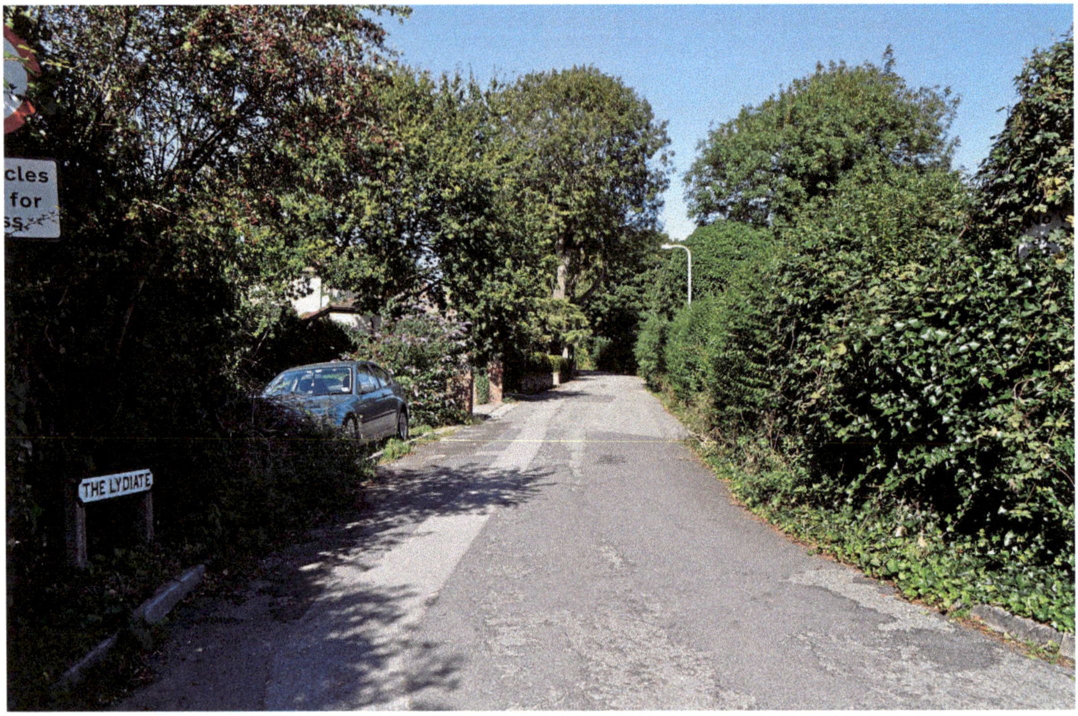

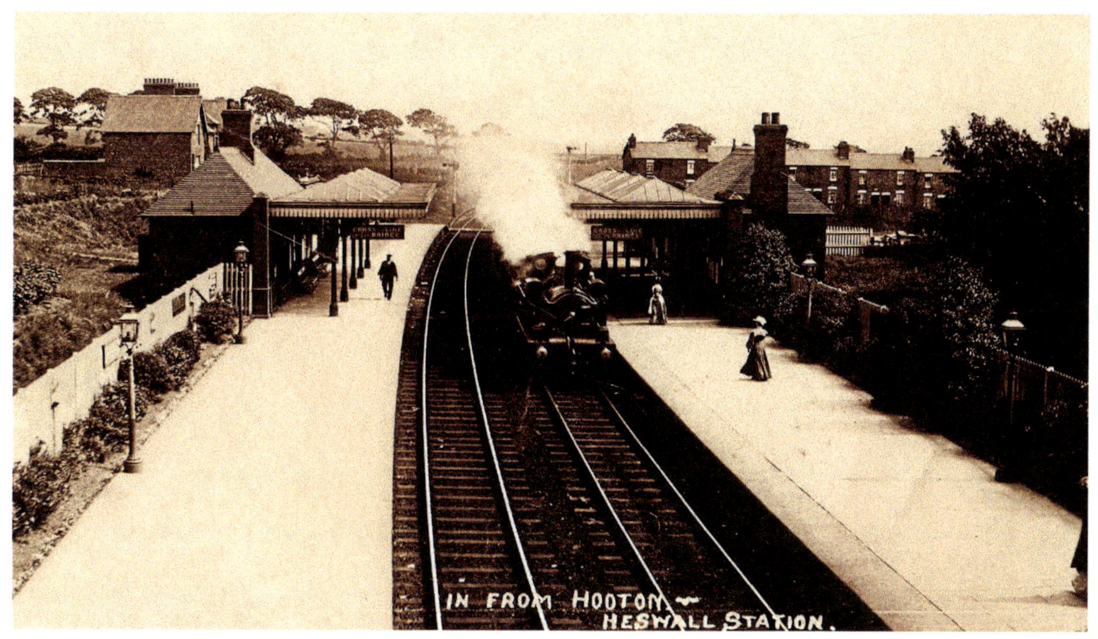

Heswall Station

The opening of the railway line from Hooton to West Kirby in 1886 triggered a rapid growth in the size of the village by enabling easy commuting to Liverpool and Chester. It was closed to passengers in 1956 and to goods in 1962. The Wirral Way Country Park now runs along the old railway track. This photograph is taken from the bridge in Station Road. The original stationmaster's house can still be seen on the left at the end of Riverbank Close.

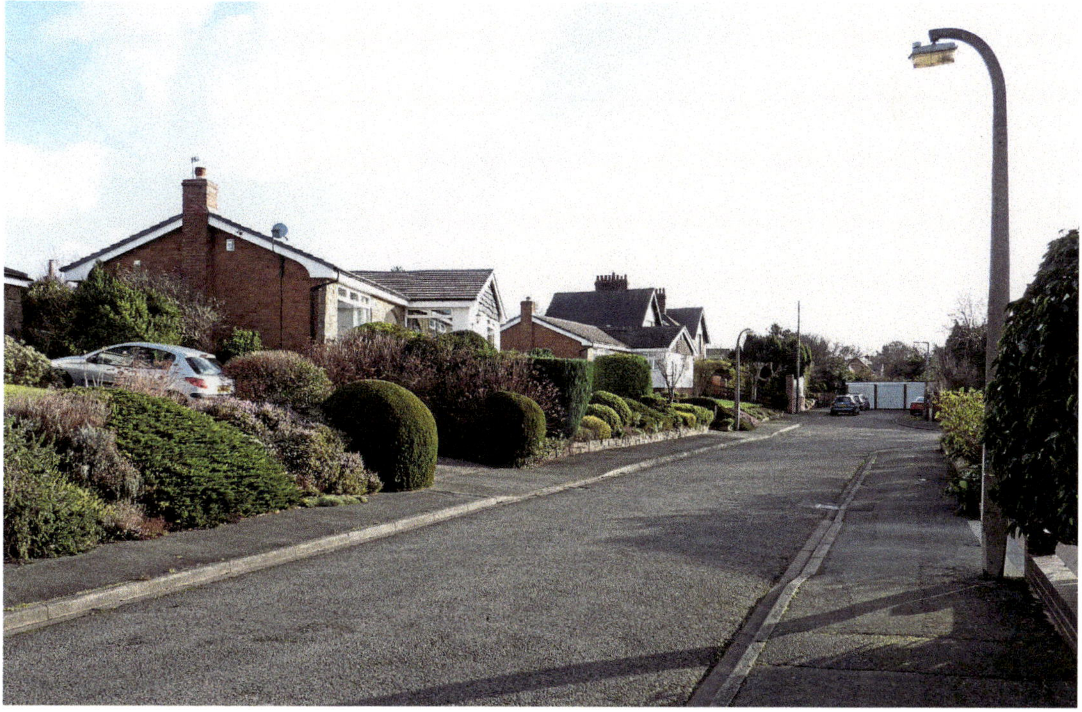

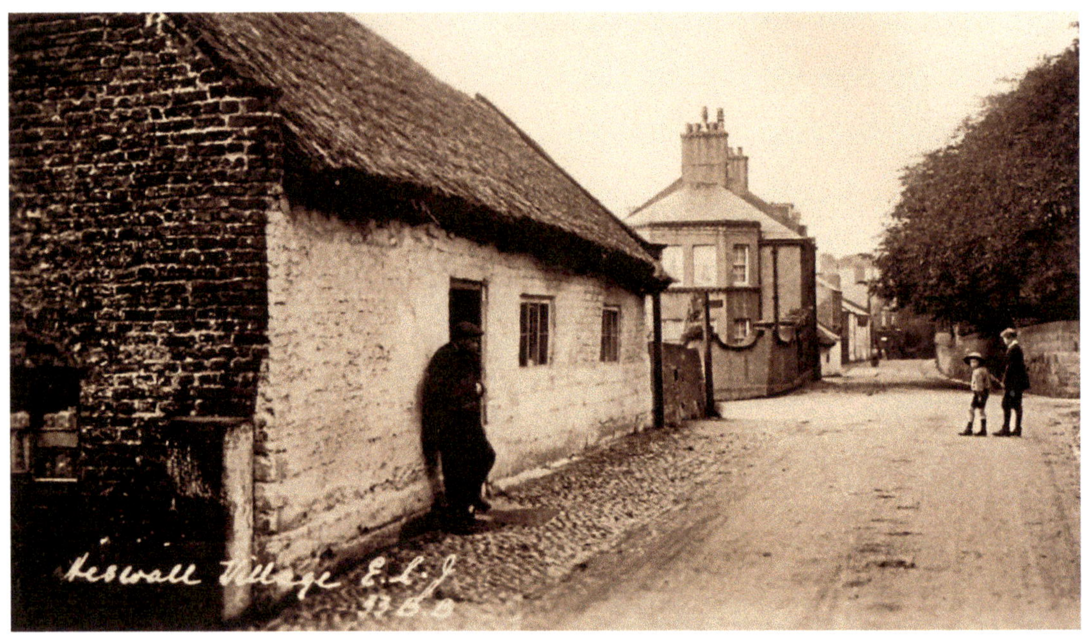

Tiger Smith's Cottage

Tiger Smith's cottage was at the junction of Wallrake, Village Road and Station Road. This area was once the Village Square and the social centre of the village. The cottage was thatched and the door opened on to the road. It was demolished in the 1930s and the site is now grassed over.

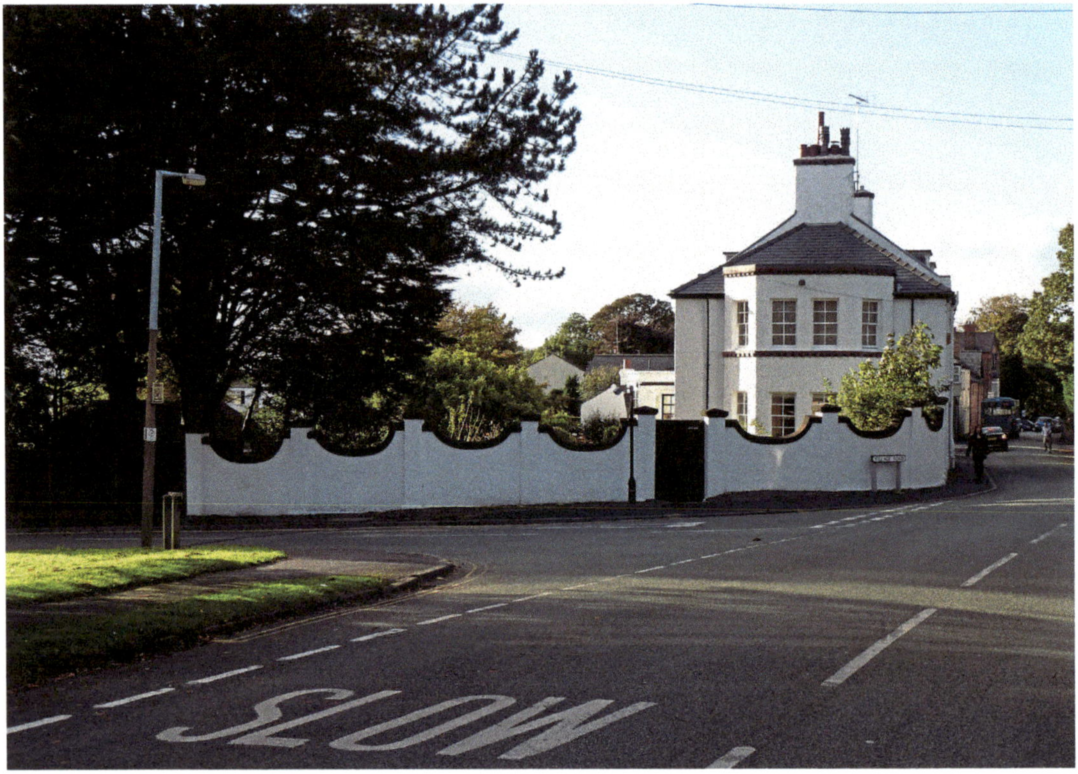

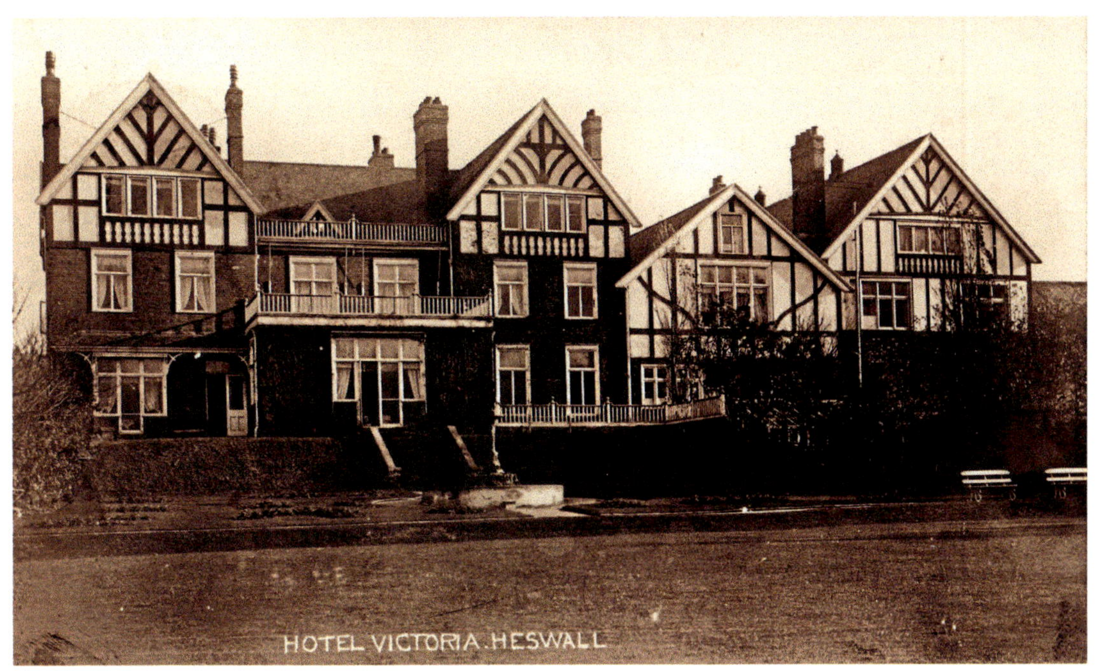

Hotel Victoria

The owner of the Black Horse, Mr Montgomery, opened the Hotel Victoria, now the site of Lapwing Rise, in 1896. The licence was granted in 1892 on the basis that those of The Ship Inn and the White Lion, also in the Lower Village, would not be renewed. The hotel was a popular venue for over 100 years until it was closed in 2002 and demolished in 2007.

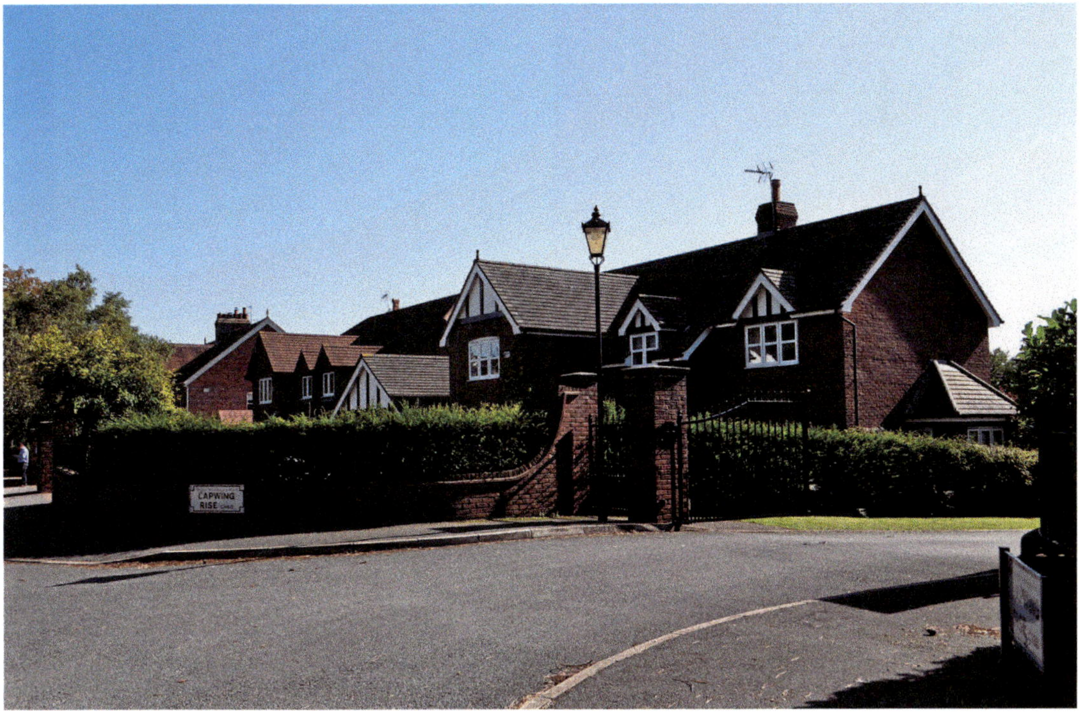

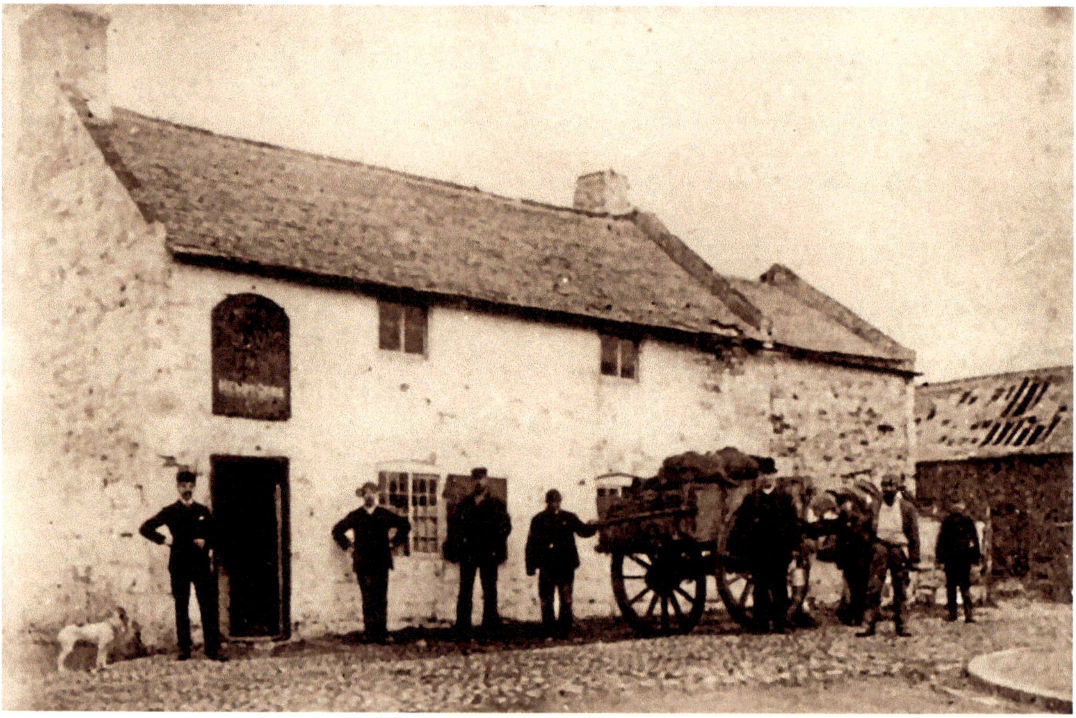

The White Lion

The White Lodge at the intersection of Wallrake and Gayton Road was originally the White Lion Inn. In 1891 the White Lion and 20 acres of land were sold for £4,700 and the licence transferred to the new Hotel Victoria. It is now converted into three houses.

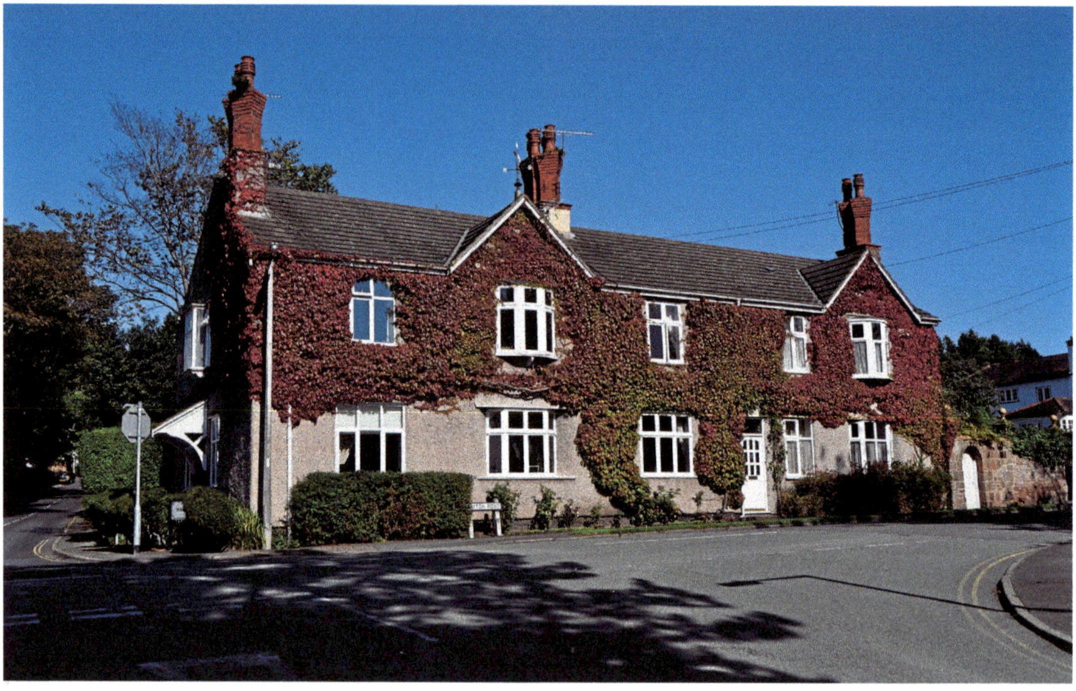

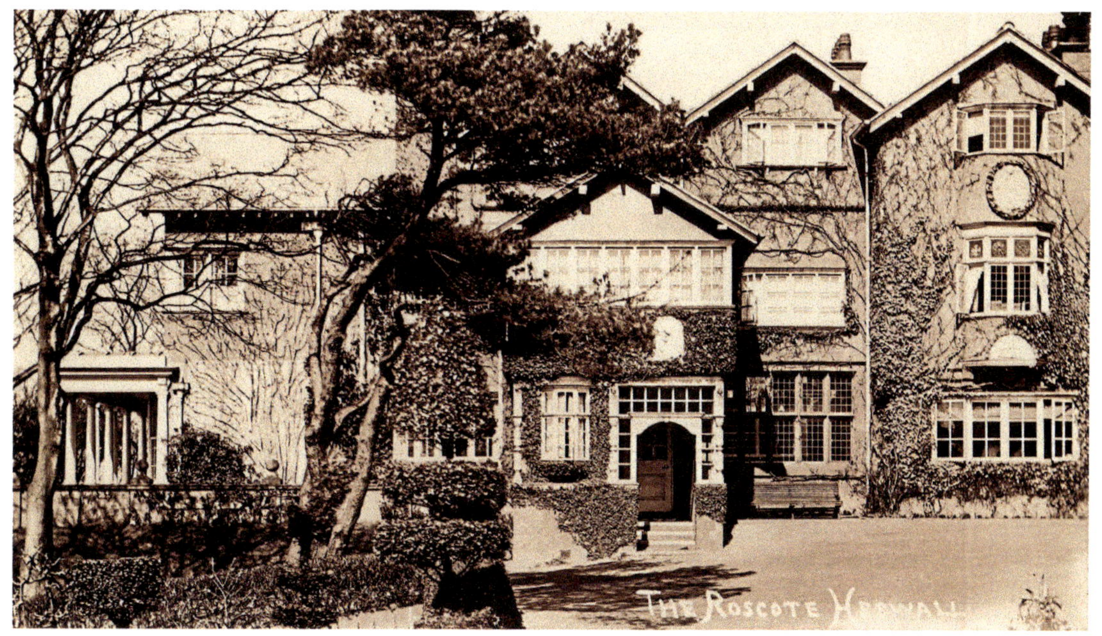

The Roscote

The first reference to this grand house in Wallrake is found in the 1850s. William Newton, Thomas Brocklebank, Thomas Guthrie and William Hannay were some of the early owners of the house, all important men in their own rights. The house was extended several times. By 1971 the Roscote had been demolished and nine houses built on the site. A few of the estate buildings remain along Wallrake, including the clock tower and two lodges.

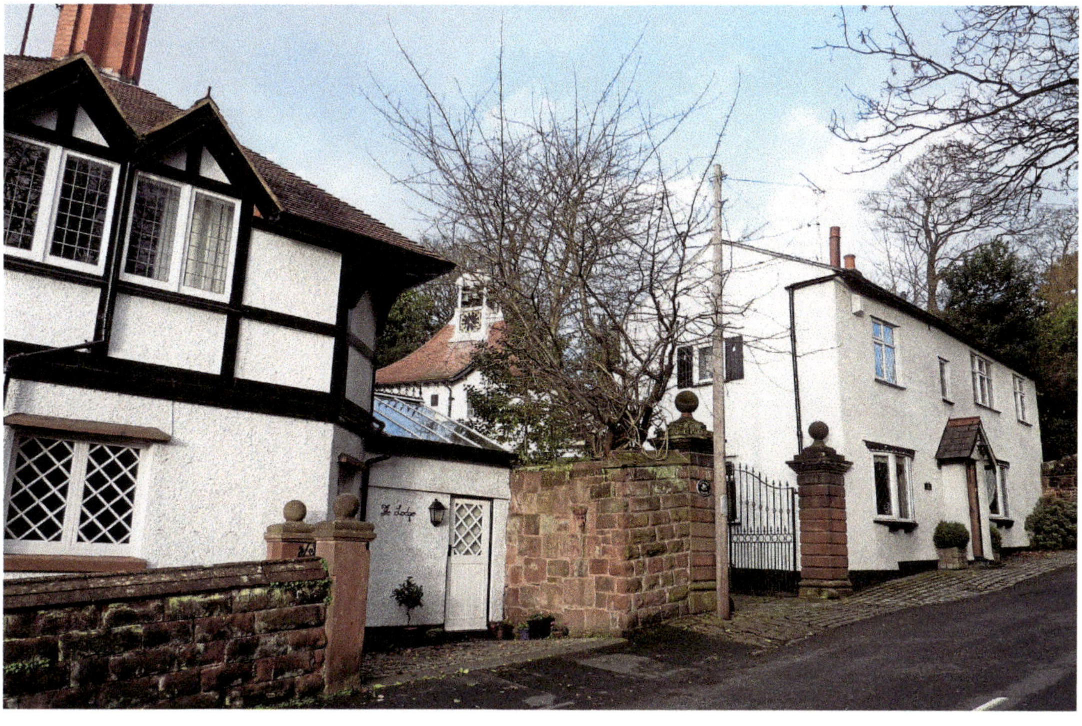

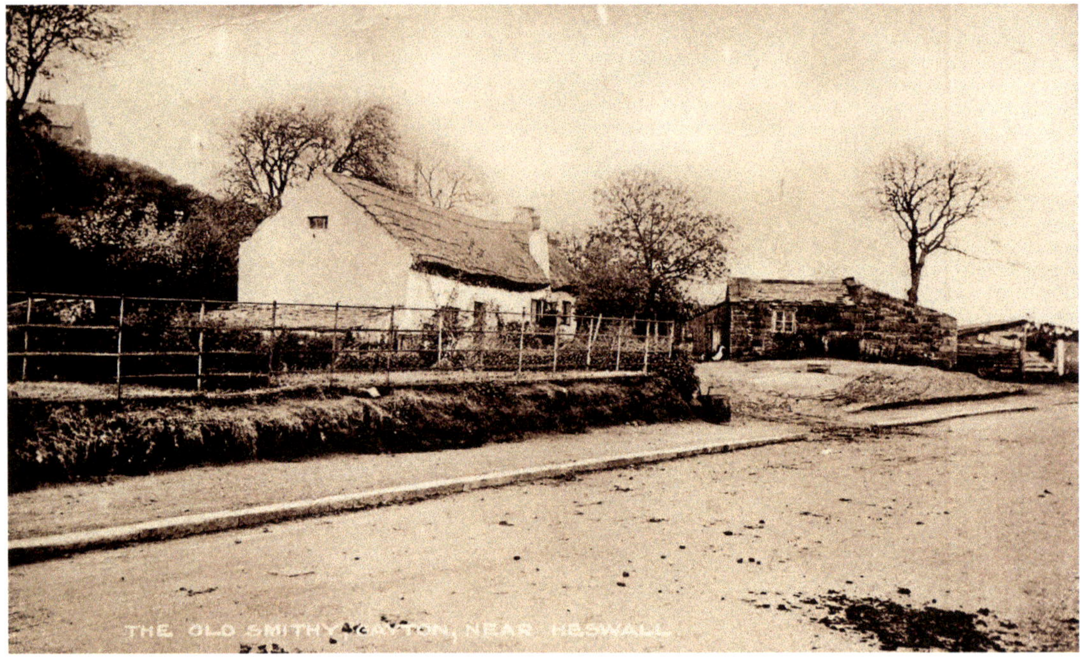

Old Smithy

Sandstone Walk, off Dawstone Road, is where Heswall smithy used to be. The smithy was on the left and the cottage on the right, and was owned by a branch of the Barlow family. Billy Barlow was the last blacksmith in 1964. One of the Barlow family is reputed to have shod King William the Third's horse when he visited Gayton Hall in 1690 en route to Ireland and the Battle of The Boyne.

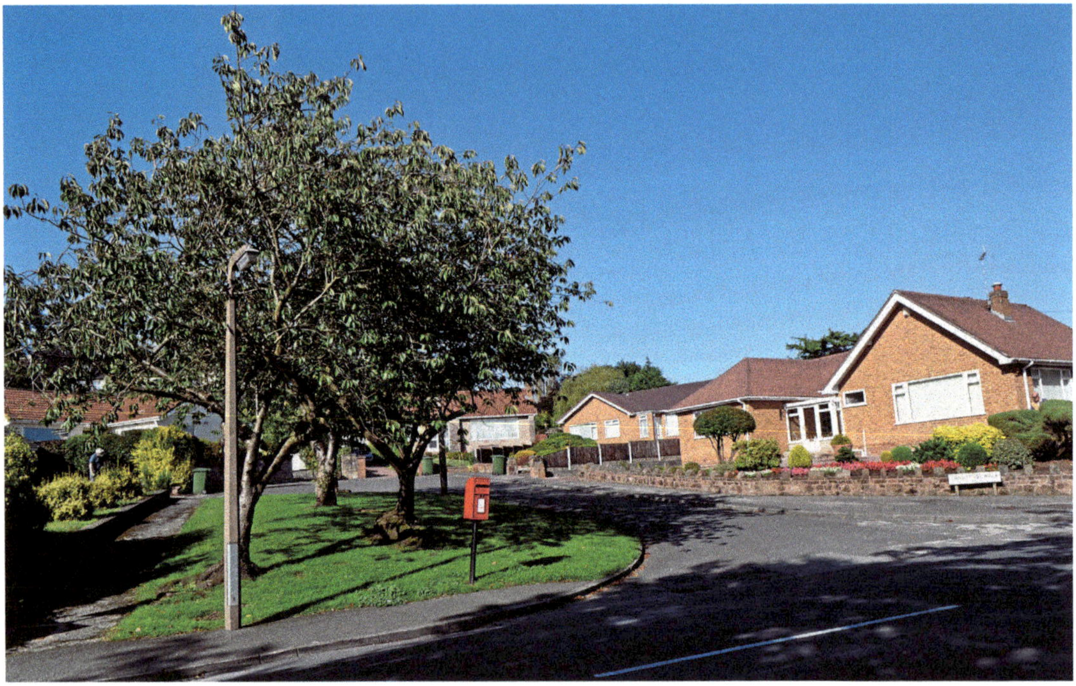

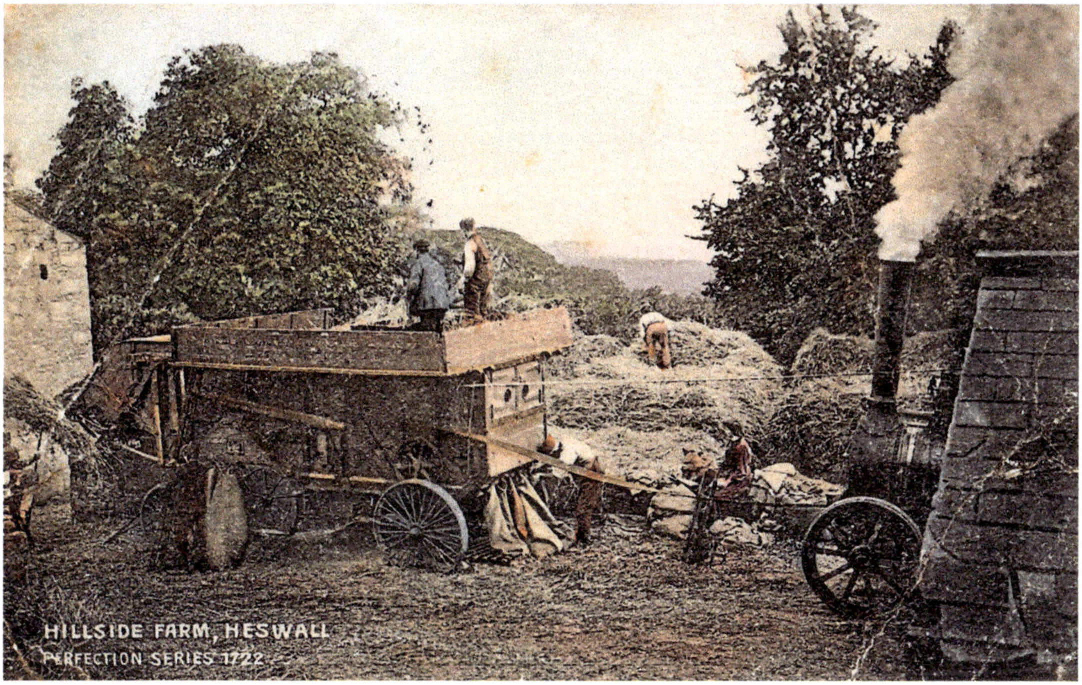

Hillside Farm

Hillside farm in Dawstone Road was tenanted by many local farmers, including the Lawtons. Part of the old farmhouse still exists within a more modern building. In common with many other local farms, the land has now been used for housing.

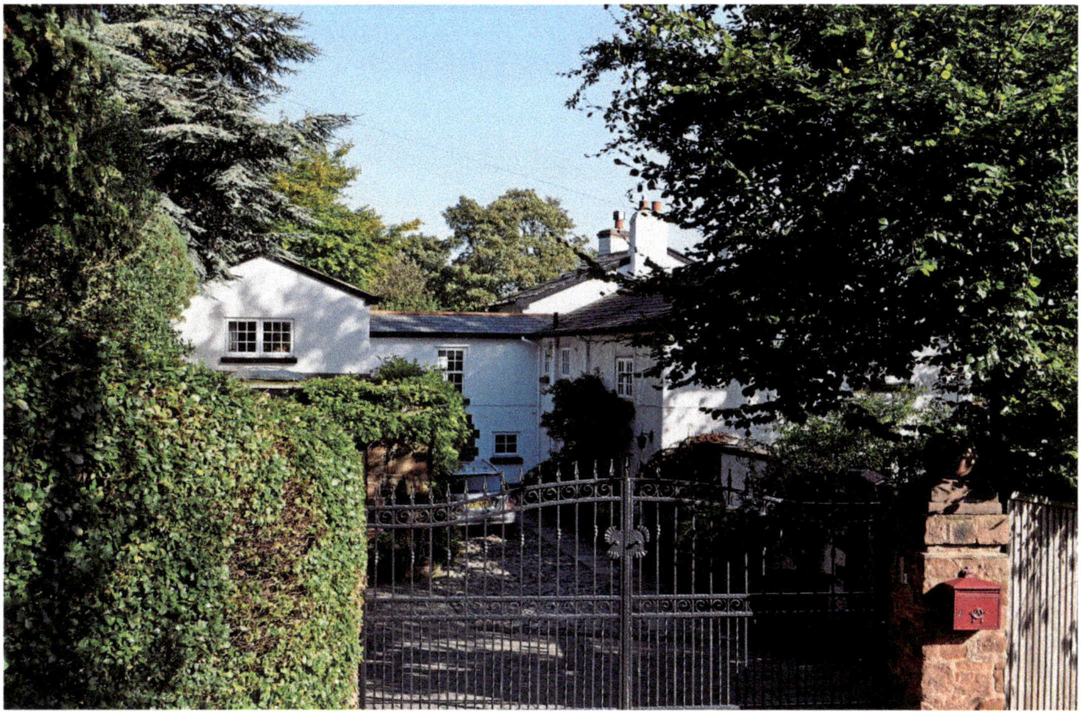

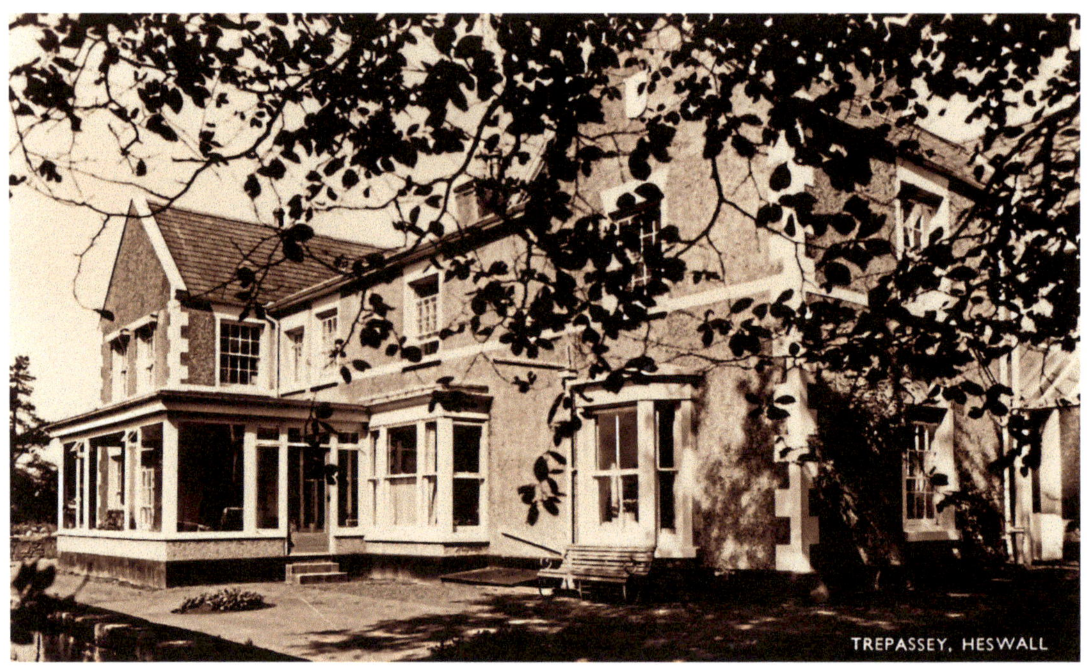

Trepassey, Hillside Road

Originally called Sunnyside, this house in 1911 had eighteen rooms and six servants when owned by Richard Brancker, a colliery owner. It was later owned by the Bowring family. Trepassey was bought for £5,600 in 1957 by the Cheshire Residential Homes Trust, and after an eight-bed extension had been built, opened in 1958 as a home for 'Persons of Limited Means' with twenty-four residents. Recently Trepassey benefitted from a most generous legacy from the estate of the late Donald Jardine, whose wife Doreen chaired the Trepassey Committee for many years, which has enabled the Trustees to embark on a major modernisation and expansion project.

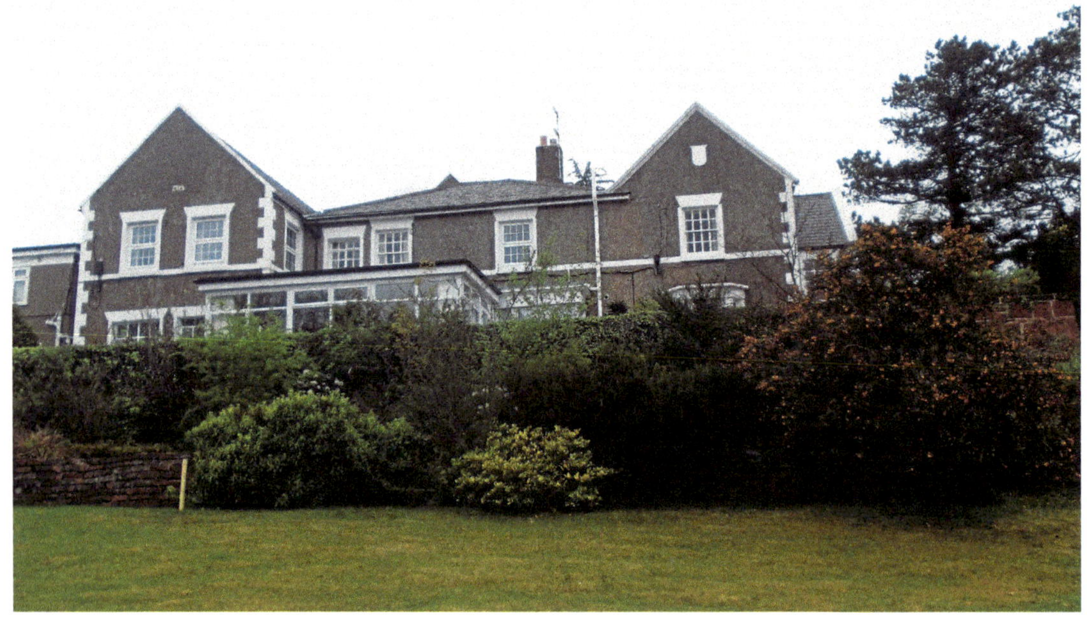

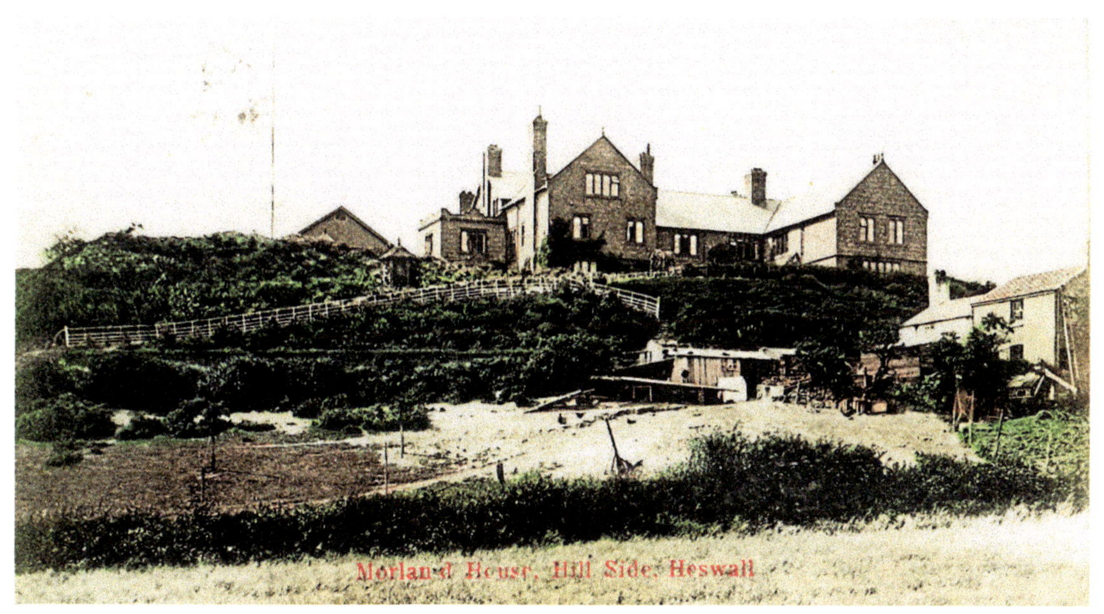

Moorland House School

Moorland House School, or Dobie's College as it was known, was in College Road, now Hillside Road, from 1893 to the 1970s. Built for Mr Leonard Dobie, the headmaster, 'For the education of the sons of Gentlemen', it was a preparatory boys' boarding school. It boasted a chapel, tennis courts, swimming pool and a science laboratory. The land in the foreground of this picture was the school playing fields, now Moorland Park.

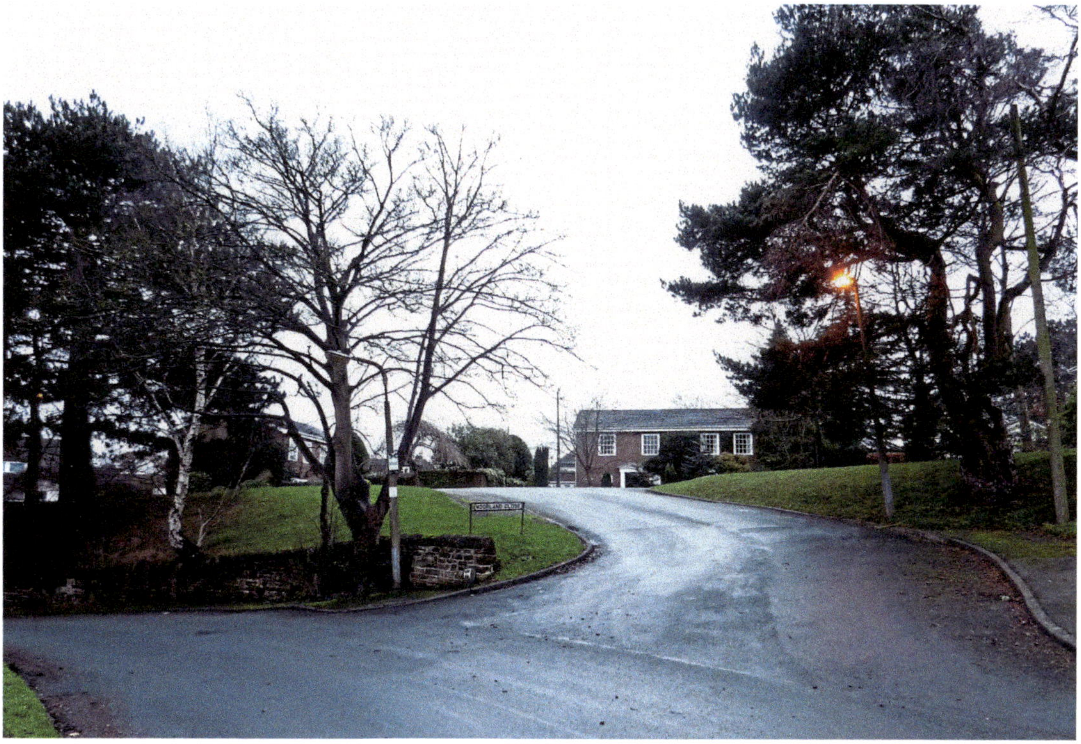

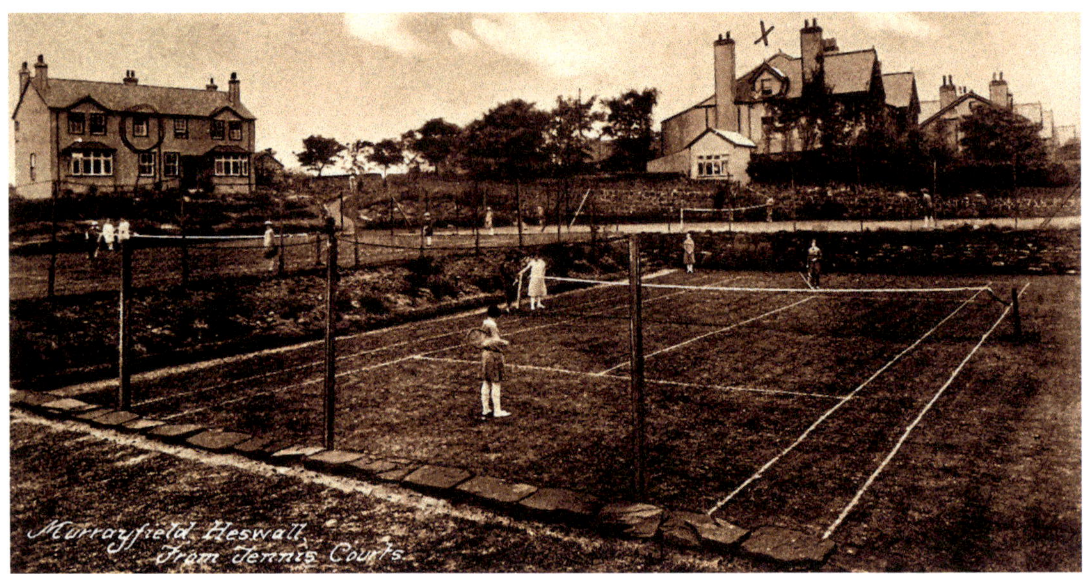

Murrayfield School

Mr Newsom lived in Brandenburgh, South Drive, and was concerned that there was no girls' boarding school in Heswall for the sisters of those boys at Moorland House. He bought the neighbouring house to his, and Murrayfield School was started in 1911. Miss Whittall was the first headmistress. The school closed in the 1970s. BUPA was interested in the site to build a hospital, but it proved to be too small, so they decided instead to build in Holmwood Drive, Thingwall, but retained the Murrayfield name. The honours board from the school can still be seen in the hospital.

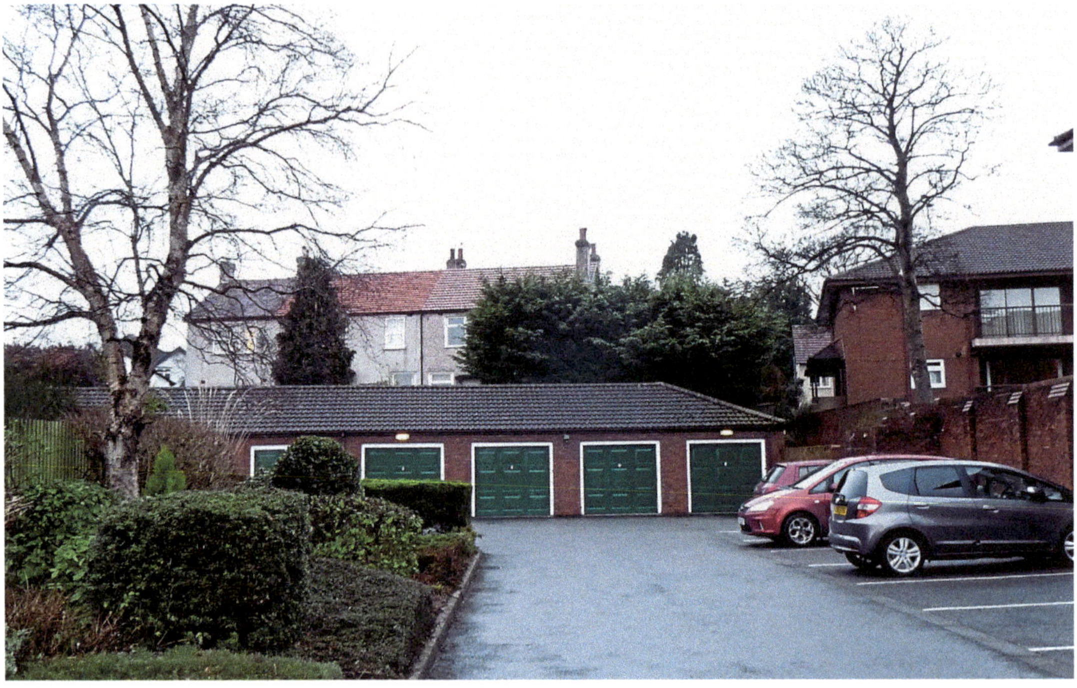

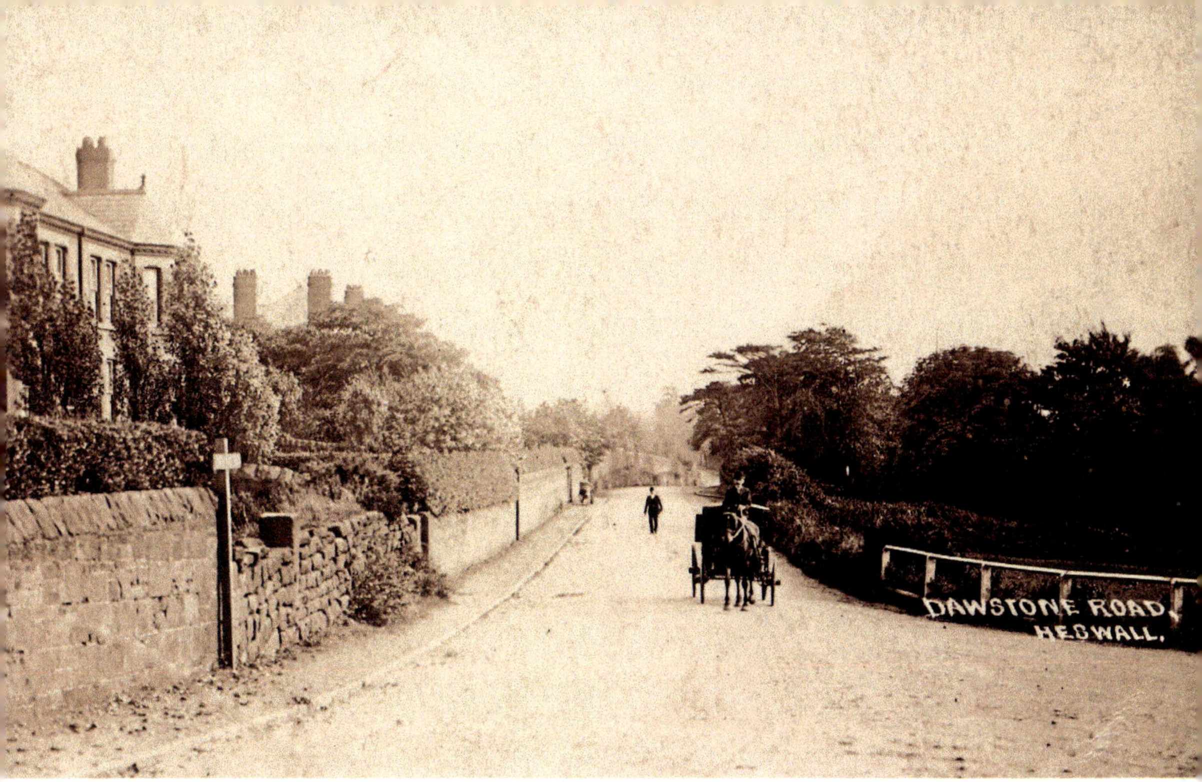

Dawstone Road

These views are separated by over a century, but apart from the mode of transport, the top end of Dawstone Road is remarkably unchanged, characterised by walls made of locally quarried red sandstone. Dawstone Park and the war memorial now lie on the right.

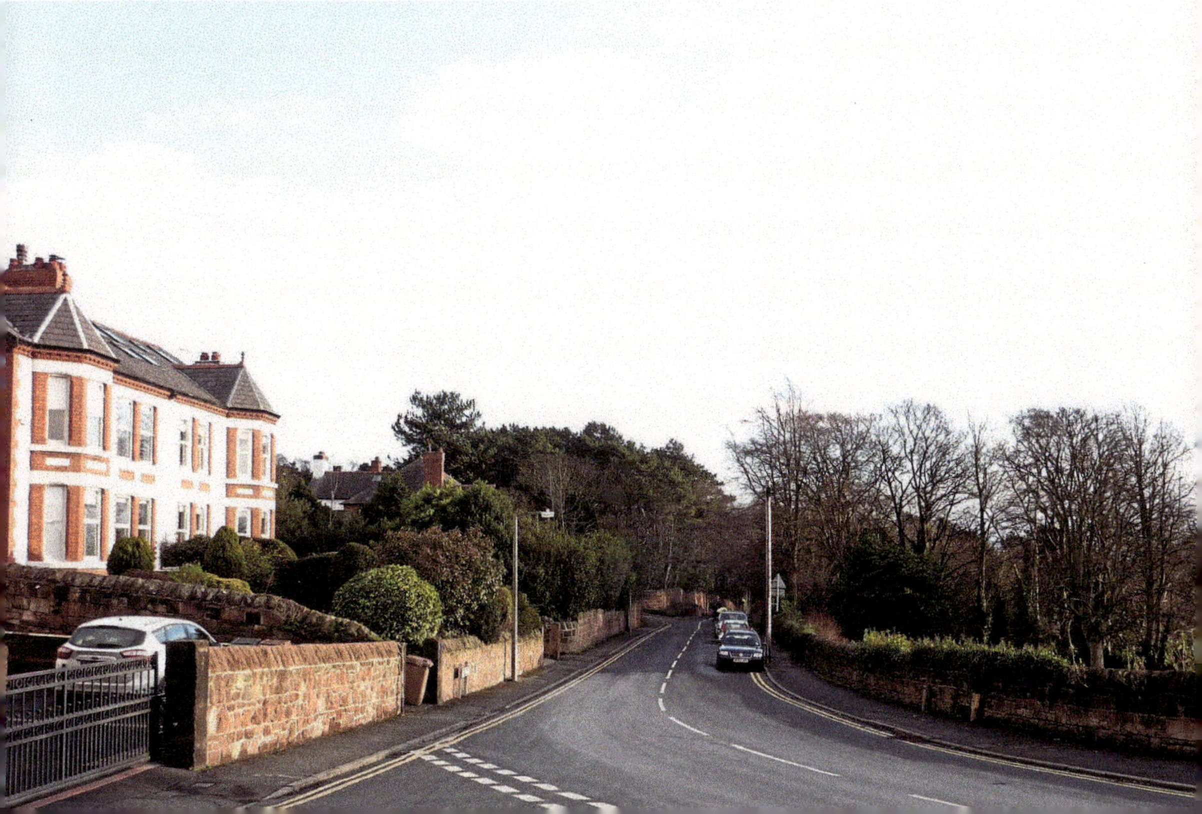

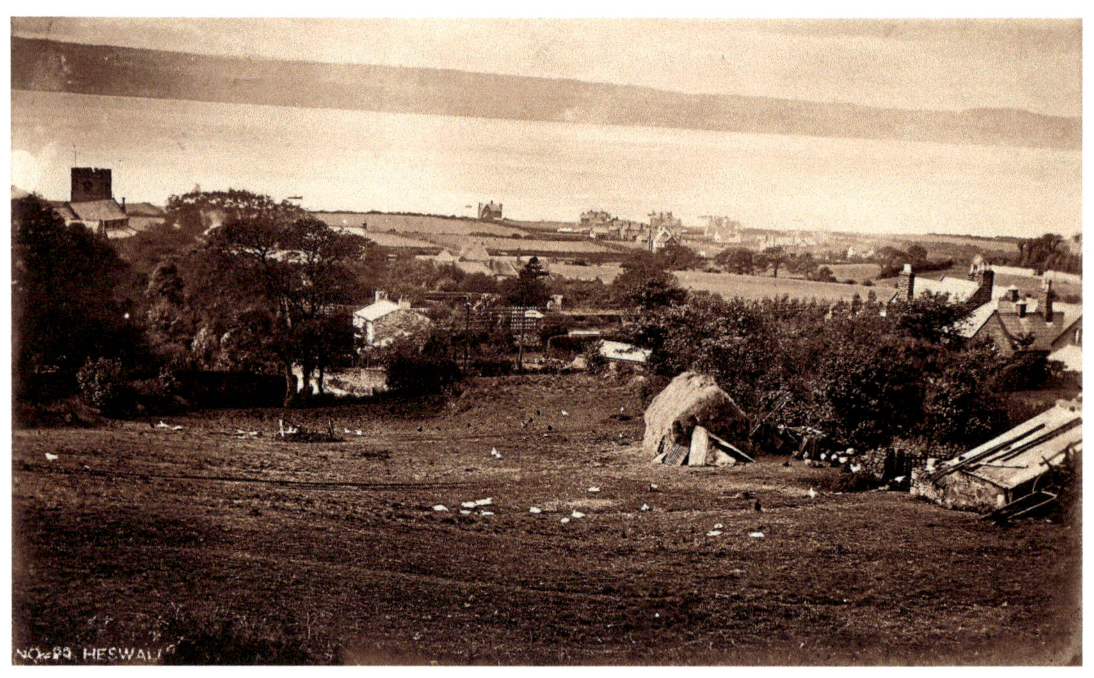

Ned Swift's Field

Named after a local man who farmed the land, the Heswall cum Oldfield Parish Council had this field made into Dawstone Park for the benefit of the people of Heswall in 1931. A commemorative stone listing the names of the council at that time can still be found in the boundary wall.

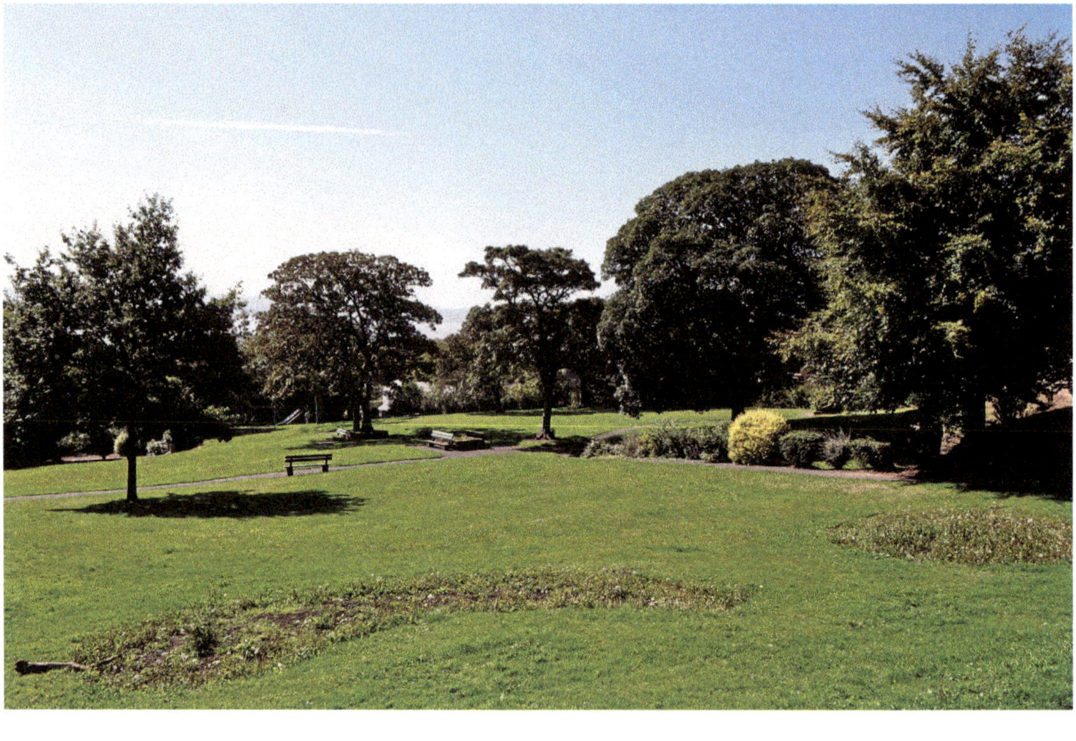

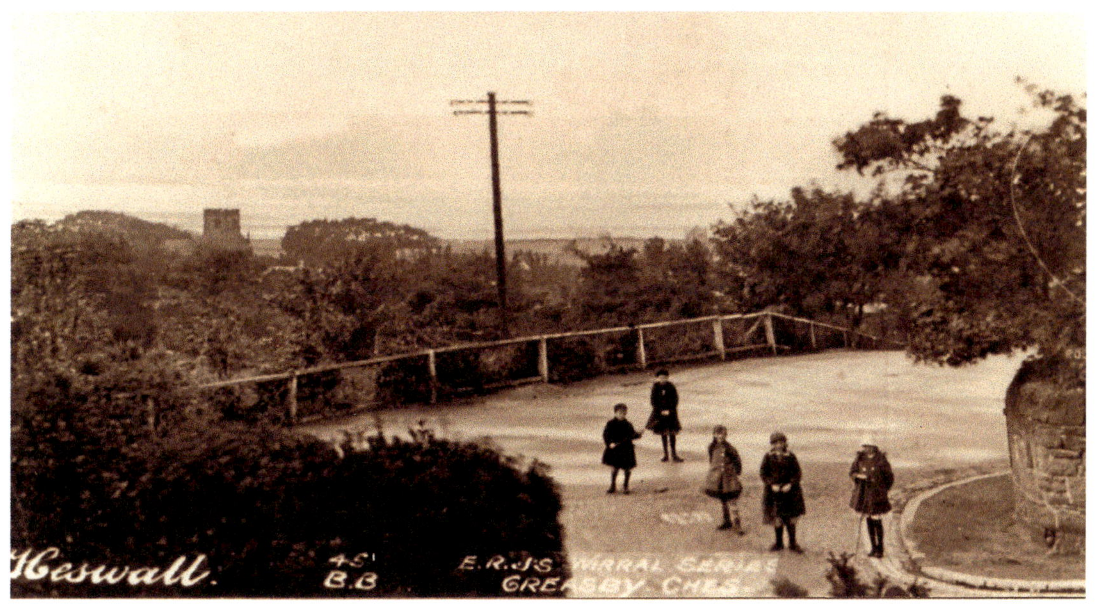

Site of the War Memorial

This old photograph was taken before 1924 when the Heswall war memorial was erected at the top of Dee View Road. It was unveiled by Mrs Peter Campbell, whose husband, along with over seventy other young men from Heswall, lost their lives in the First World War. The children are standing at the junction of Rocky Lane, Dawstone Road, Dee View Road and The Mount.

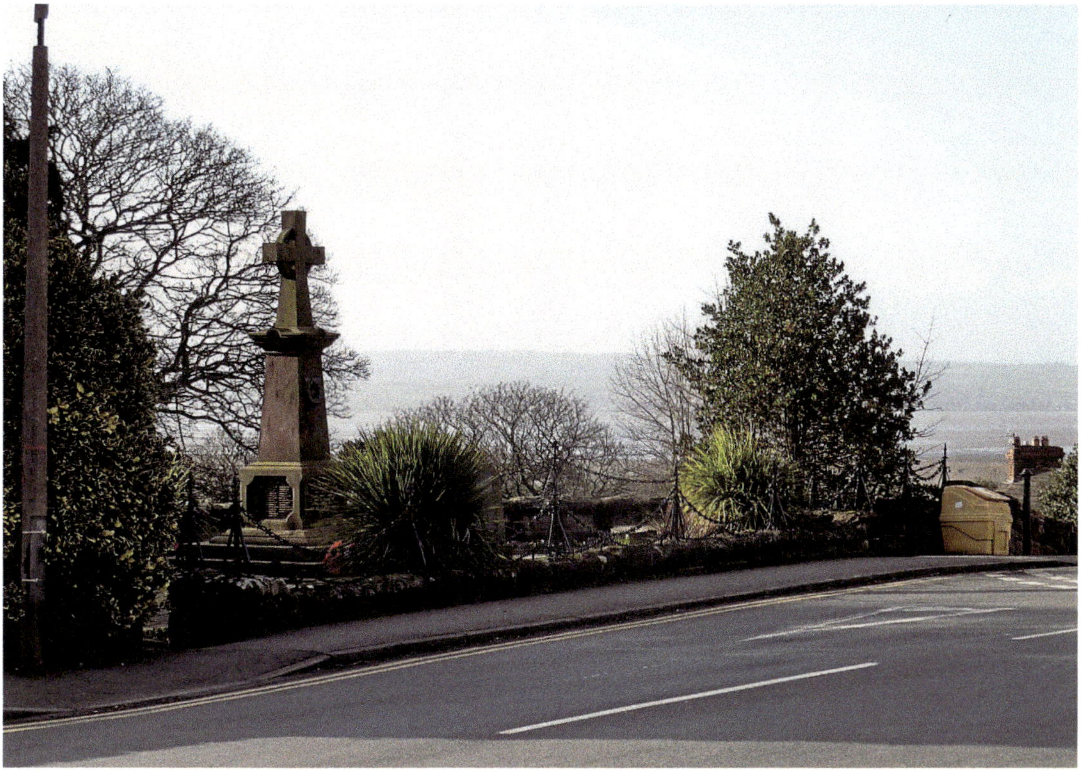

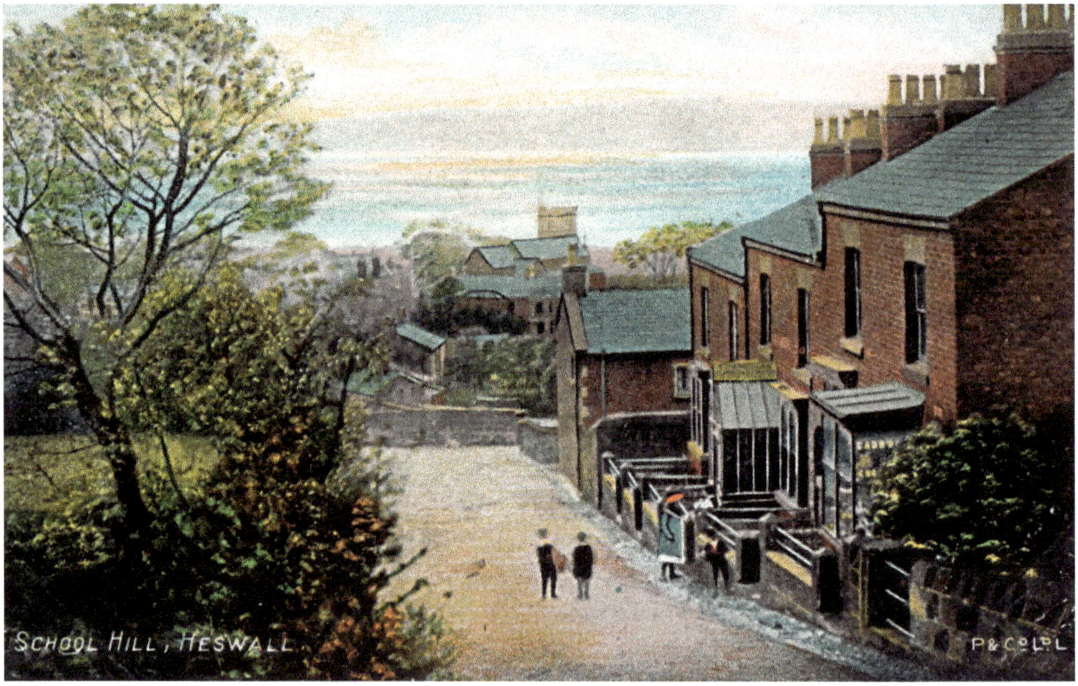

School Hill Looking Down

There is little change in this picturesque view down to the Lower Village and River Dee from the top of School Hill, except that the shop in the first cottage is no longer there.

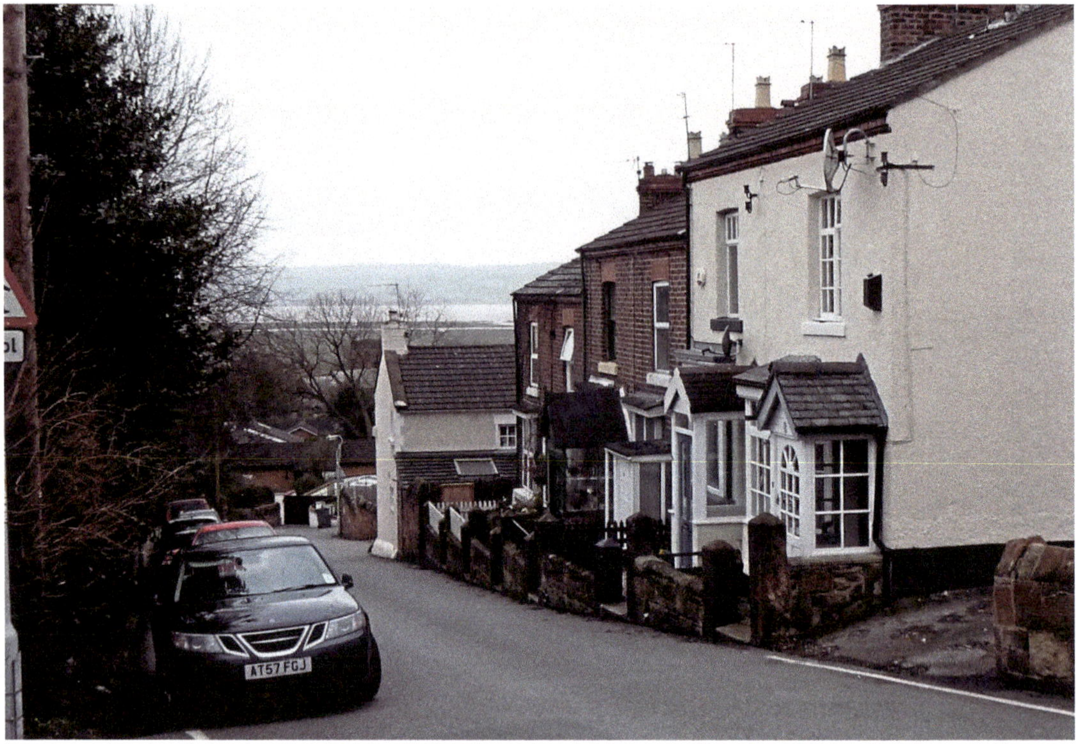

Brow Lane

Running from School Hill up to Rocky Lane, this was the original route from the Lower Village to Birkenhead. The cottage, occupied for many years by Mr Tarbuck, and the coach house beyond, were part of the 'Dawstone' estate, which originally extended to 8 acres.

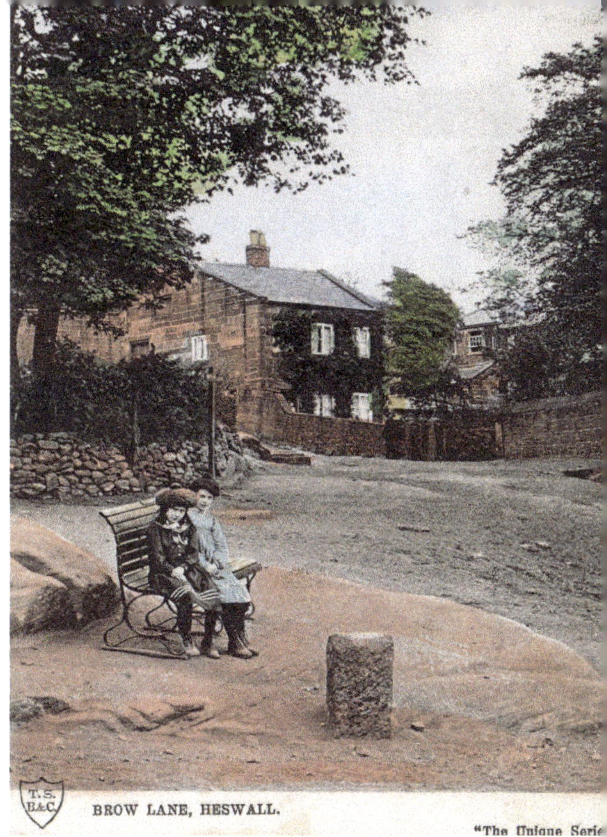

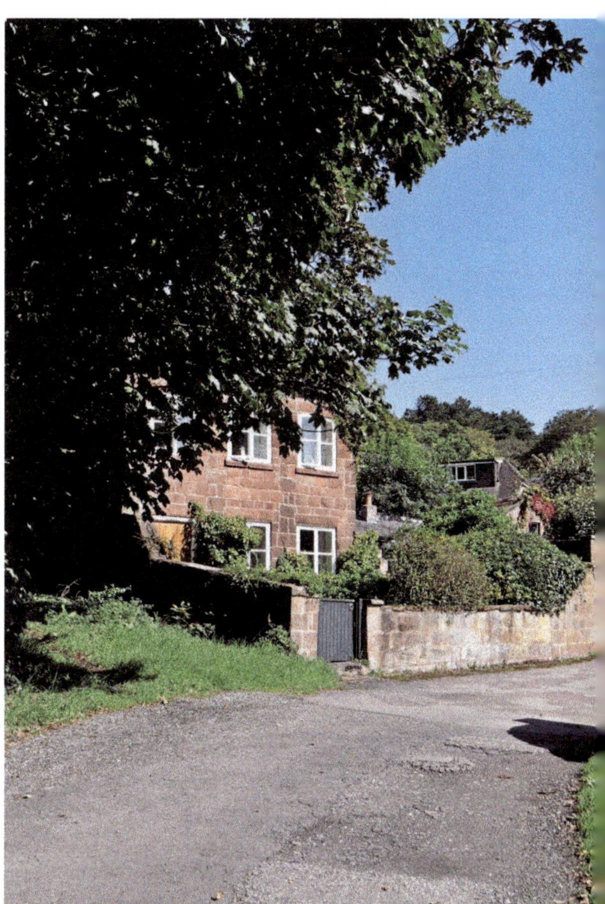

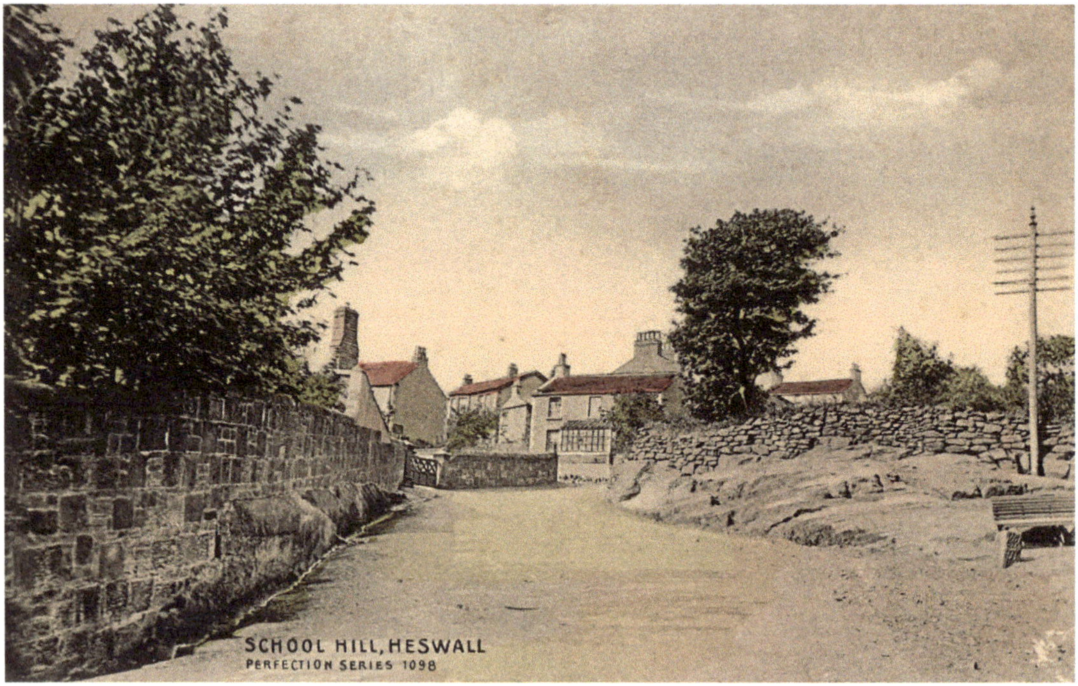

School Hill Looking Up
The stone building on the left, now known as Richmond Hall, is all that remains of the original Heswall Church School.

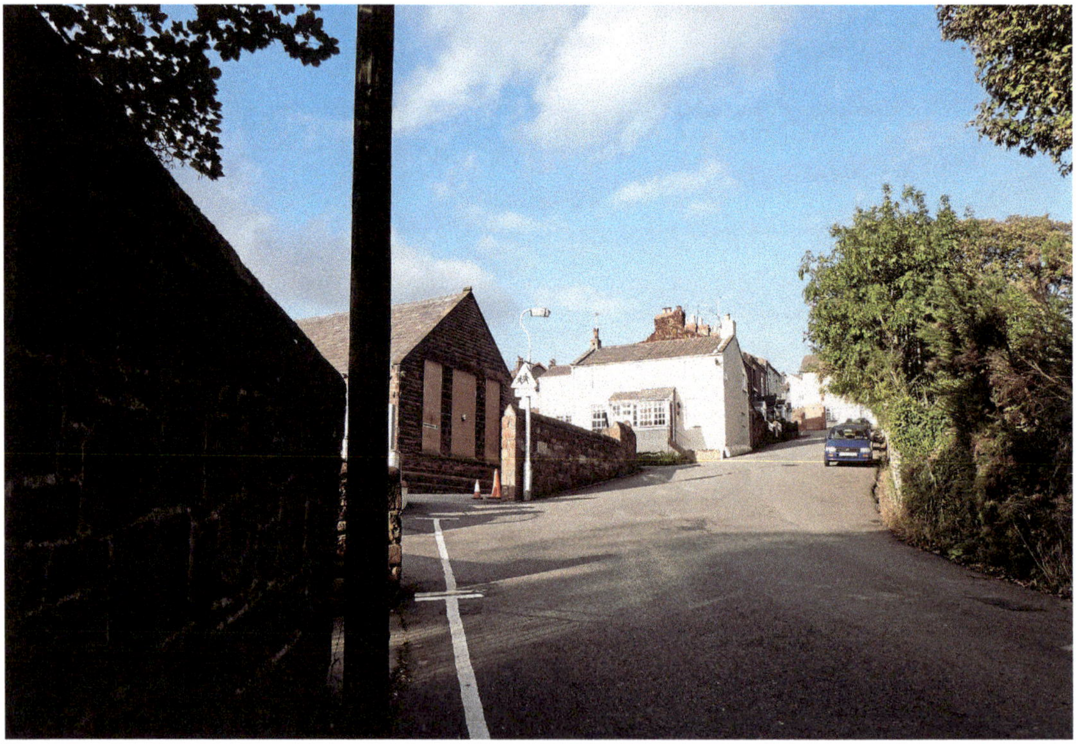

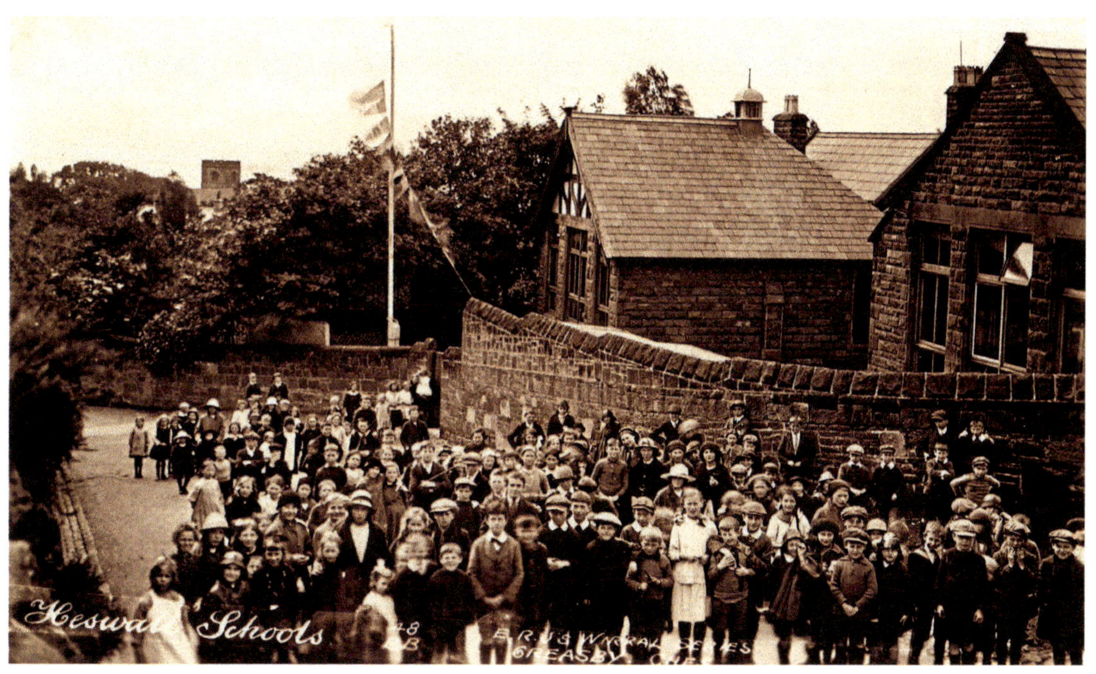

Heswall Church School, School Hill

This school replaced Elder Cottage dame school to cater for the increase in population. It was opened in 1872 on School Hill, on land donated by Sir William Bromley Davenport. In June 1941, the headmaster's house behind the school was badly damaged by a bomb and two people were killed. In 1961, a replacement church school, St Peter's Primary School, was opened in Thurstaston Road.

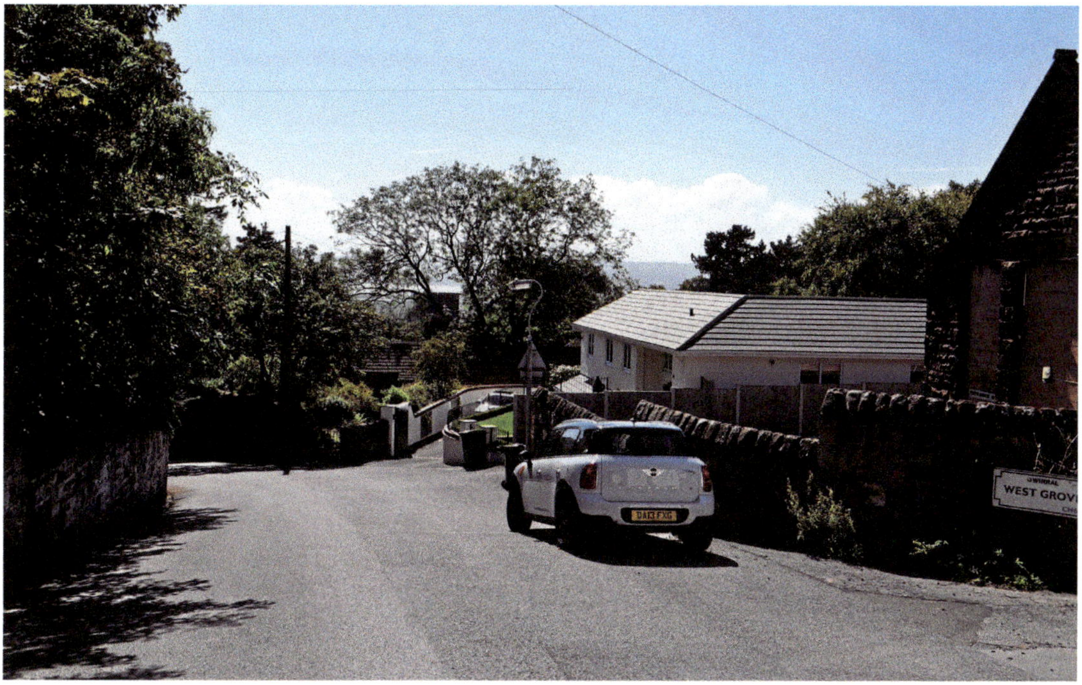

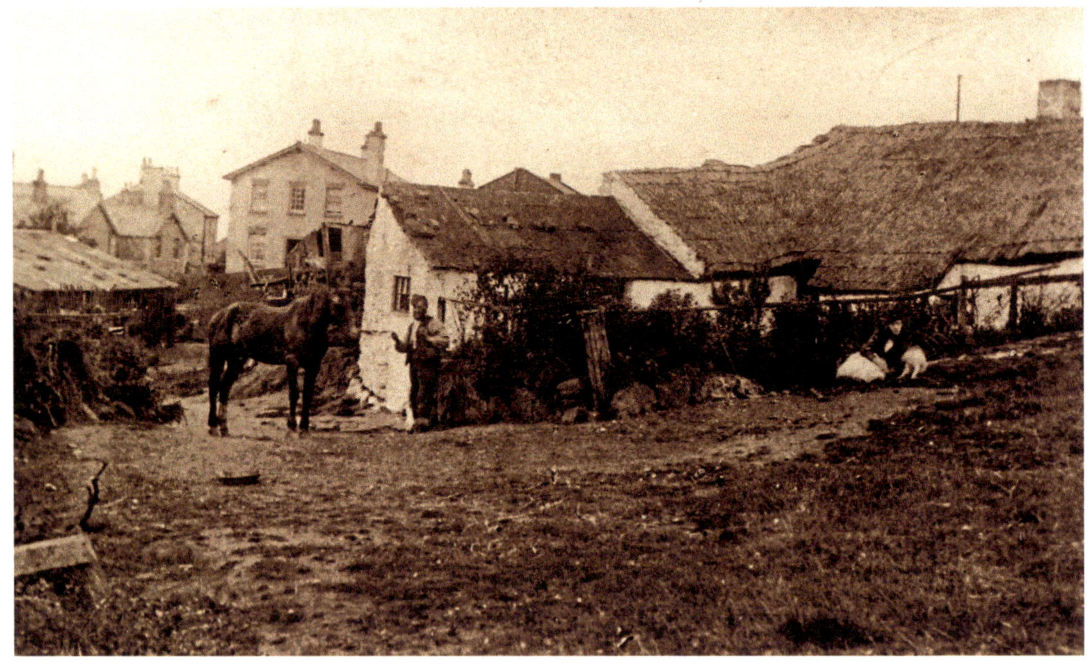

Herbert's Smallholding

This was on the corner of Rocky Lane and Dawstone Road. The roof of the Dee View Inn can be seen on the far left, with Holywell House next to it. The Herbert family also had a farm in Downham Road South. The plot is now occupied by houses.

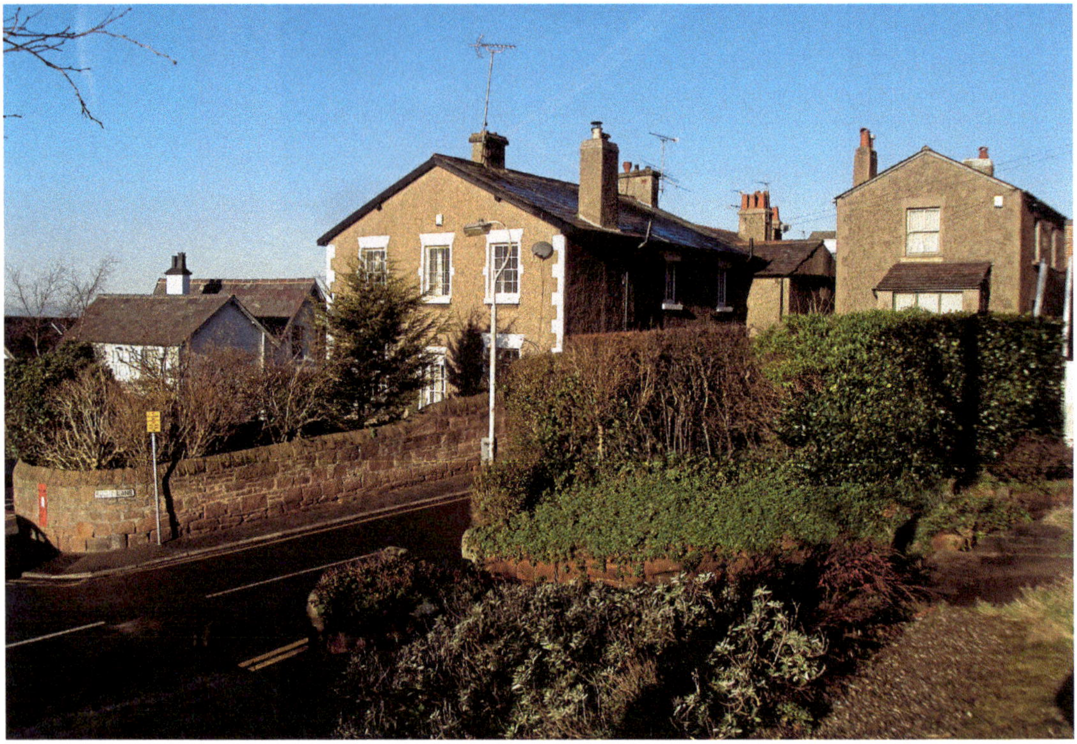

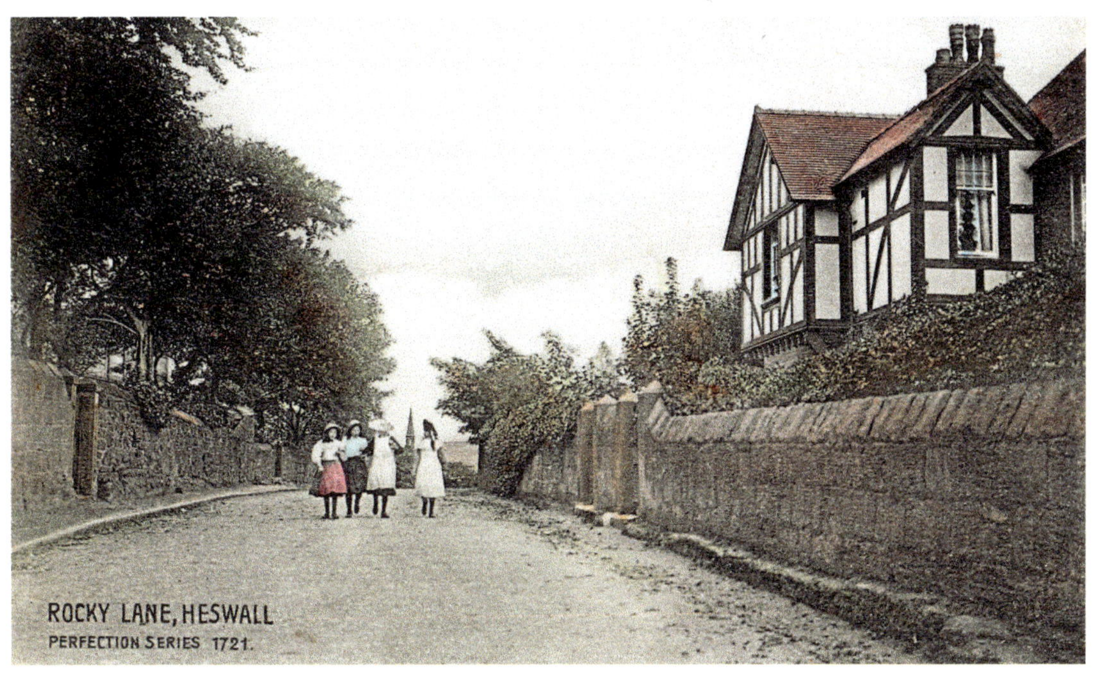

Rocky Lane

This part of Rocky Lane used to be known as Hill House Road. Hill House, now the Jug and Bottle, lies over the wall on the left. The spire of the Methodist church is just visible in both pictures.

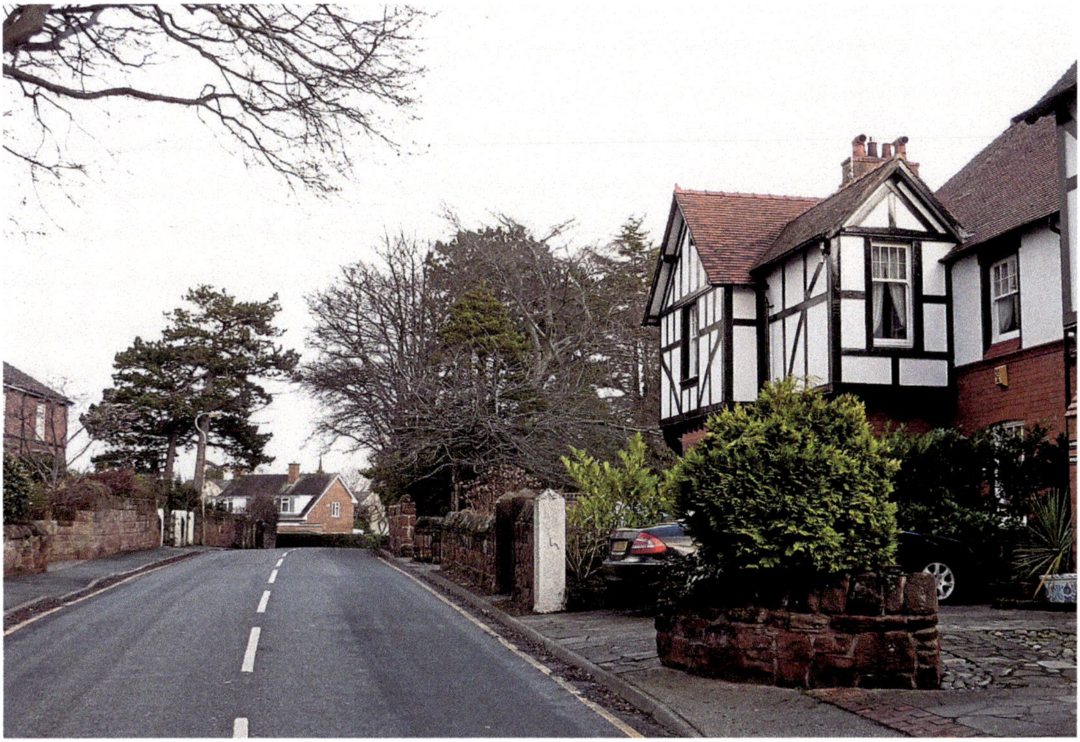

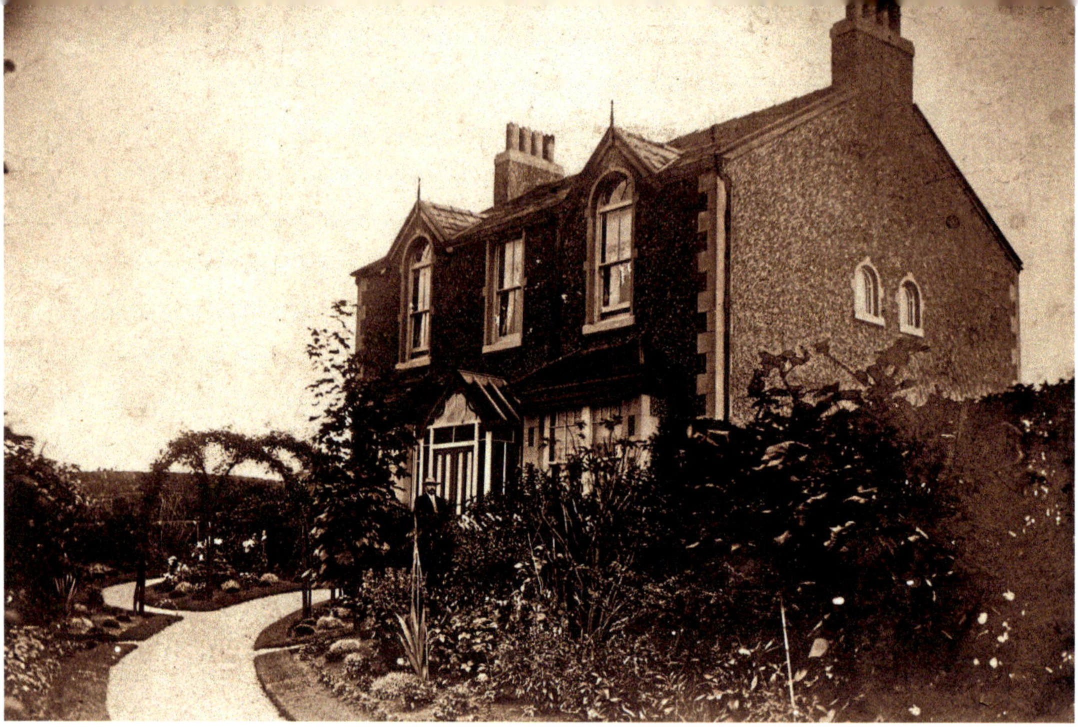

The Brambles, Rocky Lane

Situated on the corner of Rocky Lane and Beacon Lane, this house is over 100 years old and was at one time called 'Bramble Cottage'. It was the home of the Kelly family, who owned the bakery at Heswall Cross.

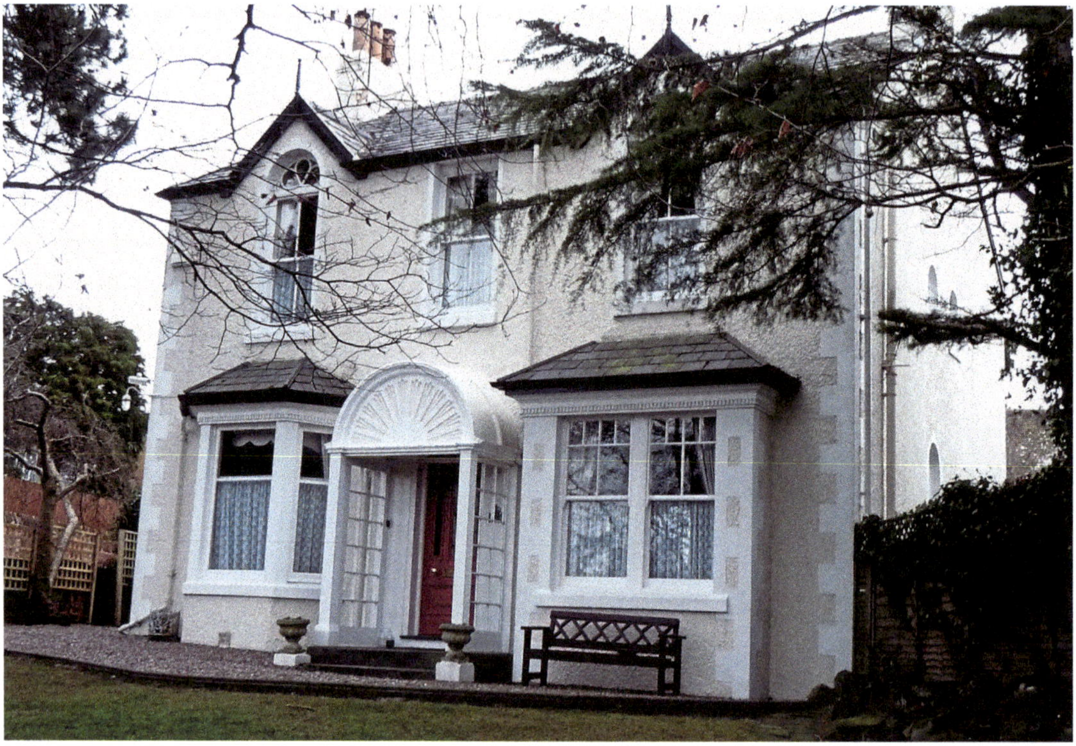

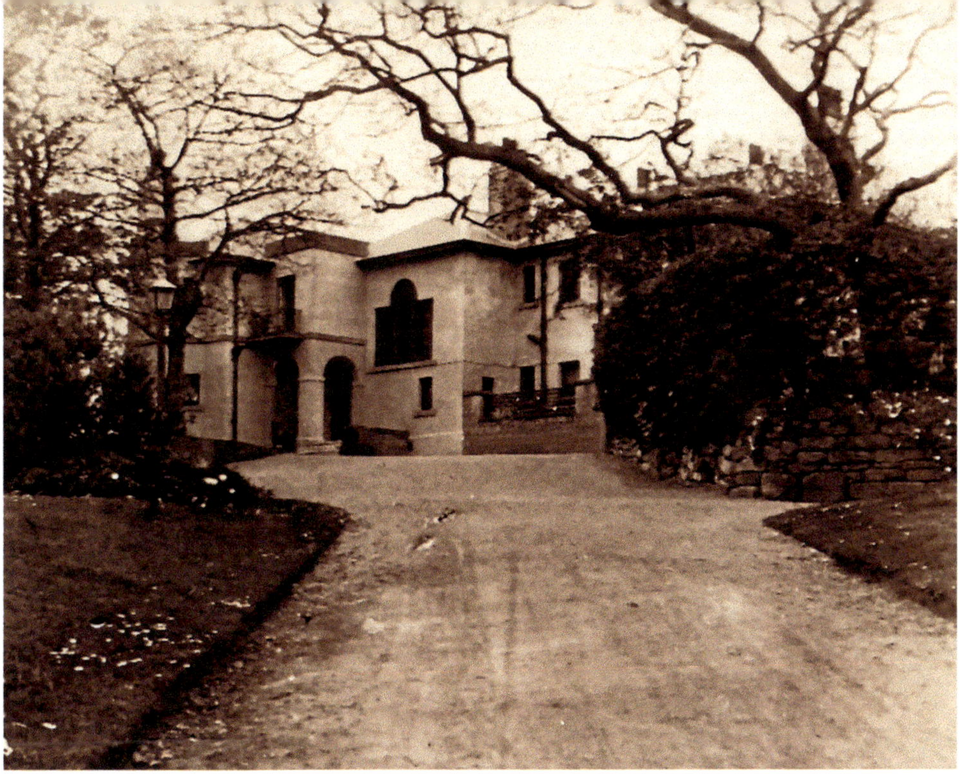

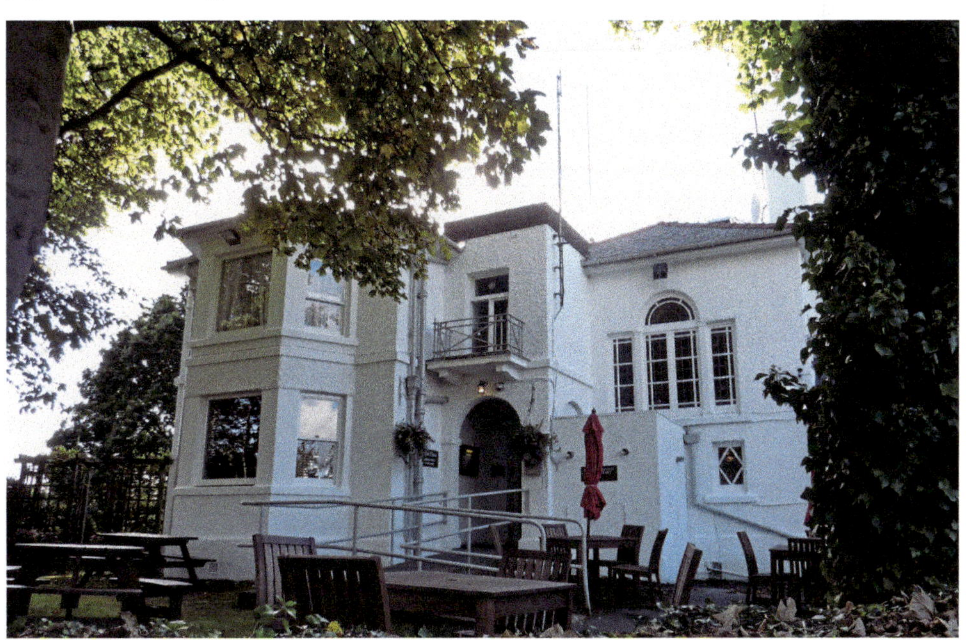

Hill House

Originally called 'Heathmount', and enjoying a commanding position with views over both the Dee and the Mersey, it was built by a Liverpool merchant in the early 1800s. Bought by Maj. Pooley in 1921, he later sold it to Wirral Urban District Council in 1935 for use as its offices. In 1985, it became a hotel called Hill House, and changed its name to the Jug and Bottle in 1992.

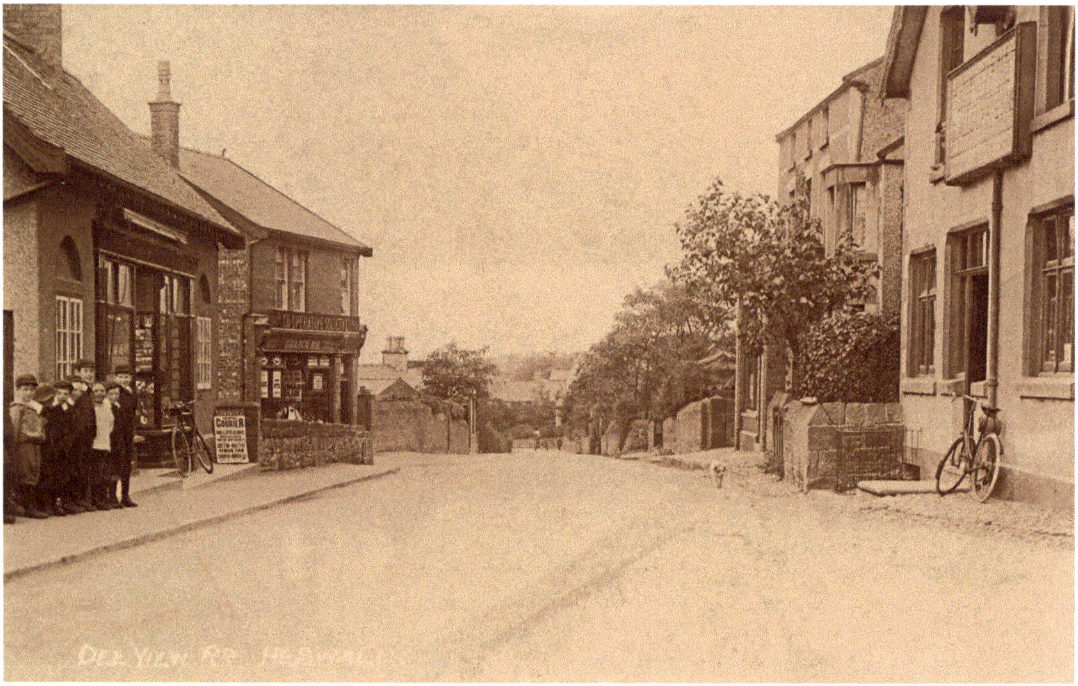

Dee View Road

On the right is the Dee View Inn, with an off licence on the site of the current car park. The newsagent and Co-operative shops opposite are now converted to private houses.

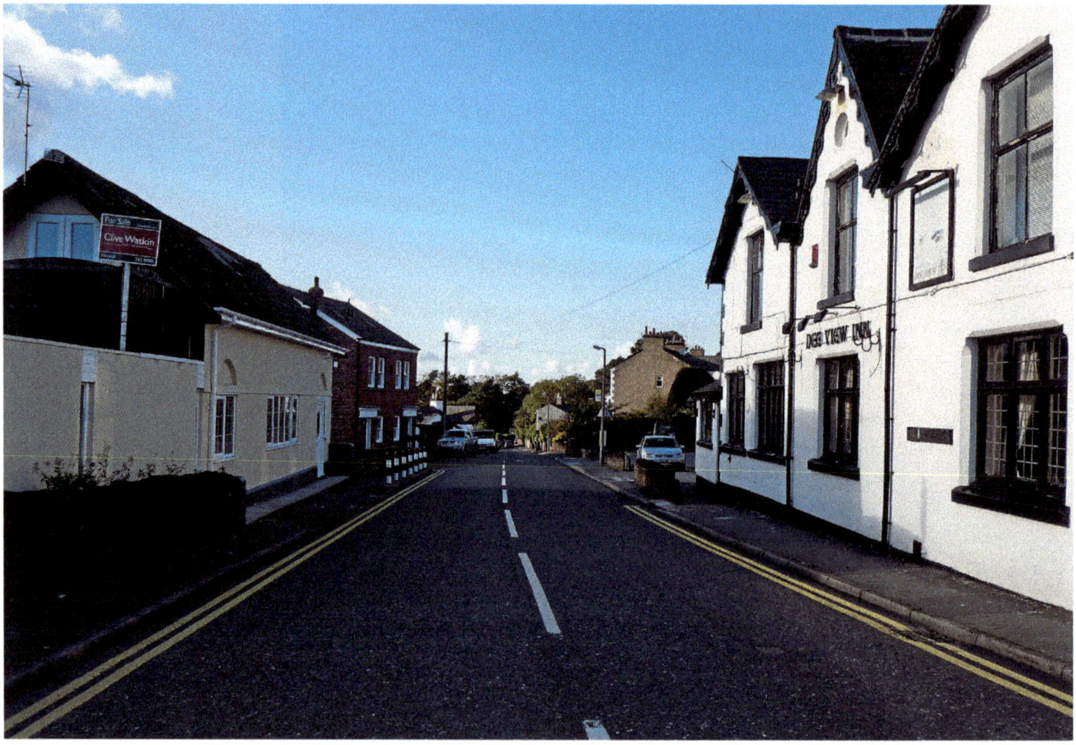

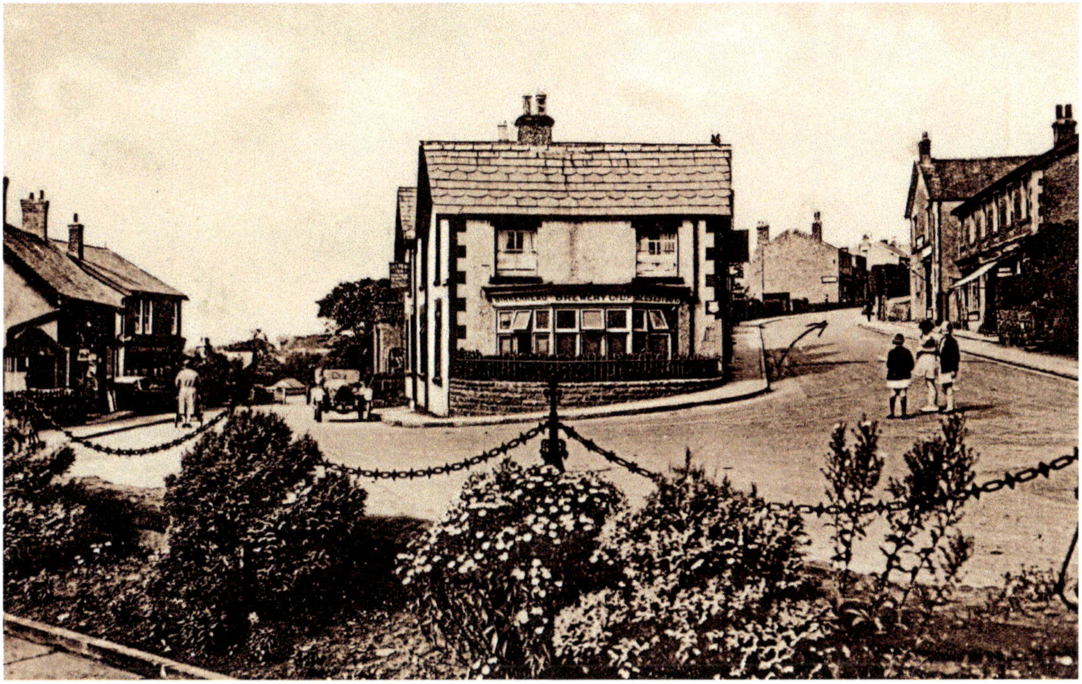

Dee View Inn and The Mount

As viewed from the war memorial, the hairpin bend required to build the road between the Lower and Top Villages is clearly visible. The Assembly Rooms, an important social venue (seen on the right), and the neighbouring shops are now private dwellings.

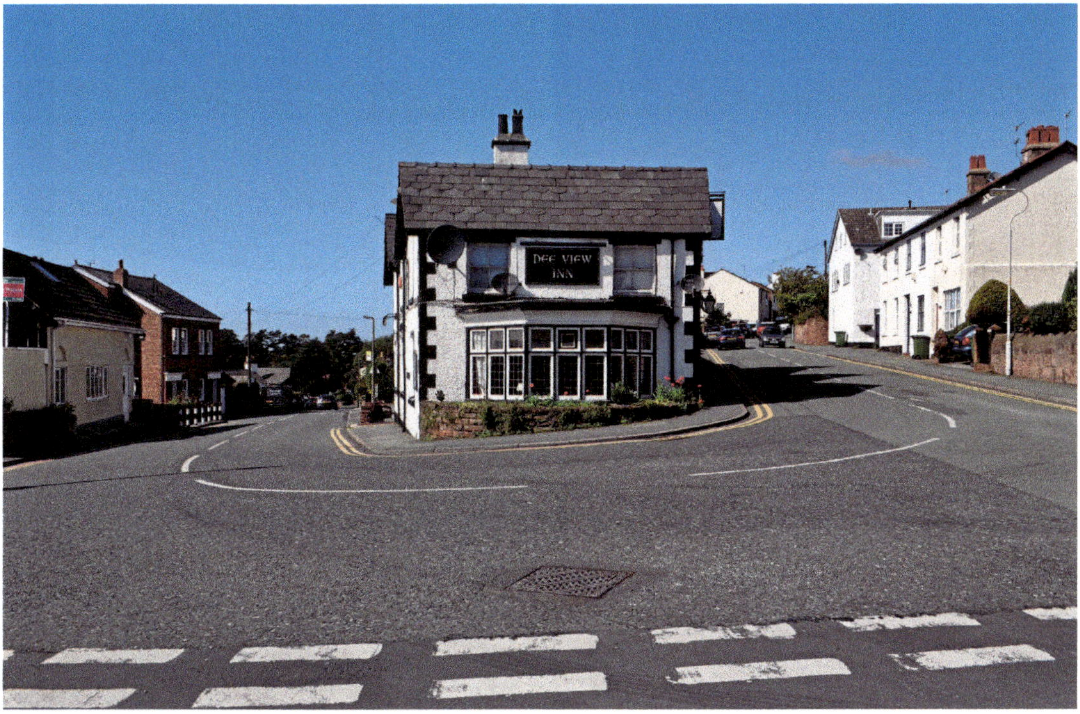

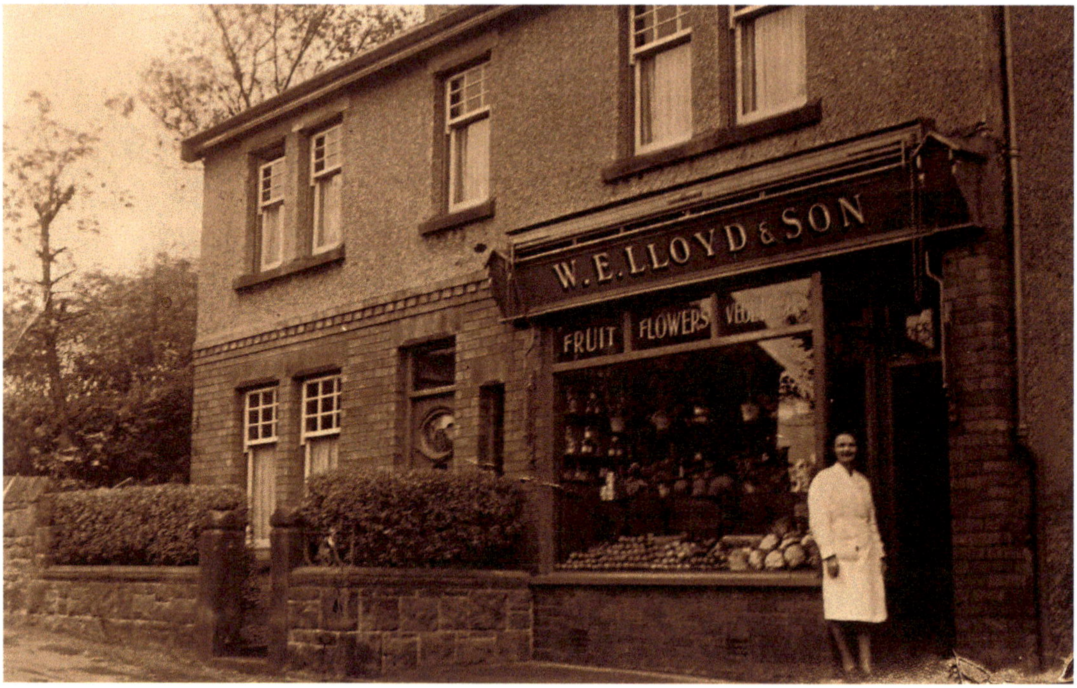

Lloyd's Shop, The Mount

Now Carlton House, this was once a greengrocer's called Lloyd's, who took over the business from the Birch family, who lost a son in the First World War.

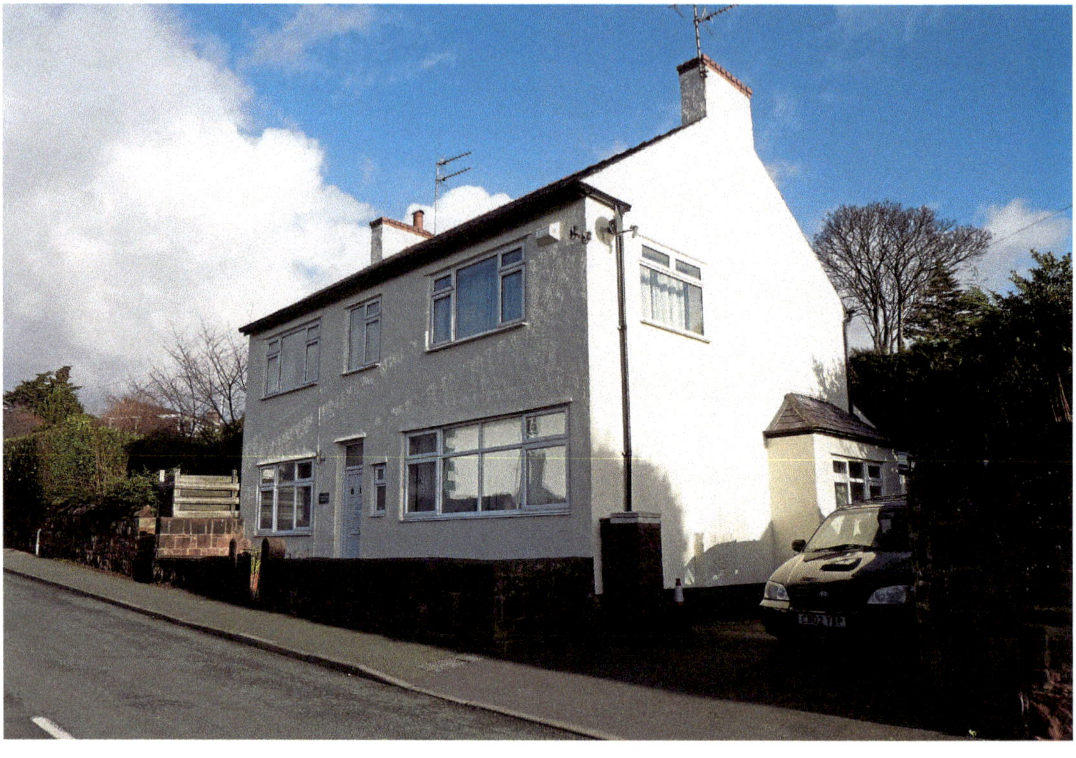

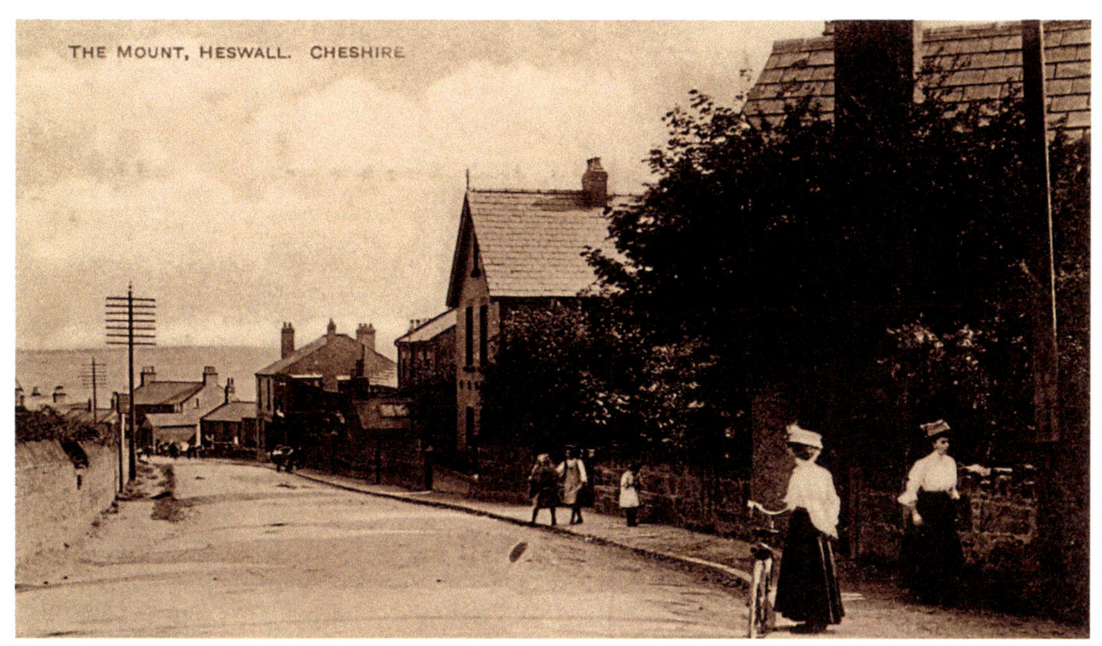

Looking Down The Mount

Looking down The Mount towards the war memorial, the buildings on the right are still easily recognisable today. Apart from the absence of cars, and the clothing of the ladies and children, little has changed.

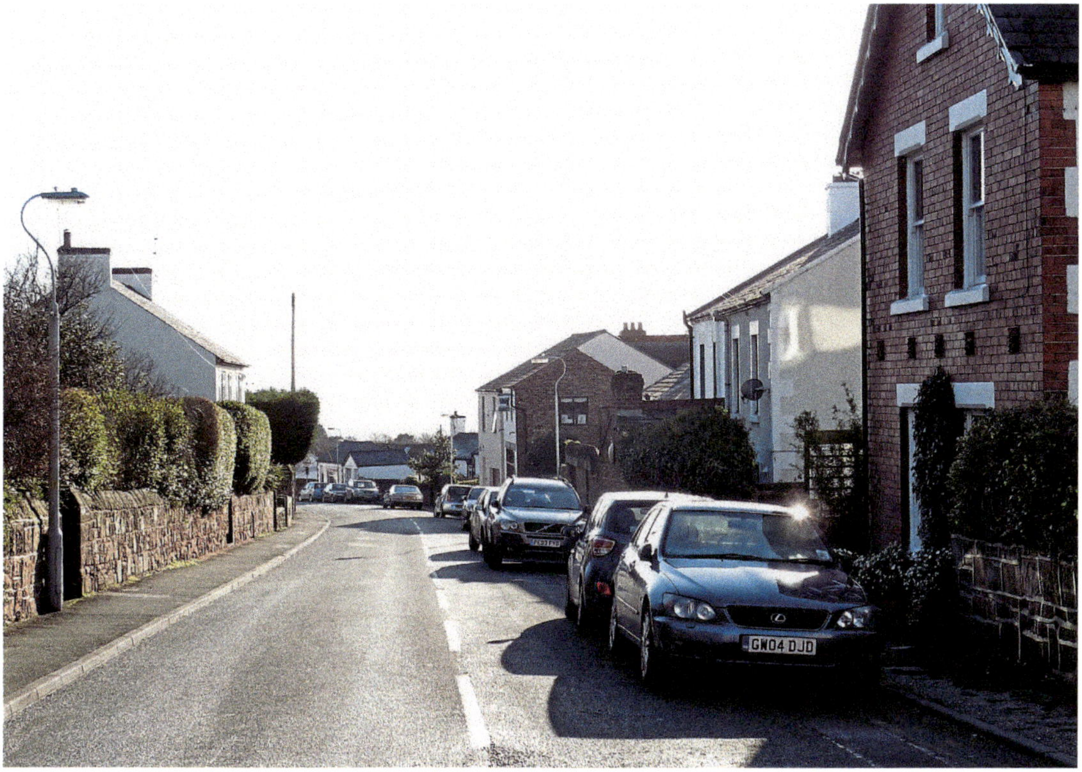

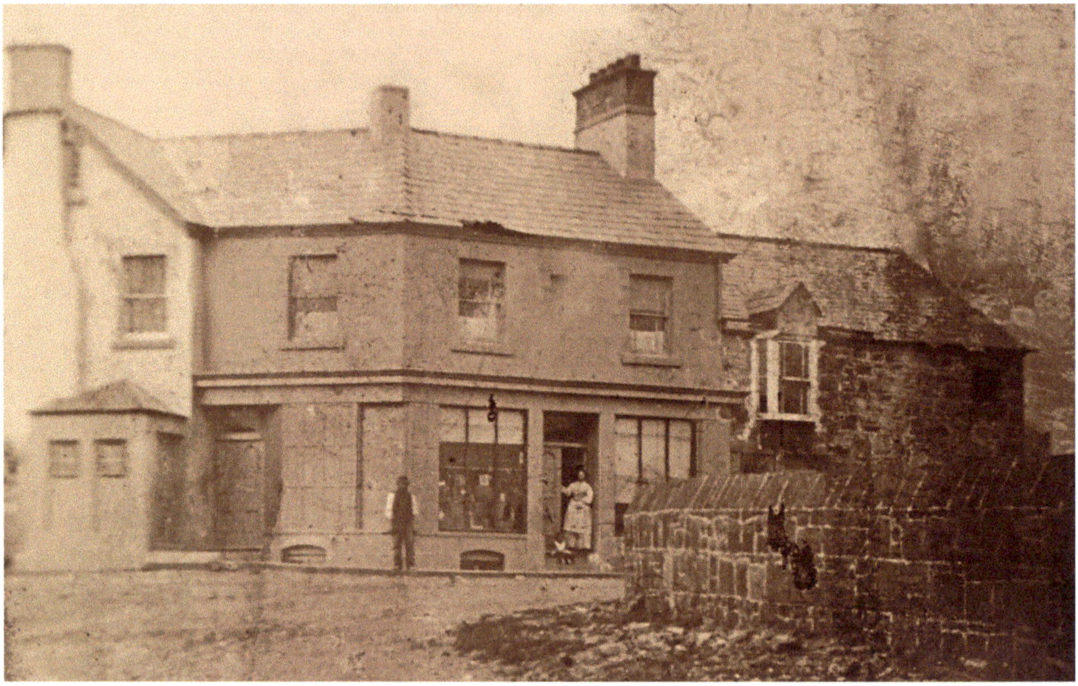

Rockland Stores, The Mount

These buildings were on the corner of The Mount and Feather Lane, and have now been replaced by a block of flats – Mount Court. It was originally Rockland Stores. In 1911, Richards & Lewis had a grocers and provision merchants here, and later it was also Swift's Coal merchants.

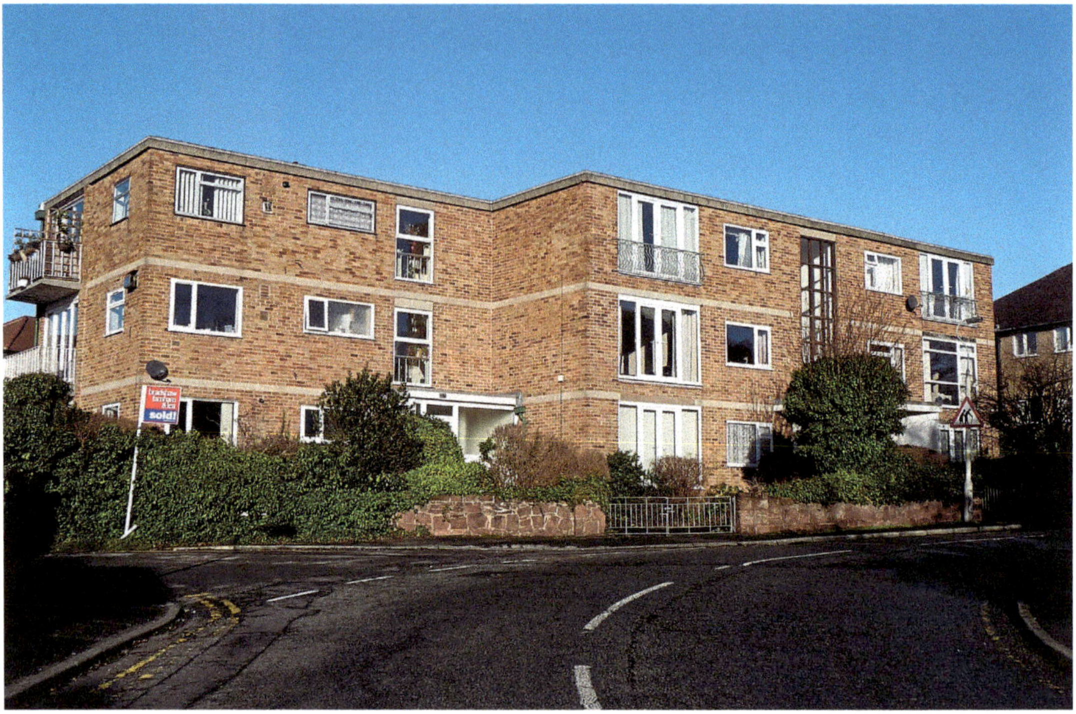

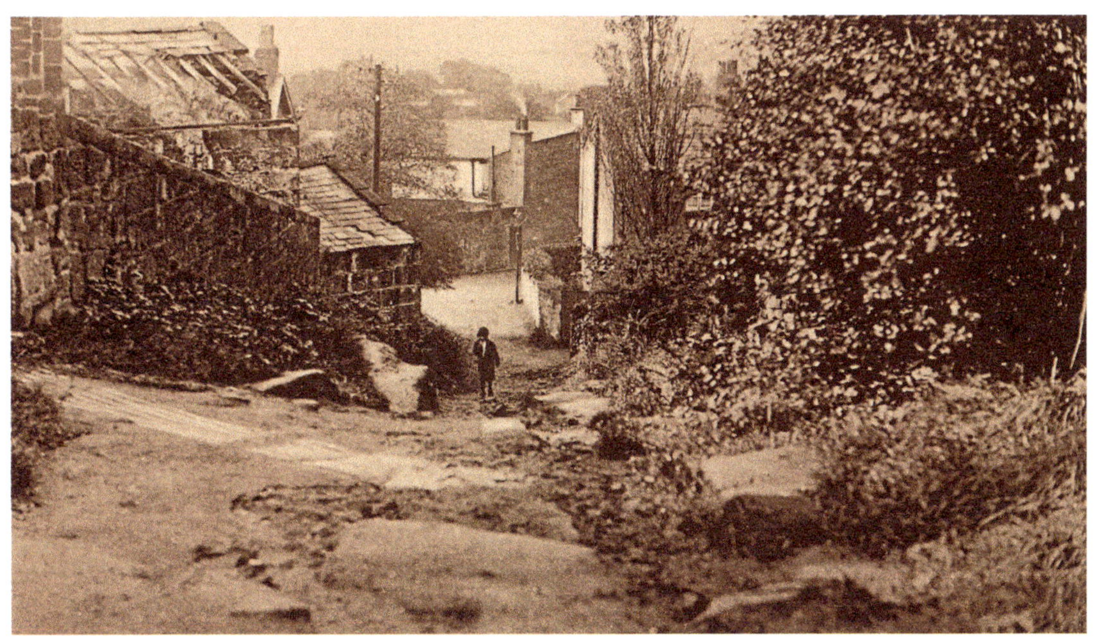

The only changes here are the modern concrete steps to make walking from The Mount to Dee View Road easier. Known locally as Swift's Rocks, after the Swift family who lived in 'The Nest' situated halfway down these steps, it was also known as Featherbed Lane, being a favourite haunt at night for itinerants.

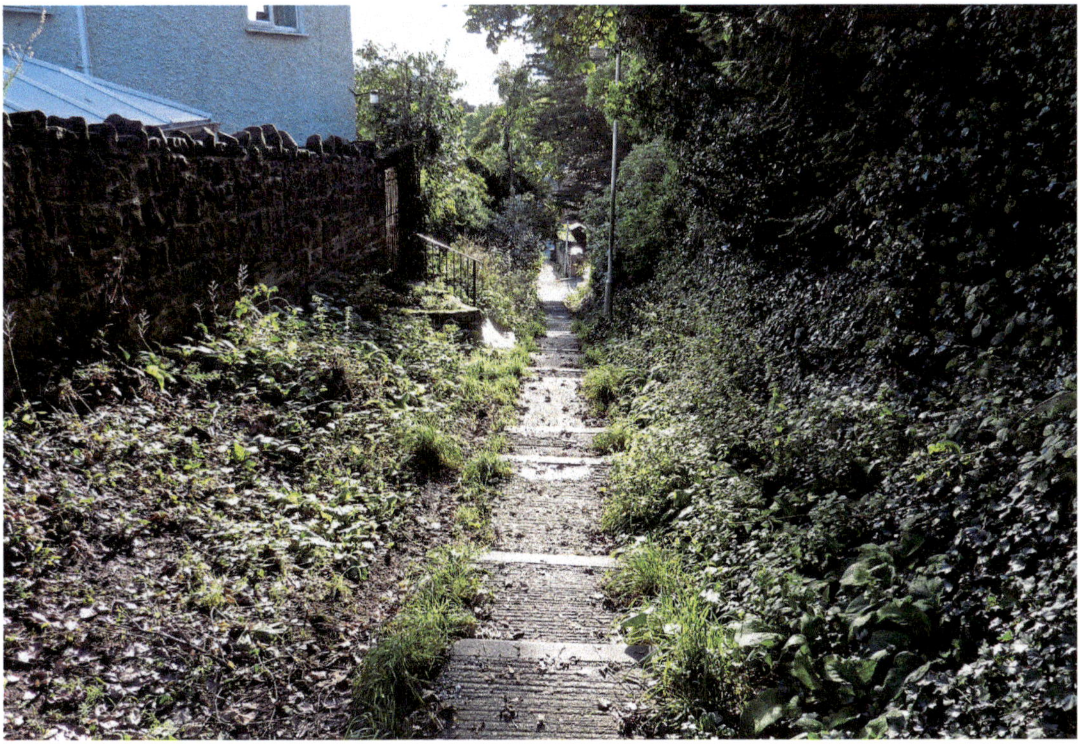

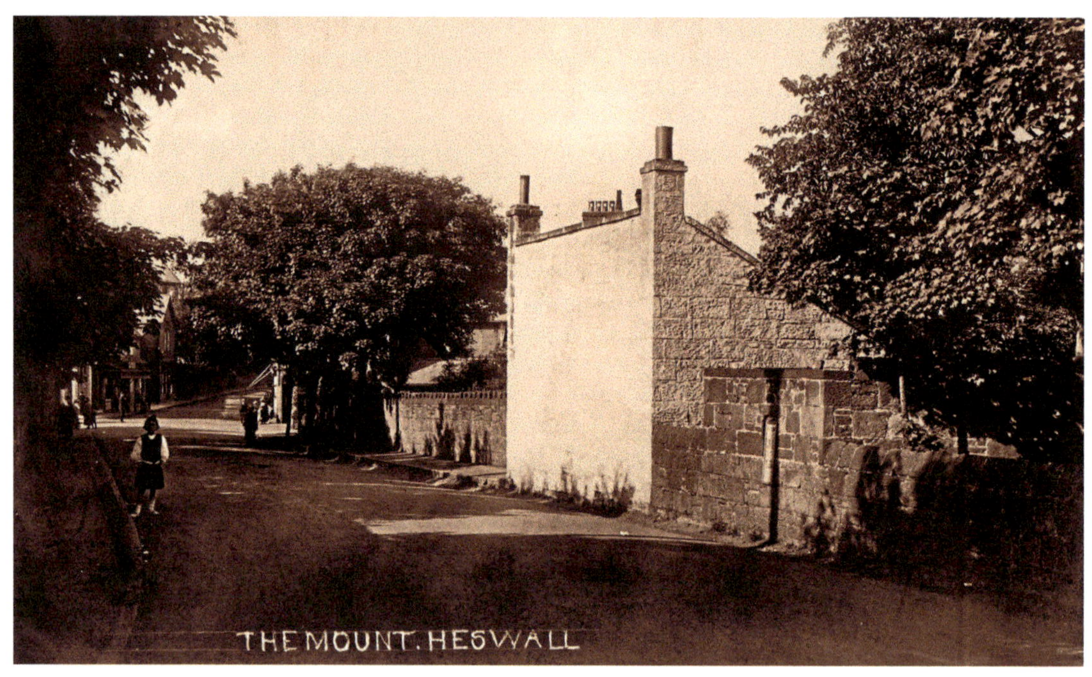

The Salt Box

This white building was given the name of the Salt Box by the locals as it resembled the shape of an old wooden salt box. It was occupied by the Hall family and was demolished between the two world wars. It was where the back entrance of Woolworths was located when it was built in the late fifties, now occupied by Gould's.

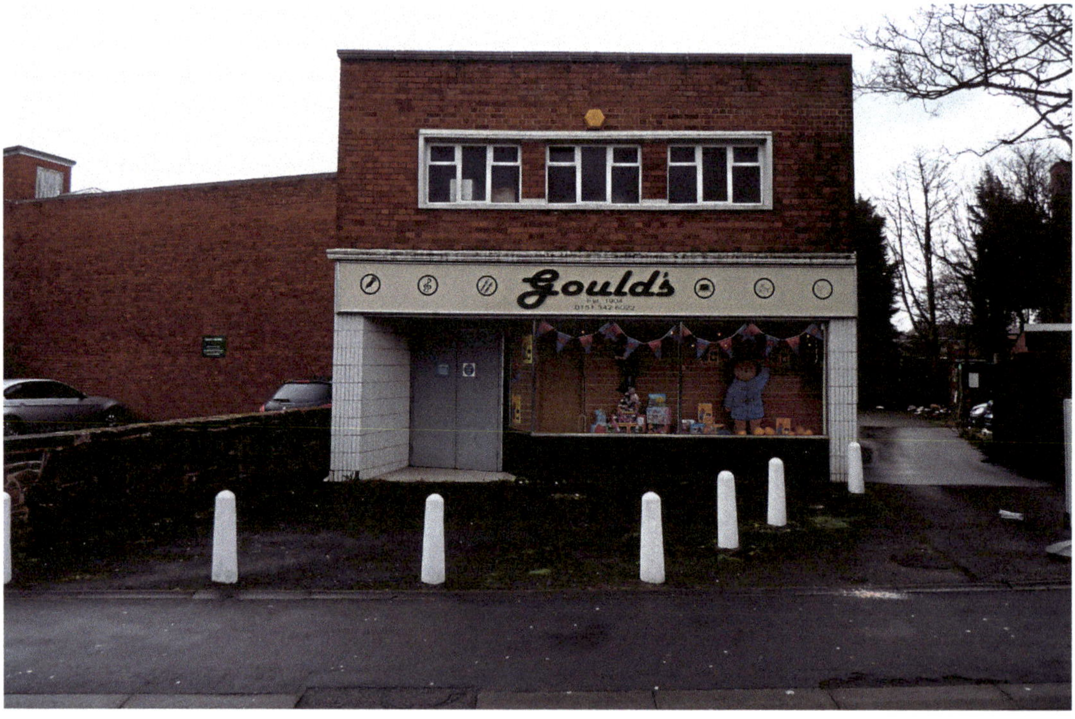

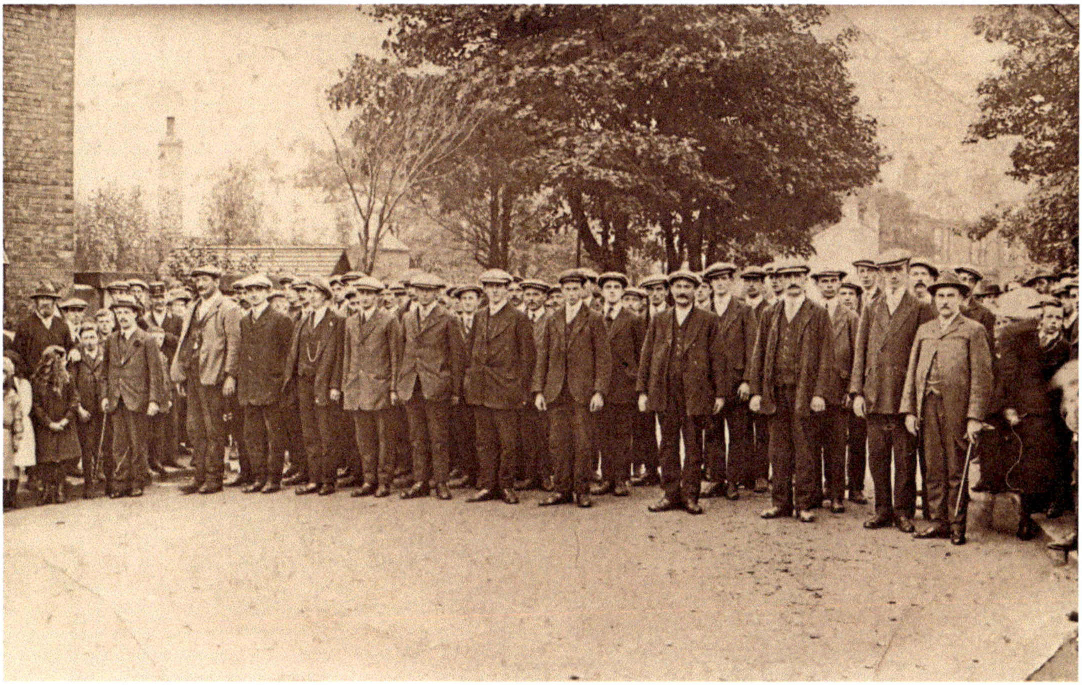

First World War Volunteers

These volunteers are standing at Heswall Cross in 1915 before leaving for the First World War. Over seventy men from Heswall lost their lives, a great loss for a small village. There are memorials to these men in most of the local churches. This one can be found in St Peter's church. Capt. Shaw, who trained them, can be seen on the right; he was also headmaster of the Heswall Church School.

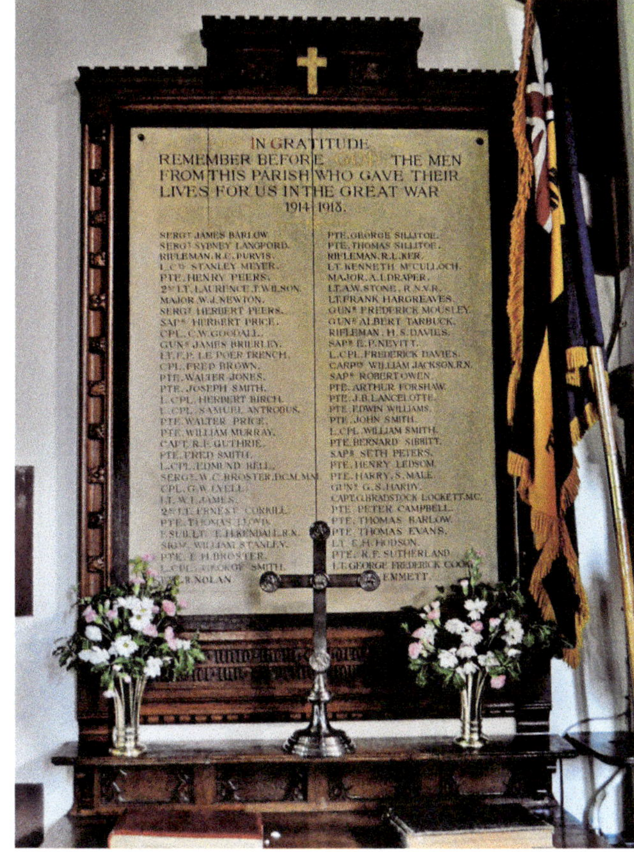

IN GRATITUDE
REMEMBER BEFORE GOD THE MEN
FROM THIS PARISH WHO GAVE THEIR
LIVES FOR US IN THE GREAT WAR
1914–1918.

SERGT. JAMES BARLOW.	PTE. GEORGE SILLITOE.
SERGT. SYDNEY LANGFORD.	PTE. THOMAS SILLITOE.
RIFLEMAN. R.C. PURVIS.	RIFLEMAN. R.L. KER.
L.C'L. STANLEY MEYER.	LT. KENNETH M'CULLOCH.
PTE. HENRY PEERS.	MAJOR. A.L. DRAPER.
2ND LT. LAURENCE J. WILSON.	LT. A.W. STONE. R.N.V.R.
MAJOR. W.J. NEWTON.	LT. FRANK HARGREAVES.
SERGT. HERBERT PEERS.	GUNR. FREDERICK MOUSLEY.
SAPR. HERBERT PRICE.	GUNR. ALBERT TARBUCK.
CPL. C.W. GOODALL.	RIFLEMAN. H.S. DAVIES.
GUNR. JAMES BRIERLEY.	SAPR. E.P. NEVITT.
LT. F.P. LE POER TRENCH.	L.CPL. FREDERICK DAVIES.
CPL. FRED BROWN.	CARPR. WILLIAM JACKSON. R.N.
PTE. WALTER JONES.	SAPR. ROBERT OWEN.
PTE. JOSEPH SMITH.	PTE. ARTHUR FORSHAW.
L.CPL. HERBERT BIRCH.	PTE. J.B. LANCELOTTE.
L.CPL. SAMUEL ANTROBUS.	PTE. EDWIN WILLIAMS.
PTE. WALTER PRICE.	PTE. JOHN SMITH.
PTE. WILLIAM MURRAY.	L.CPL. WILLIAM SMITH.
CAPT. R.F. GUTHRIE.	PTE. BERNARD SIBBITT.
PTE. FRED SMITH.	SAPR. SETH PETERS.
L.CPL. EDMUND BELL.	PTE. HENRY LEDSOM.
SERGT. W.C. BROSTER. DCM. MM.	PTE. HARRY. S. MALE.
CPL. G.W. LYELL.	GUNR. G.S. HARDY.
LT. W.L. JAMES.	CAPT. C. BRADSTOCK LOCKETT. MC.
2ND LT. ERNEST CORKILL.	PTE. PETER CAMPBELL.
PTE. THOMAS LLOYD.	PTE. THOMAS BARLOW.
E. SUB.LT. E.H. KENDALL. R.N.	PTE. THOMAS EVANS.
SIGN. WILLIAM STANLEY.	LT. E.H. HODSON.
PTE. E.H. BROSTER.	PTE. R.F. SUTHERLAND.
L.CPL. GEORGE SMITH.	LT. GEORGE FREDERICK COOK.
PTE. R. NOLAN.	EMMETT.

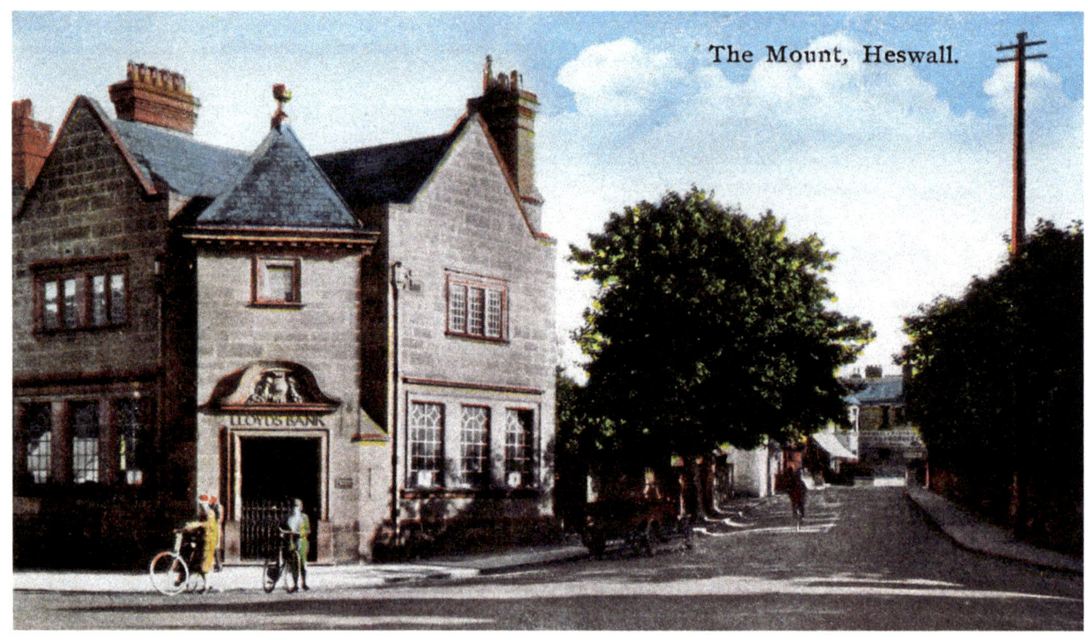

Heswall Cross Looking Down The Mount

Looking down The Mount, a taxi rank was situated below the trees on the left for many years, two of which still remain. The castle walls on the right are now shops, but from the 1940s to the 1960s this area was used as a car park.

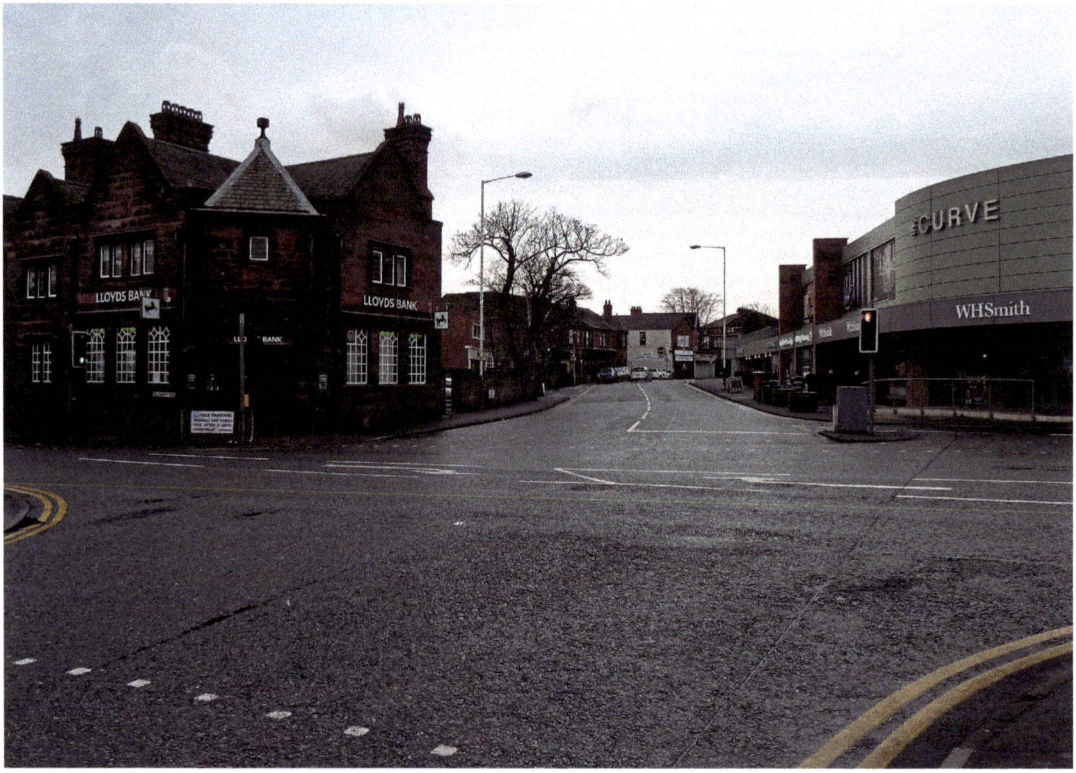

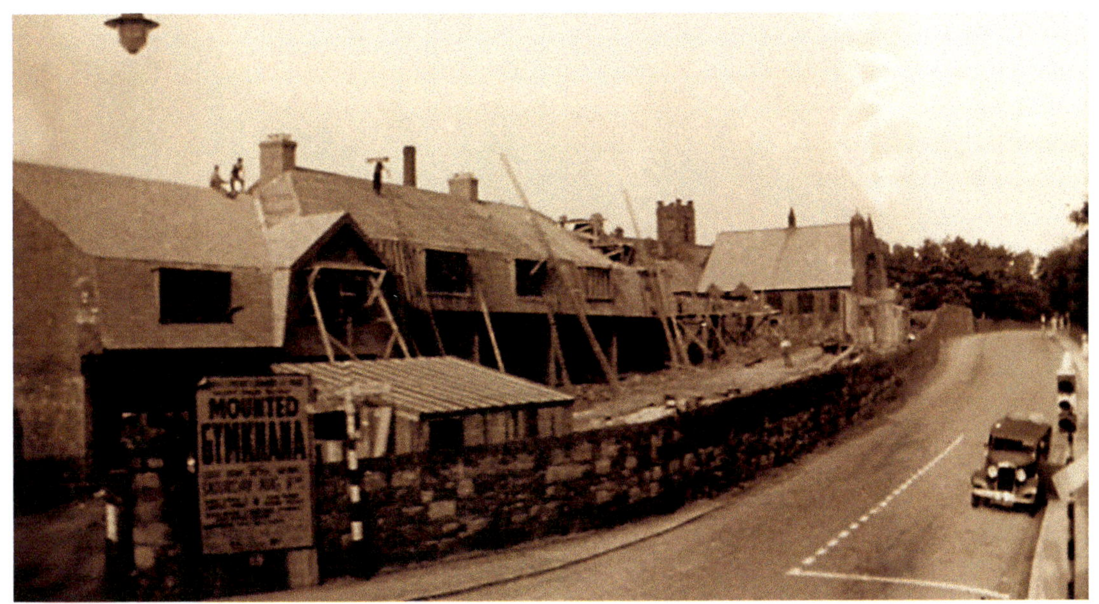

Castle Buildings

The original wall from the castle has not yet been demolished as Castle Buildings were being built around 1935. The land had to be levelled and the spoil was taken to Elmwood Drive, where builder Charlie Peers was building more houses. The Presbyterian church and the hospital can be seen in the background. The shops in Castle Buildings opened in 1936 and were very popular as they sold a wider variety of goods than those available at the time in the other local shops.

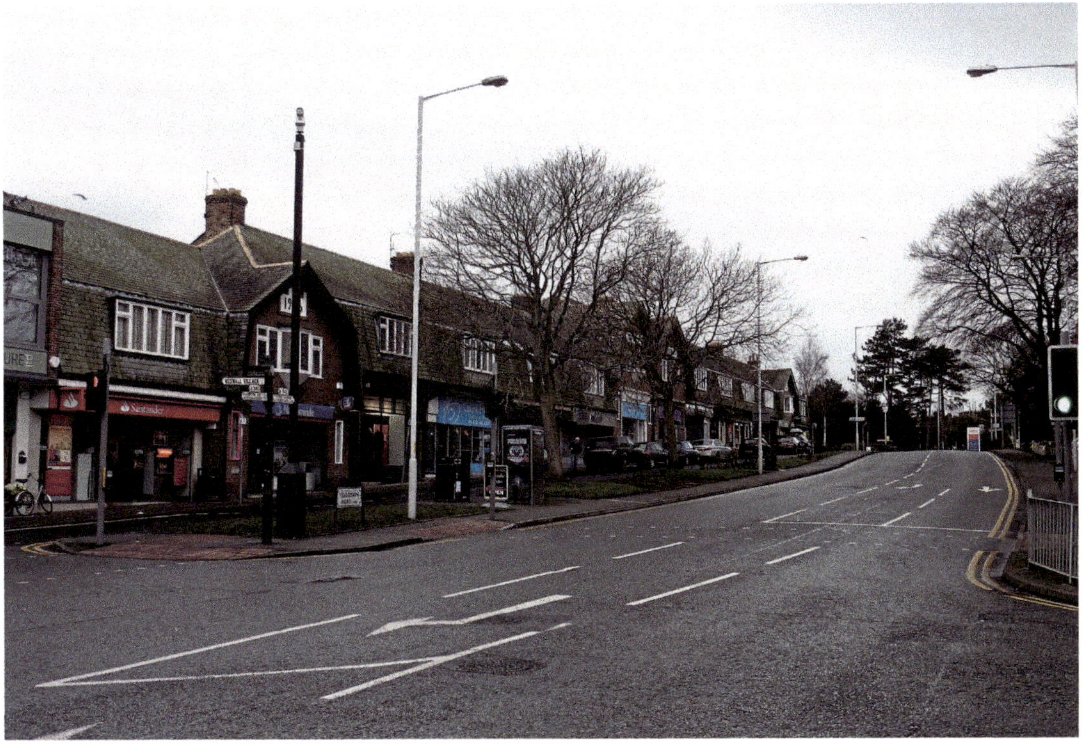

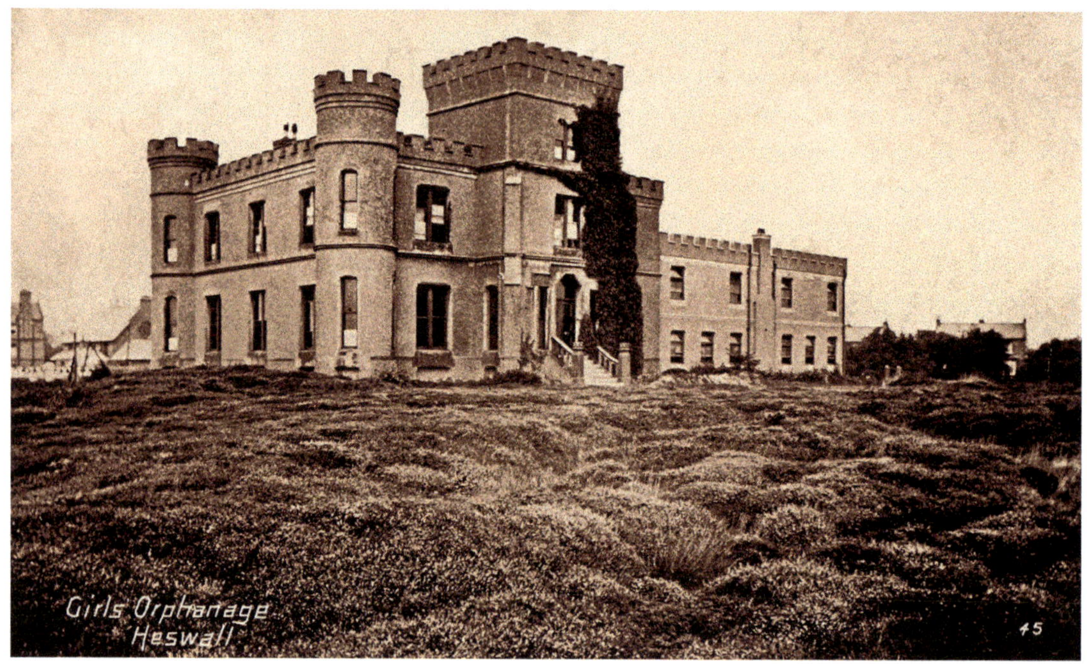

The Castle

Built on high ground on Telegraph Road in 1870 by Mr Titherington, The Towers soon became known as 'Titherington's folly', as he never lived there. Money was raised to buy it for a summer home for the Liverpool Myrtle Street Orphans' Asylum and in July 1891 the grand opening of the Heswall Home of the Liverpool Female Orphan Asylum took place. The very distinctive castellated architecture led to it being known locally as 'The Castle', a name that lives on in Castle Buildings and Drive. In the 1930s, after an unsuccessful proposal to convert it into offices for the Wirral Urban District Council, the Castle was demolished.

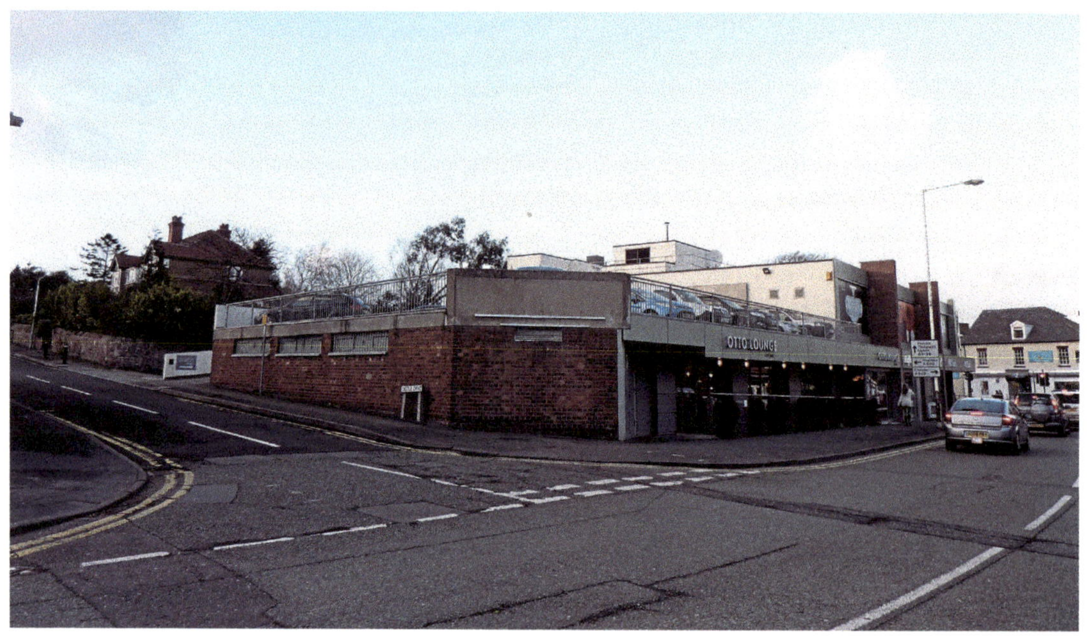

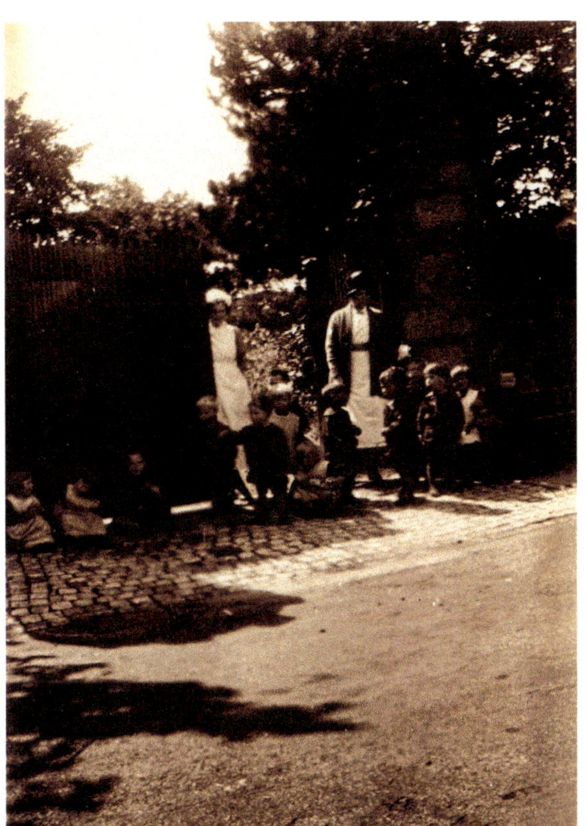

Castle Gates

The Castle was used by the
Orphan Asylum from Liverpool
as a country retreat in the
summer months. The children
are standing by the back gate of
the Castle grounds. The turrets
either side of the gateway can
still be seen incorporated into
a private garden wall at the
junction of Castle Drive and
Feather Lane.

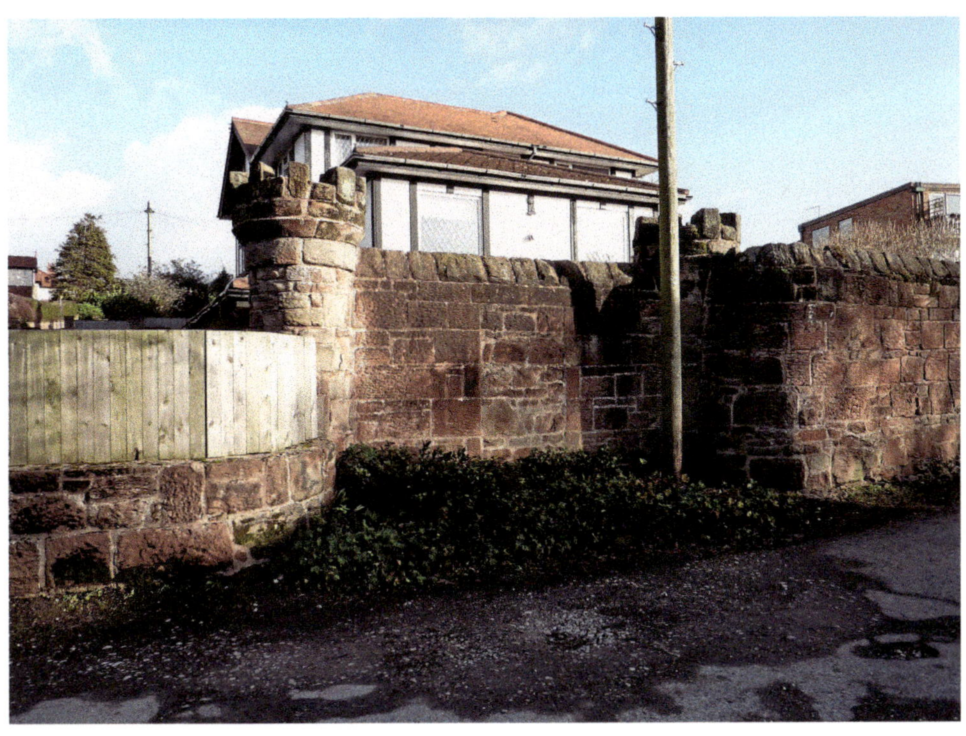

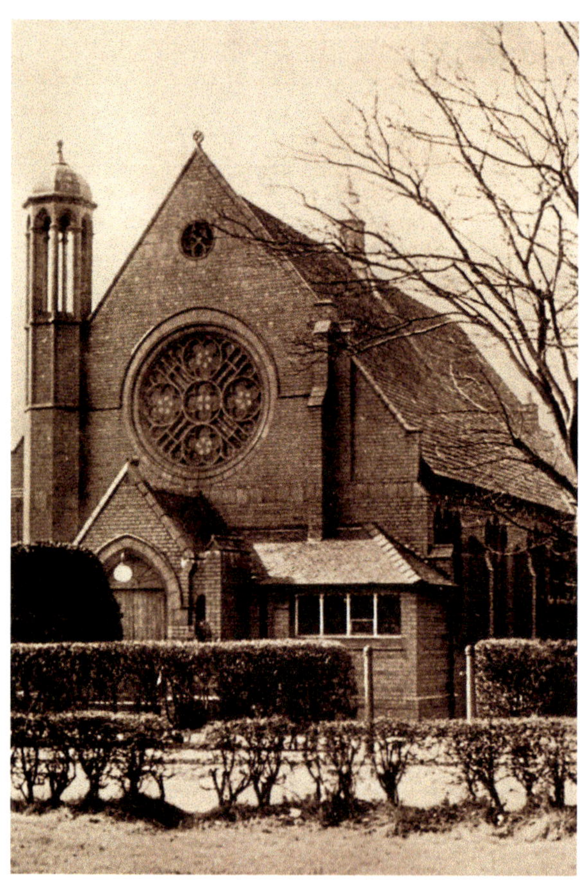

Presbyterian Church

Now the United Reformed church, there have been three churches on this site. The first was 'the Tin Tabernacle', built at a cost of £600. The second, which appears in the photograph, had the foundation stone laid in June 1908. The current church was completed in 1970. The church celebrated its centenary in 1995, having started in a cottage in Sandy Lane. Services were held in Grange Hall in Grange Mount, before the Tin Tabernacle was erected in Telegraph Road.

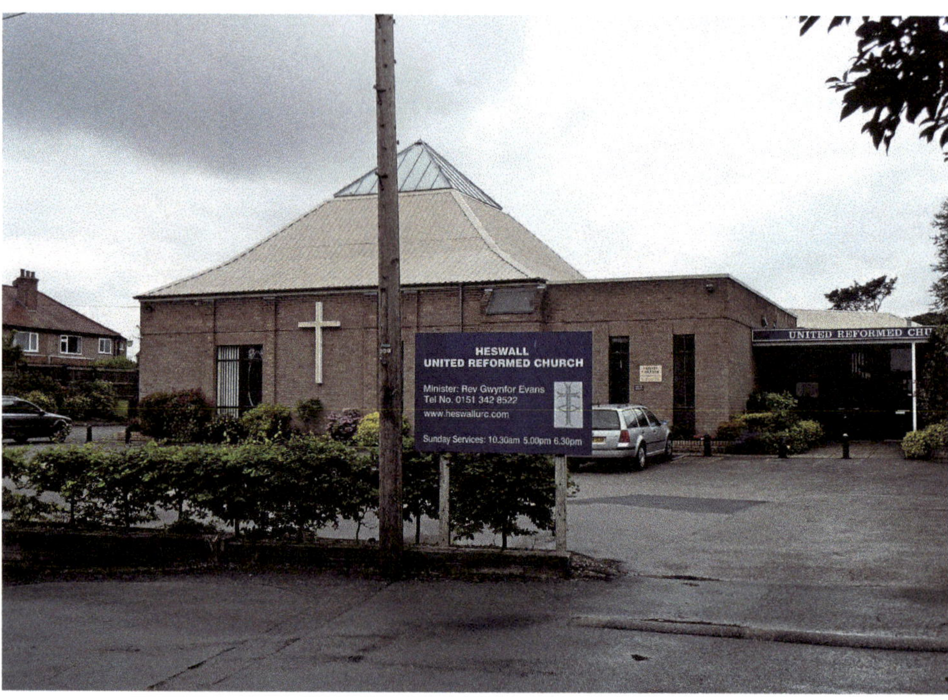

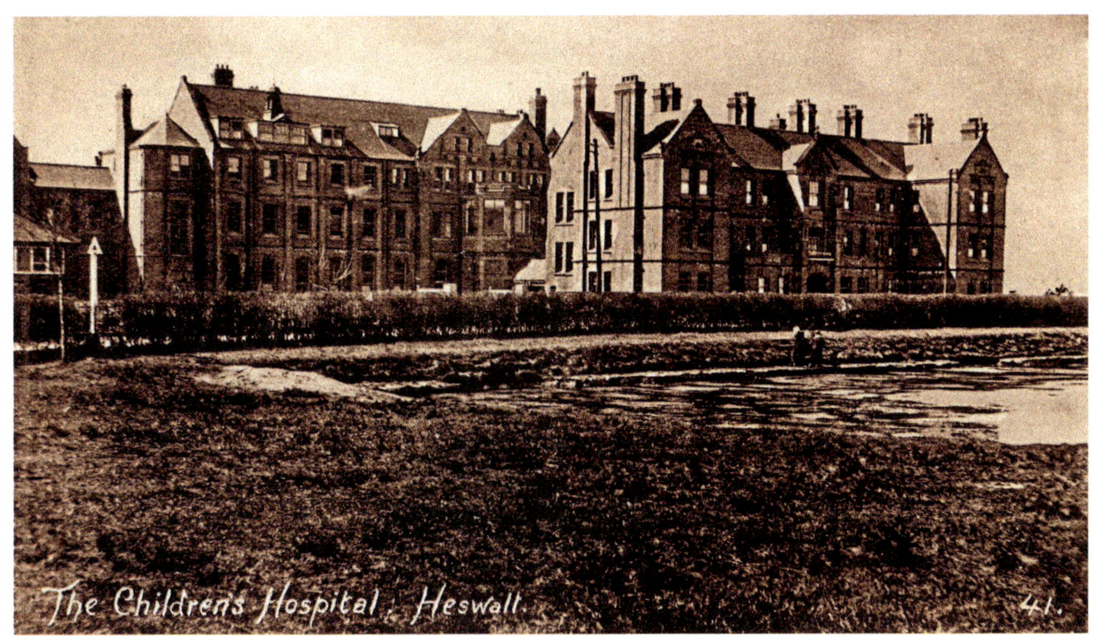

The Royal Liverpool Children's Hospital

Tesco's Supermarket now occupies the site of the Royal Liverpool Children's Hospital, which was demolished in 1989. The 4-acre site was purchased for the hospital in 1900 for £2,500. The hospital opened in February 1909, incorporating open-air wards to take advantage of the healthy sea air to alleviate respiratory disorders. This view was taken looking across the pond on the Puddydale.

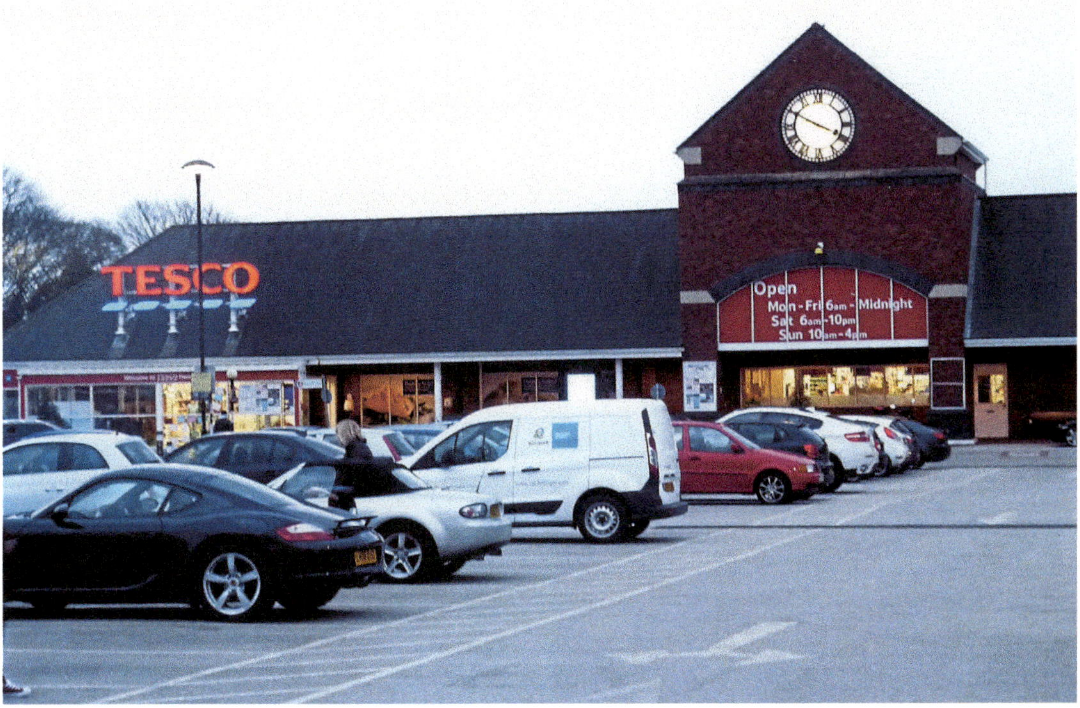

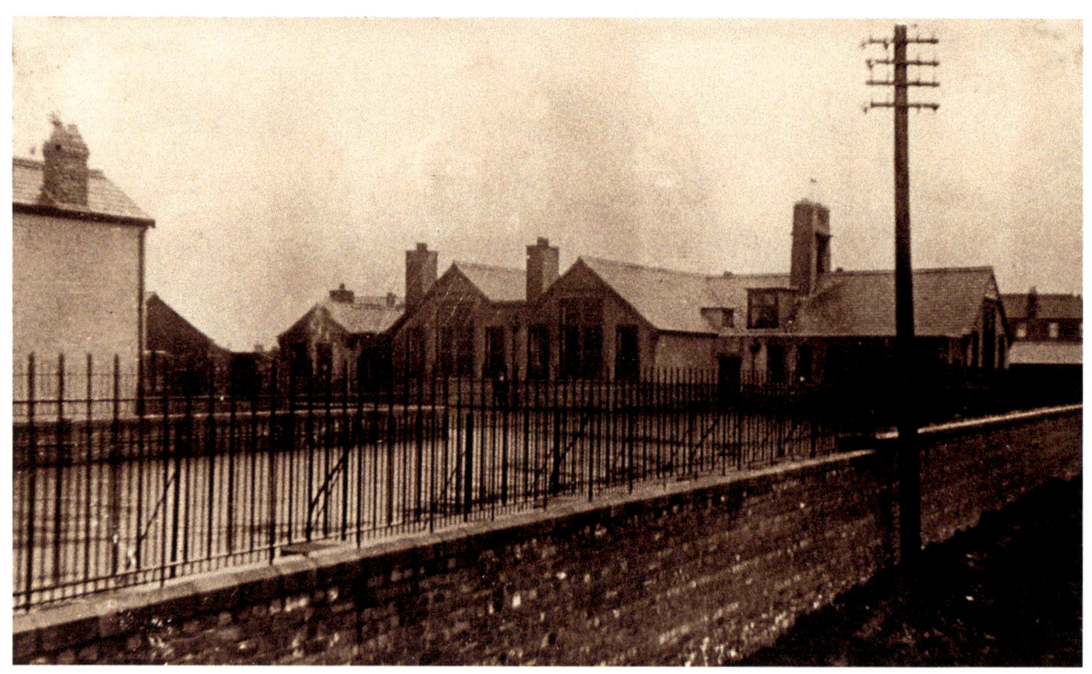

The Puddydale School

The 4-acre site of the Puddydale was given to Heswall Parish by the Enclosure Commissioners in 1855. In the 1890s, the pond on it was drained and filled to provide a recreation ground. The Heswall cum Oldfield Council School, known as 'The Puddydale', was built in 1909 and a school remained there until 1980, when all pupils were moved to its present site in Whitfield Lane. Red Dale apartments now occupy the site.

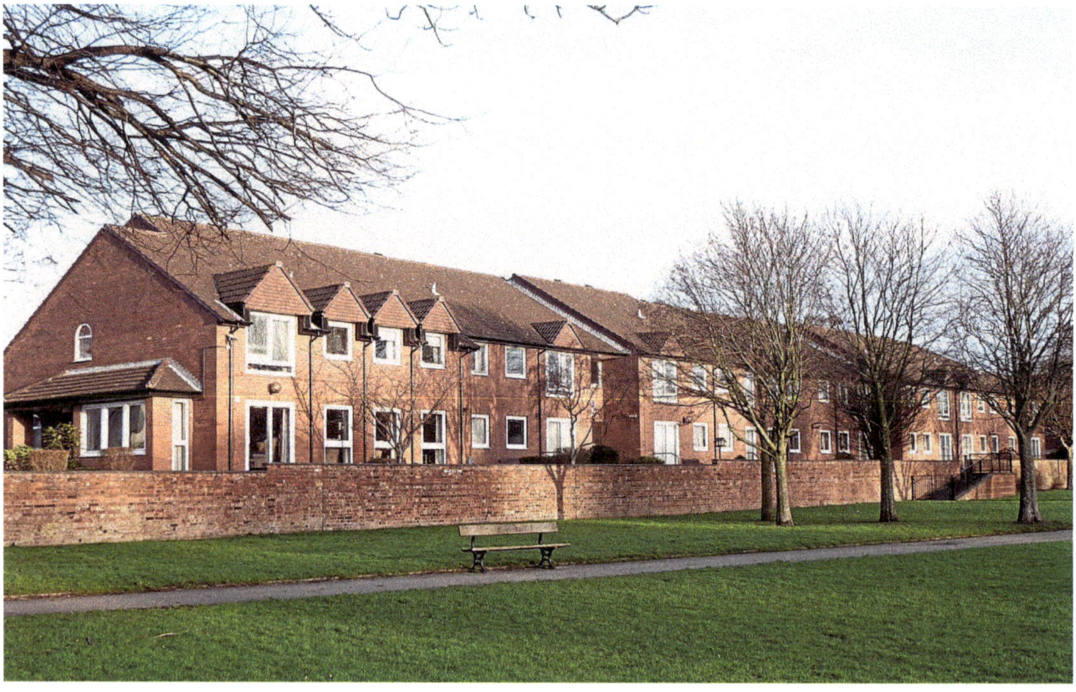

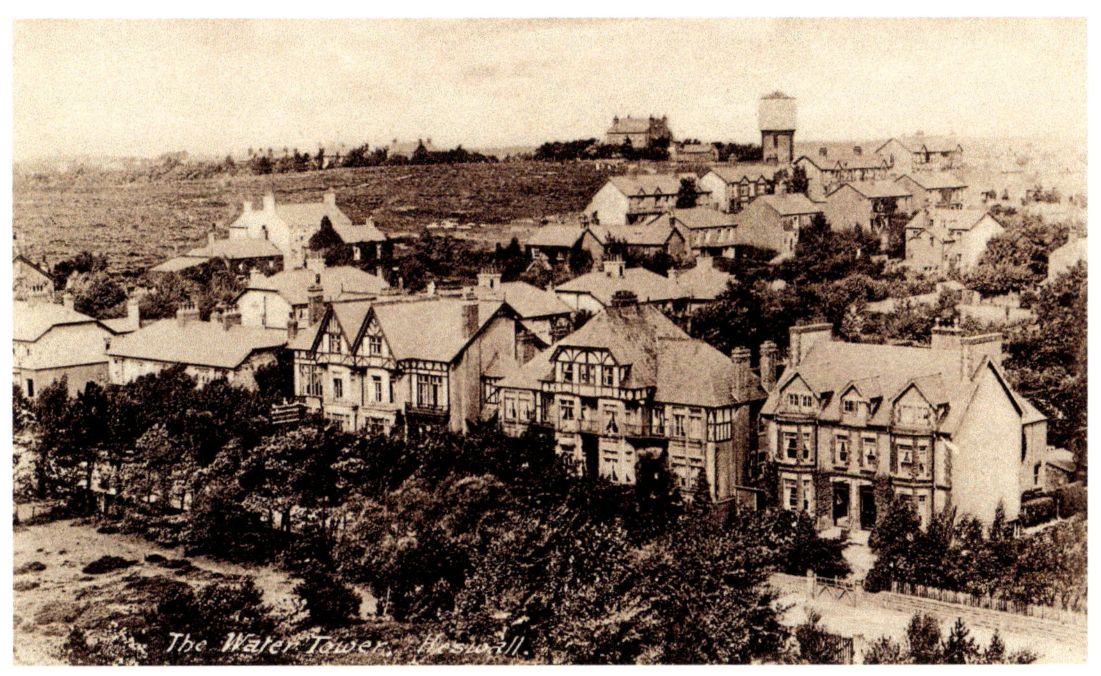

Bombed Houses, Telegraph Road

On the site that today contains the ambulance station, the Heswall Centre and the Pensby and Heswall Medical Centre, there were six large three-storey houses. In 1941, the centre houses were destroyed by bombing and one was person killed. Glendower Boarding House was the house on the far right.

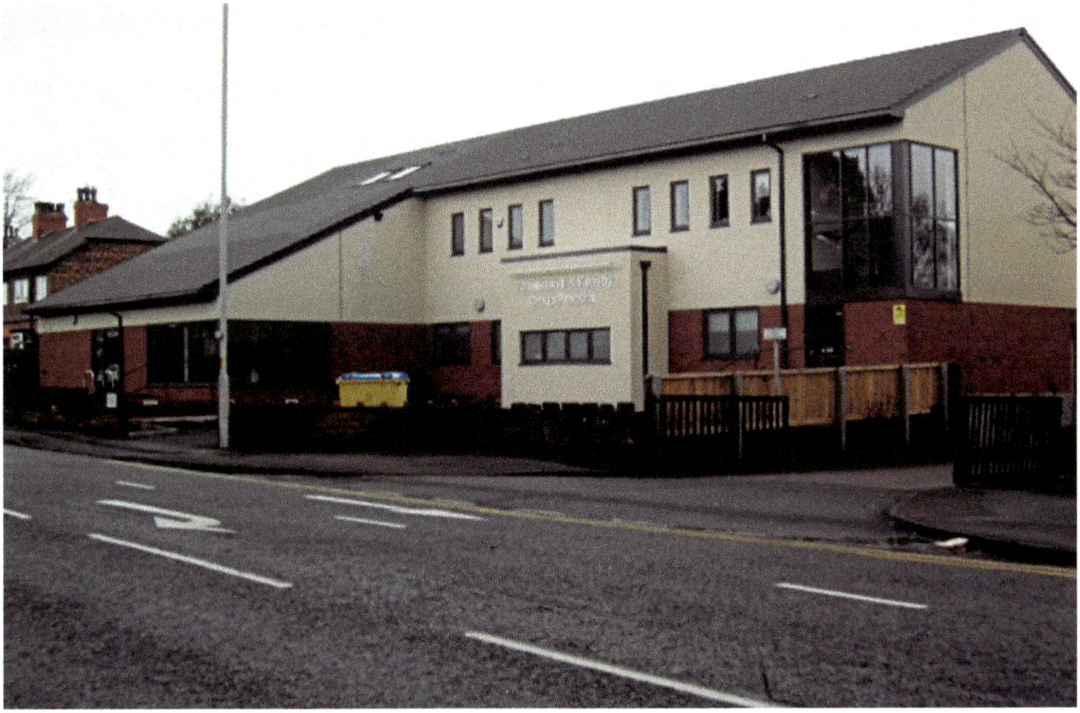

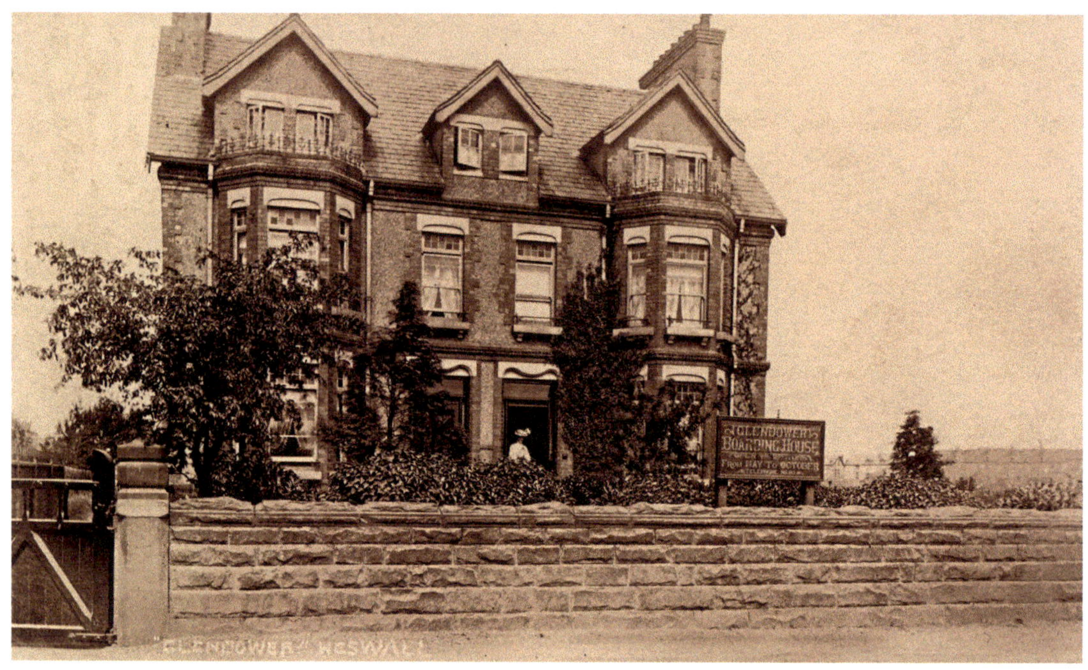

Glendower

Glendower Boarding House was once the home of the Reddy family, who ran the butcher's in Pensby Road. At the time of this picture, it was a boarding house and was demolished in the 1960s to make space for the ambulance station.

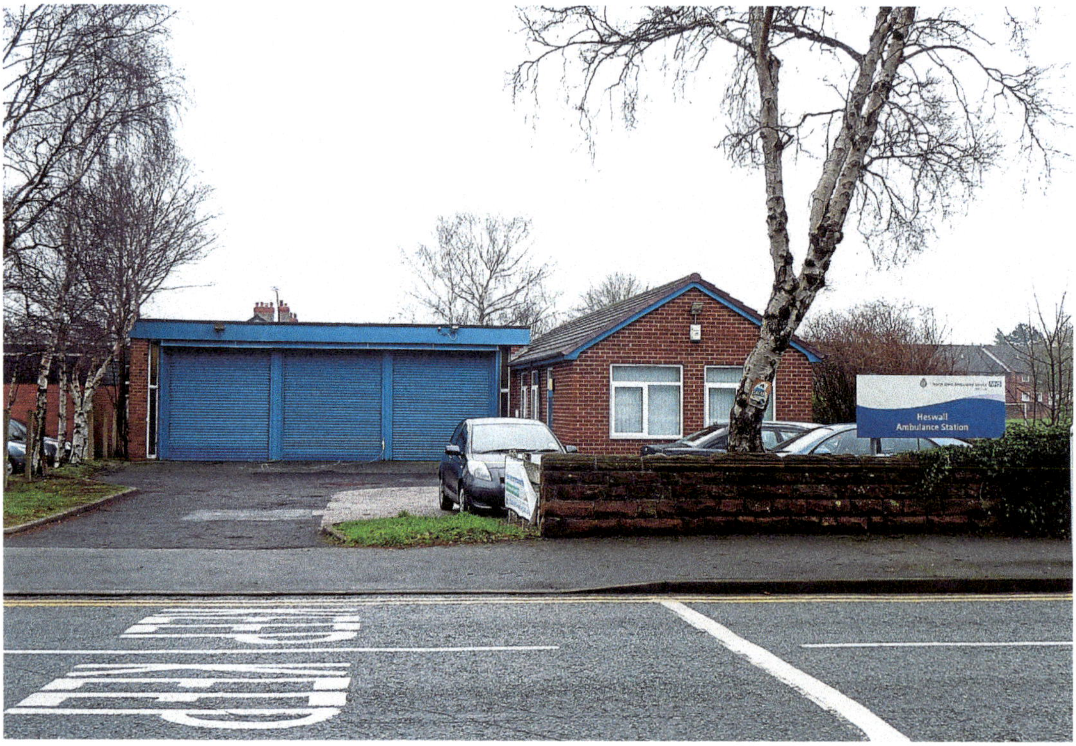

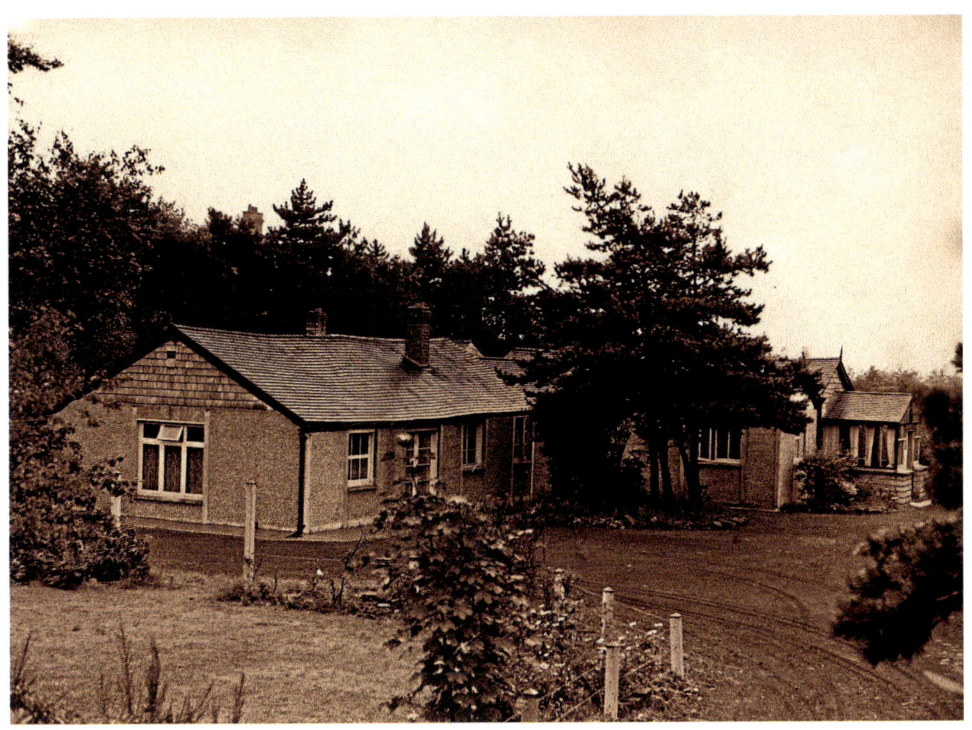

Sundial Roadhouse

Dale Court now occupies the site where the Sundial Roadhouse was situated, next to the Children's Hospital in Telegraph Road. A popular café, it was also used for social events after the Second World War until it was demolished in the 1950s.

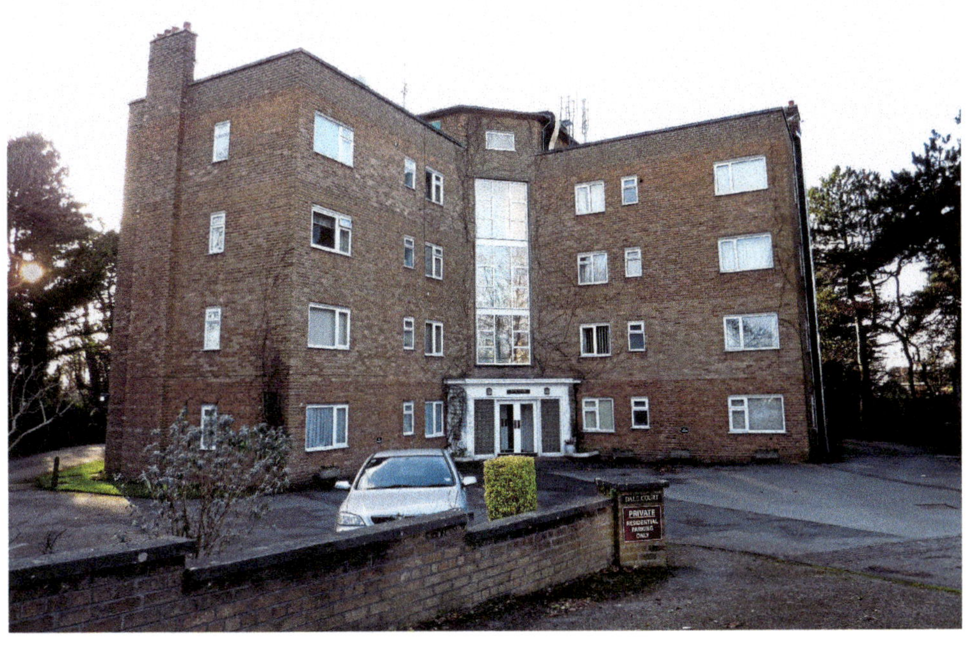

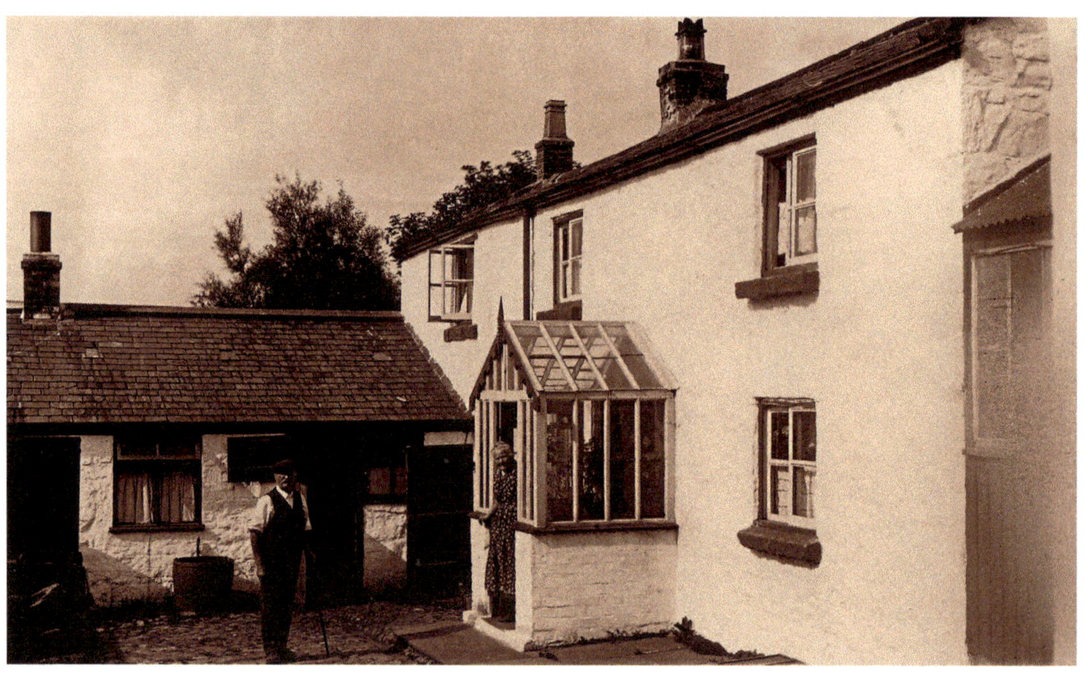

White Farm

This farm was in Telegraph Road and was owned by a branch of the Totty family. Its cows grazed in fields along Telegraph Road. A cul-de-sac of houses called Highfields now occupies the site.

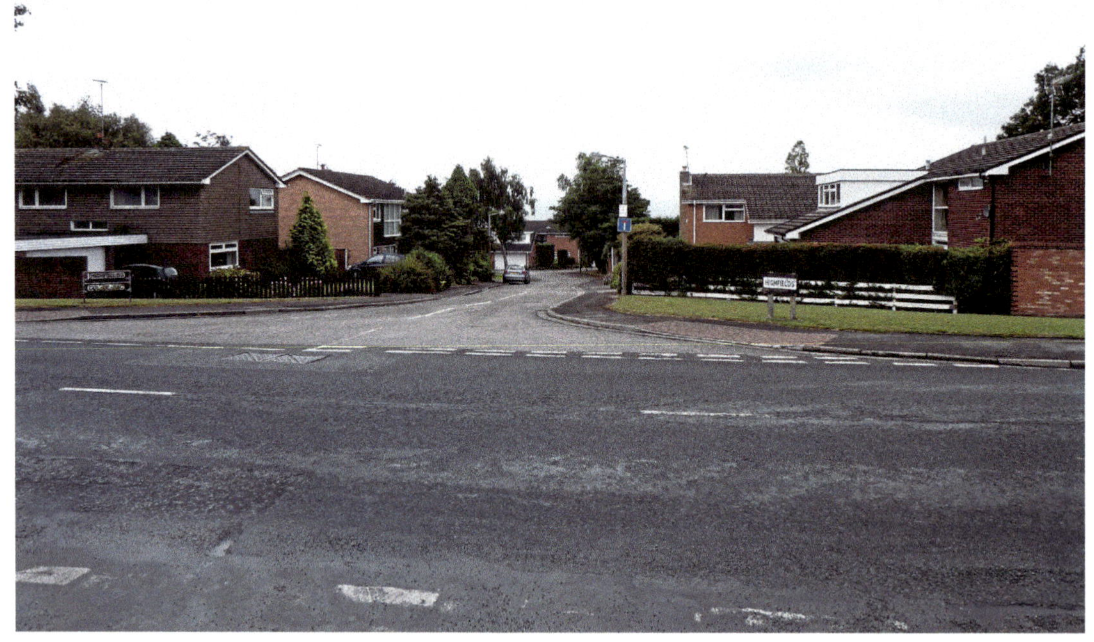

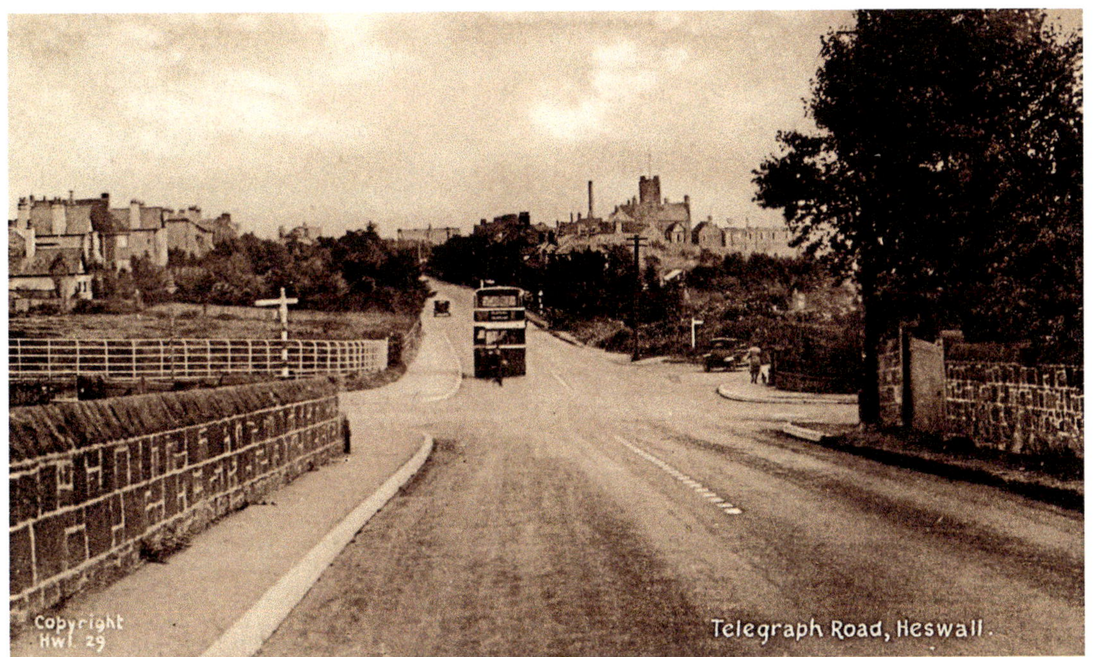

Quarry Hill

This area of Telegraph Road was known as Quarry Hill, as it was surrounded by quarries providing the characteristic red sandstone building stone. Smallwood's Quarry was on the corner on the left, and on the right there were further quarries in Quarry Road West (now Laurelbanks) and in Thurstaston Road. The hospital can be seen in the distance.

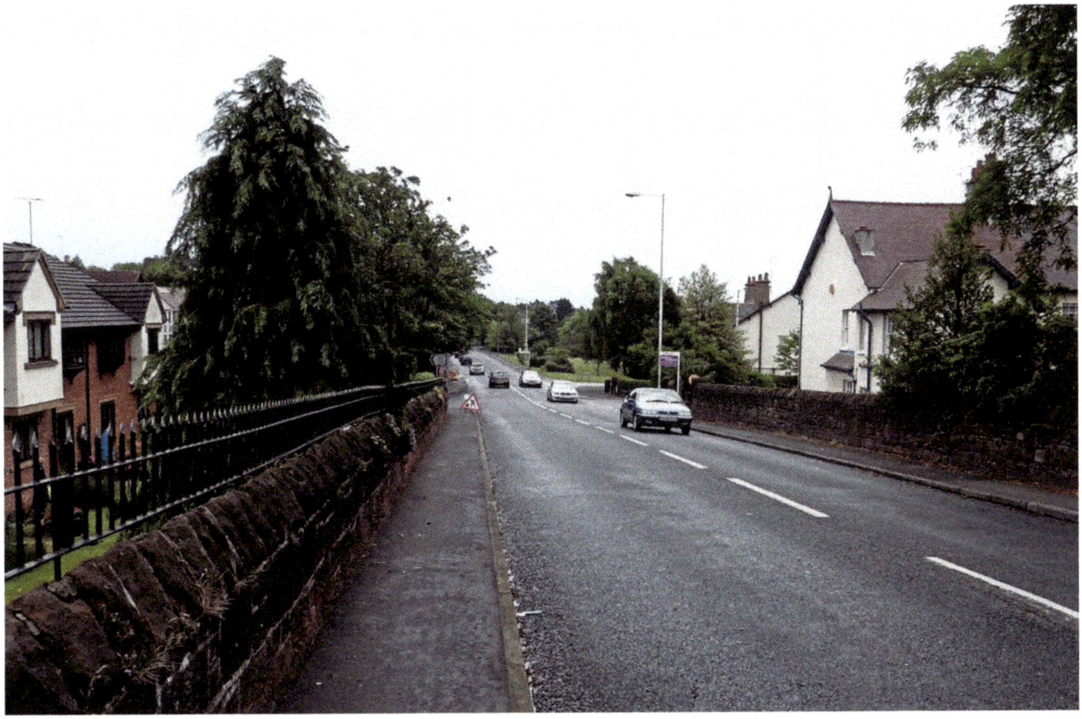

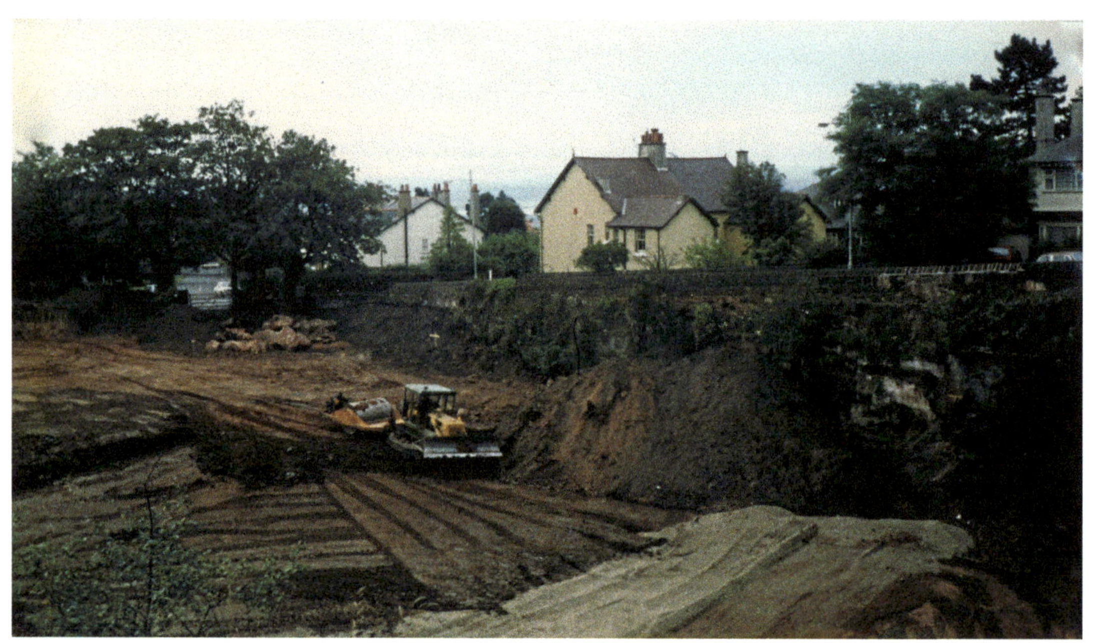

Smallwood's Quarry

A more detailed view of Smallwood's Quarry, which stood at the corner of Quarry Road East and Telegraph Road, as Smallwood Mews and Erica Court were being constructed on the site in 1986.

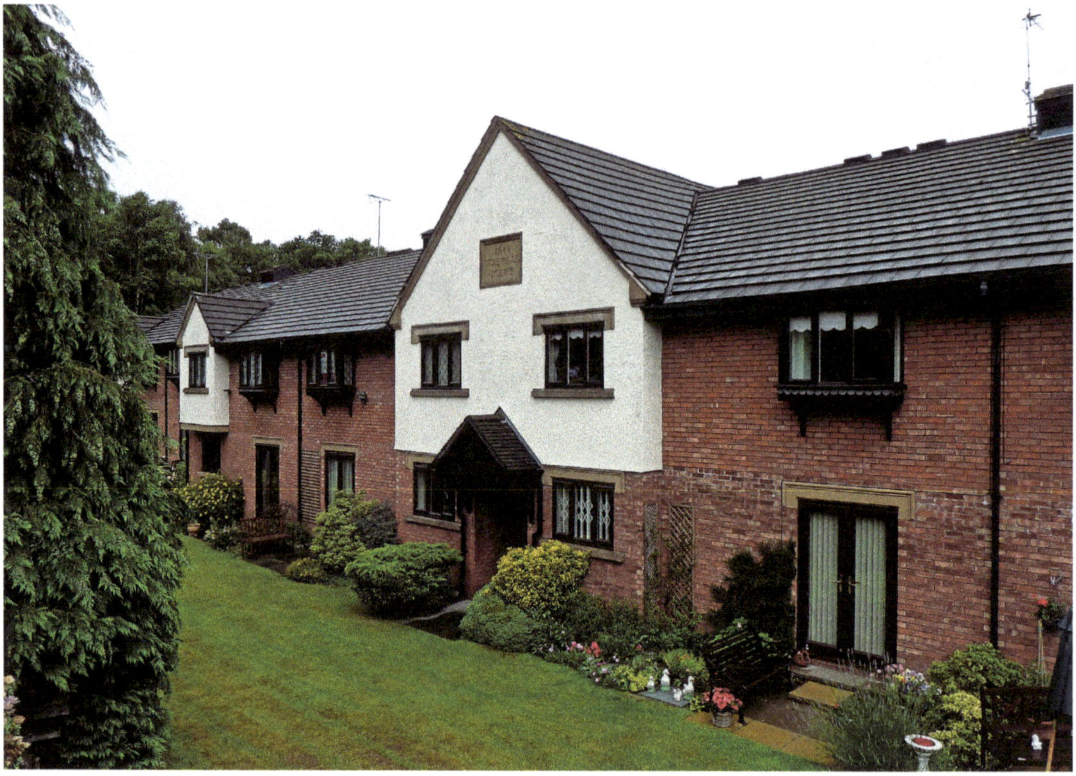

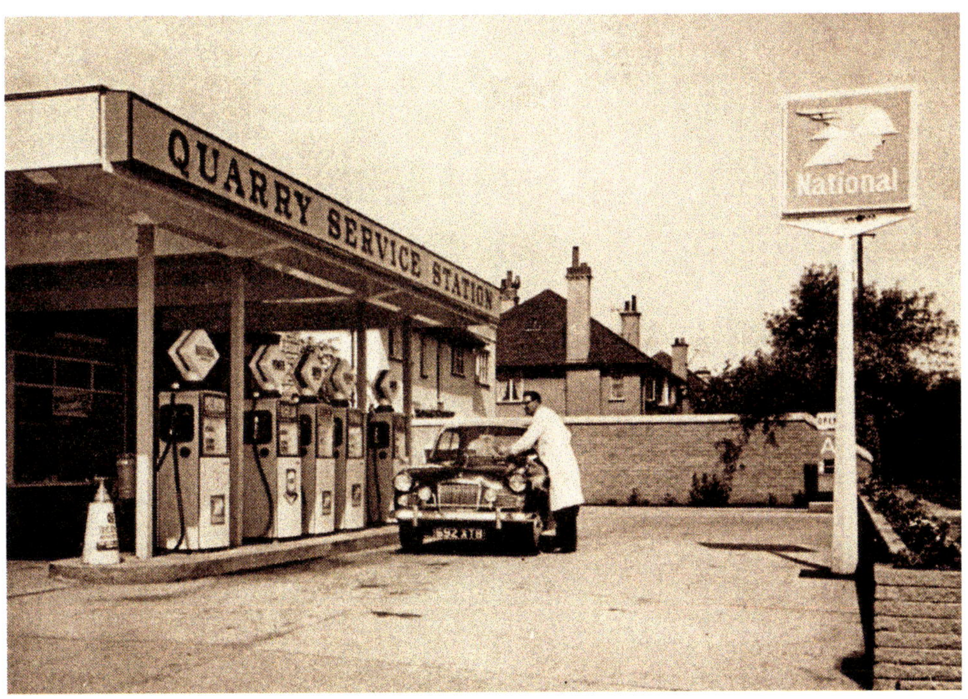

Quarry Service Station

Originally the premises of Jones and Hough, who built many houses in Heswall, it was later opened as a garage and served the community for several decades until it closed in the 1980s. Quarry Court apartments now occupy the site.

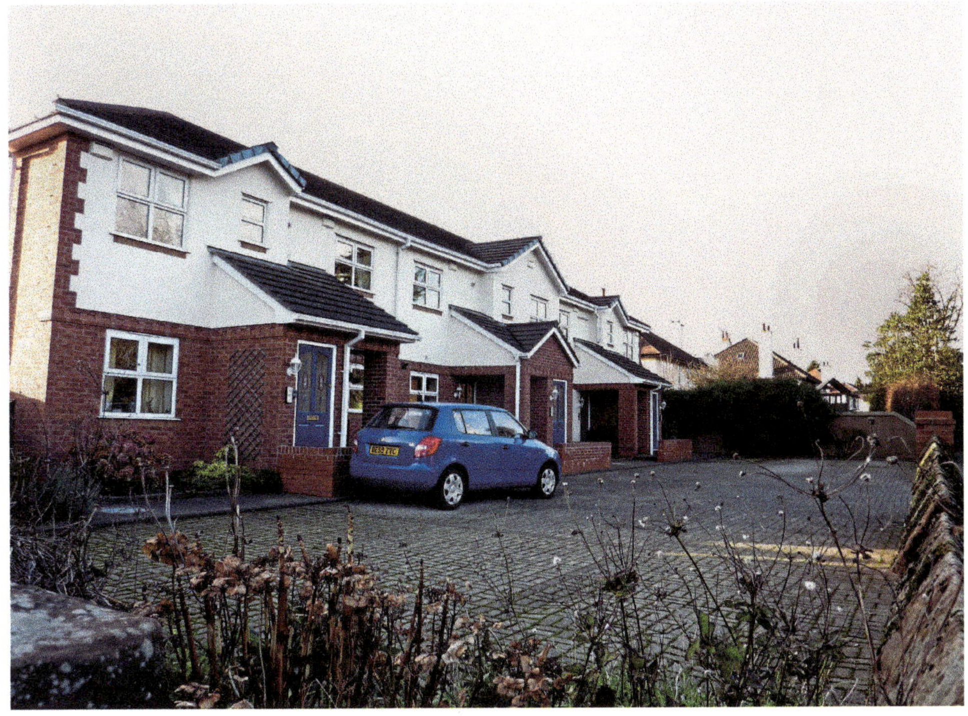

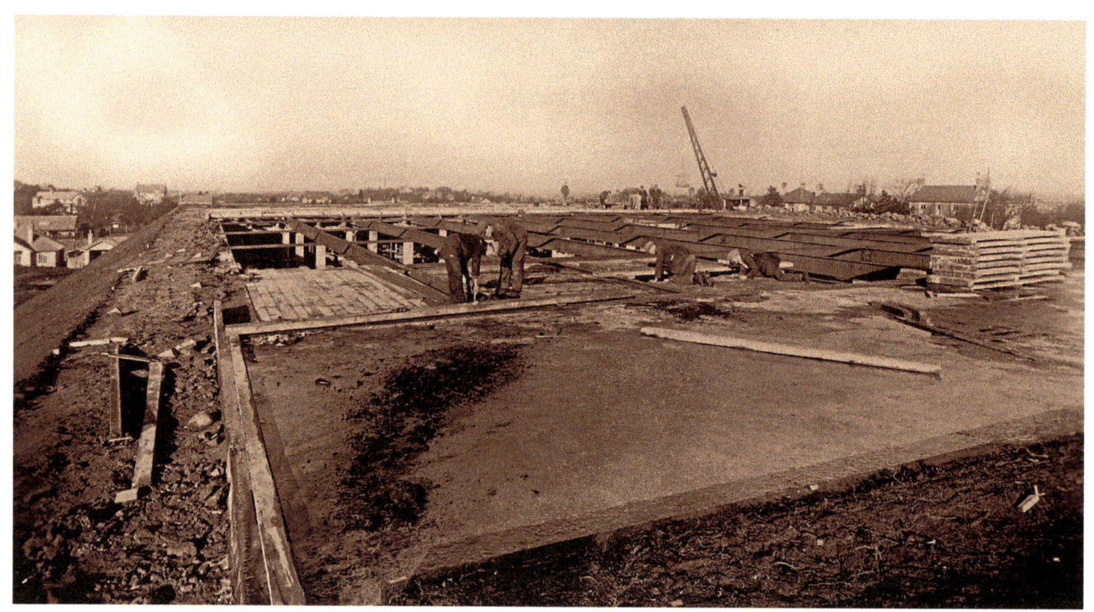

Poll Hill Reservoir

Built in 1928, this reservoir is situated at the highest point on Wirral and contains 2 million gallons of water in a rectangular concrete structure (now grassed over). It supplemented the water tower, commissioned in 1887, which was a very prominent landmark until demolished and replaced by telecommunications masts. Houses in Quarry Road East and Tower Road North can be seen in the background.

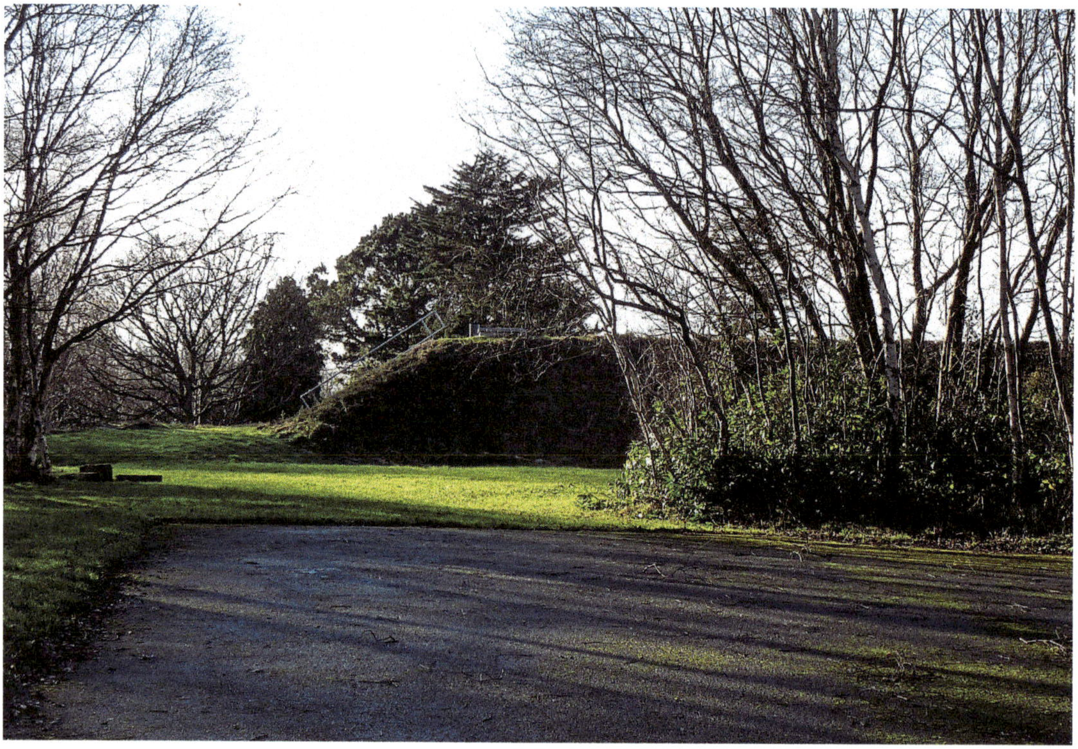

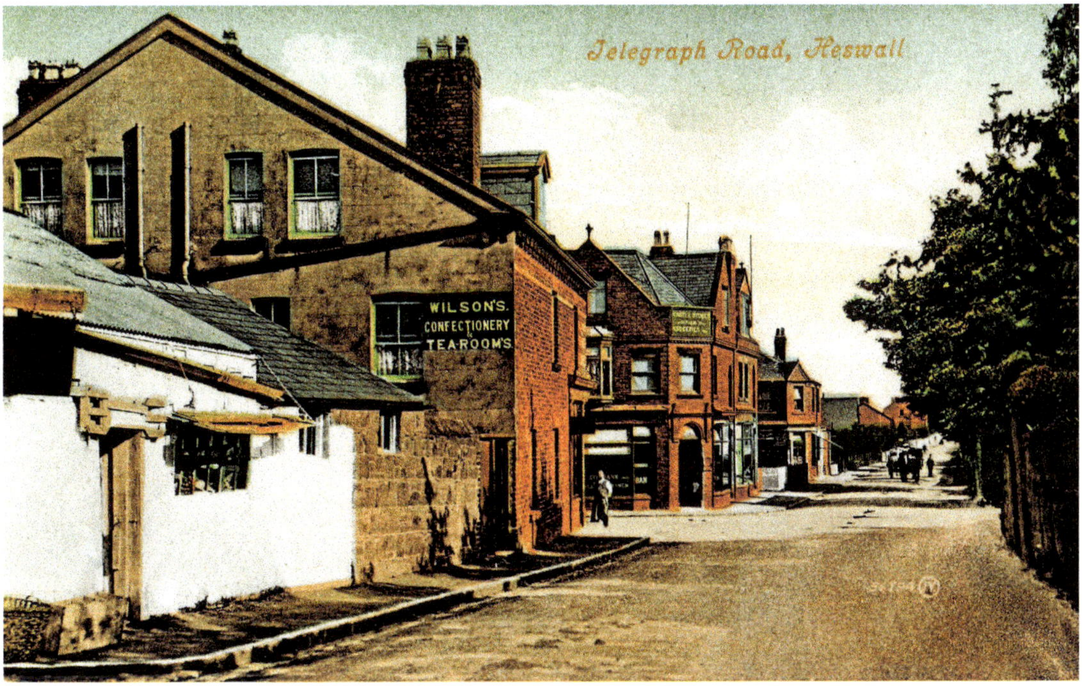

Looking Down Telegraph Road Towards Gayton

In the foreground is Wilson's Bakery, which became Kelly's Bakery and is now an optician. On the corner opposite, Castle Stores can be seen, now NatWest Bank. The Castle walls are on the right, and Lloyds Bank has not yet been built.

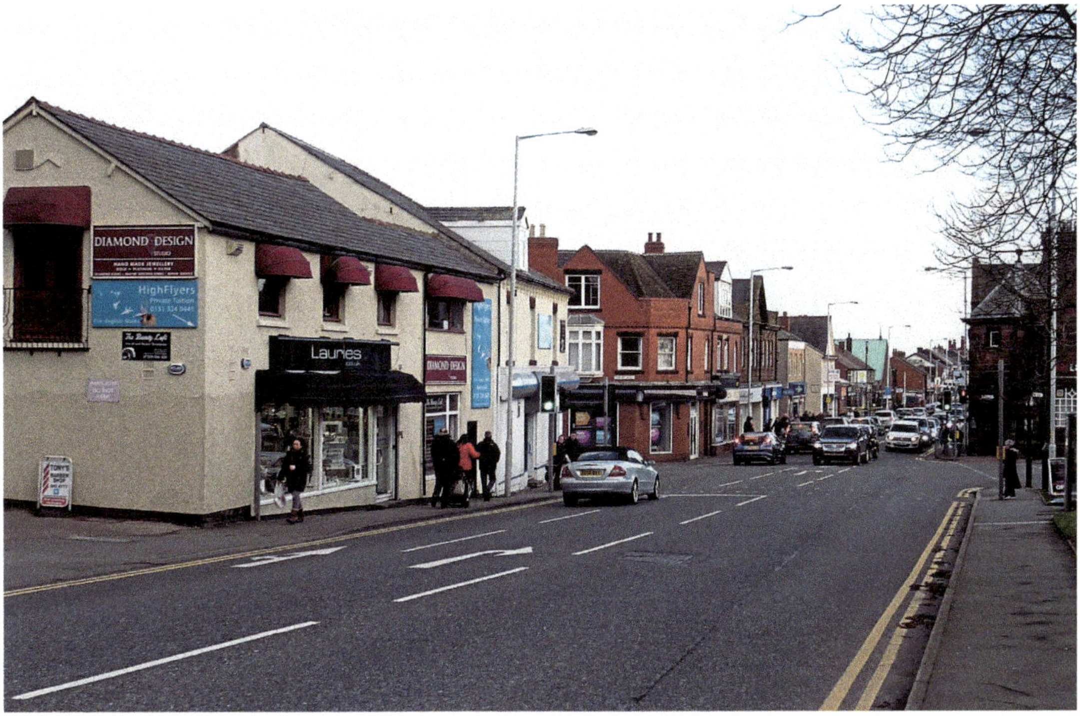

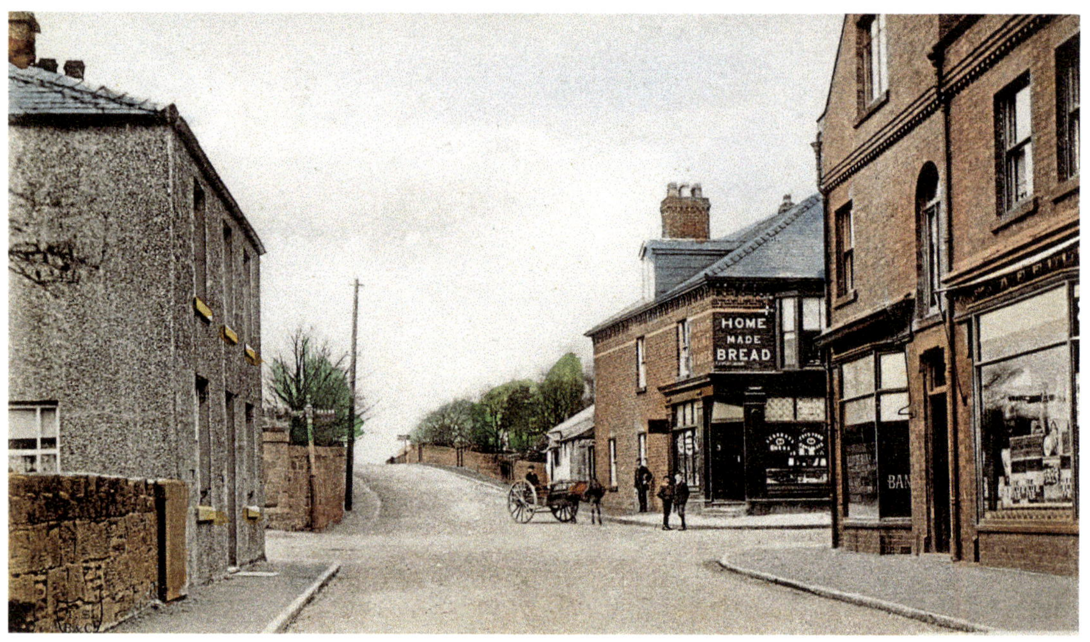

Looking Up Telegraph Road Towards West Kirby

On the left stands the building which was replaced in 1907 by Lloyds Bank. In the centre a delivery cart can be seen outside Wilson's Bakery. There was a tea room and café upstairs in this building for many decades. The entrance to the Castle can just be glimpsed on the left, and the Penneswelle, one of Heswall's many wells, was located on the right under the trees and in front of the Penneswelle Cottages (now shops).

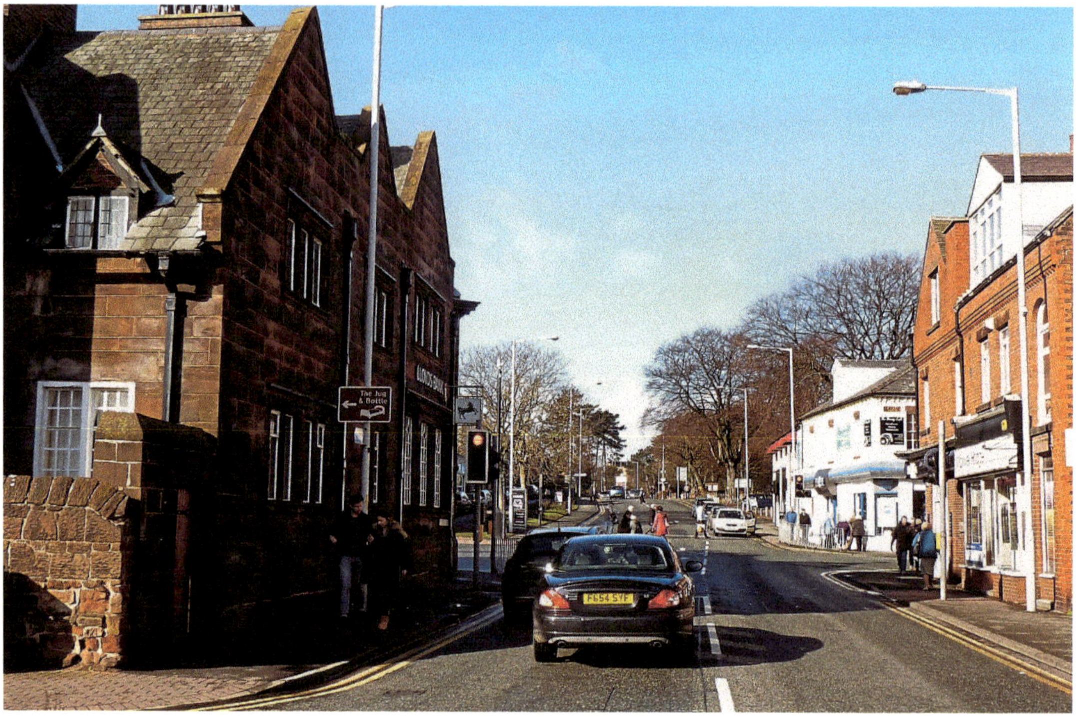

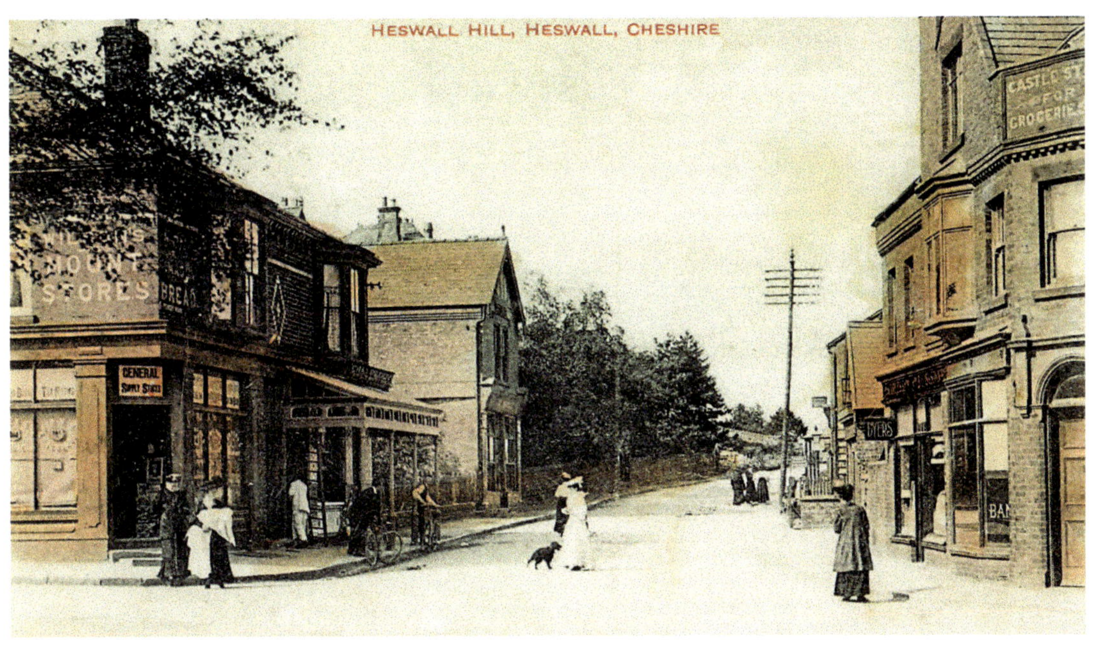

Looking Up Pensby Road from Heswall Cross

Beyond Wilson's Bakery on the corner was Reddy's butcher's, which was in business until the 1960s. Whole sides of meat would be hanging up outside, which attracted all the local dogs. The fishmonger's shop, the third building on the left, was owned by Mr Reddy's brother-in-law.

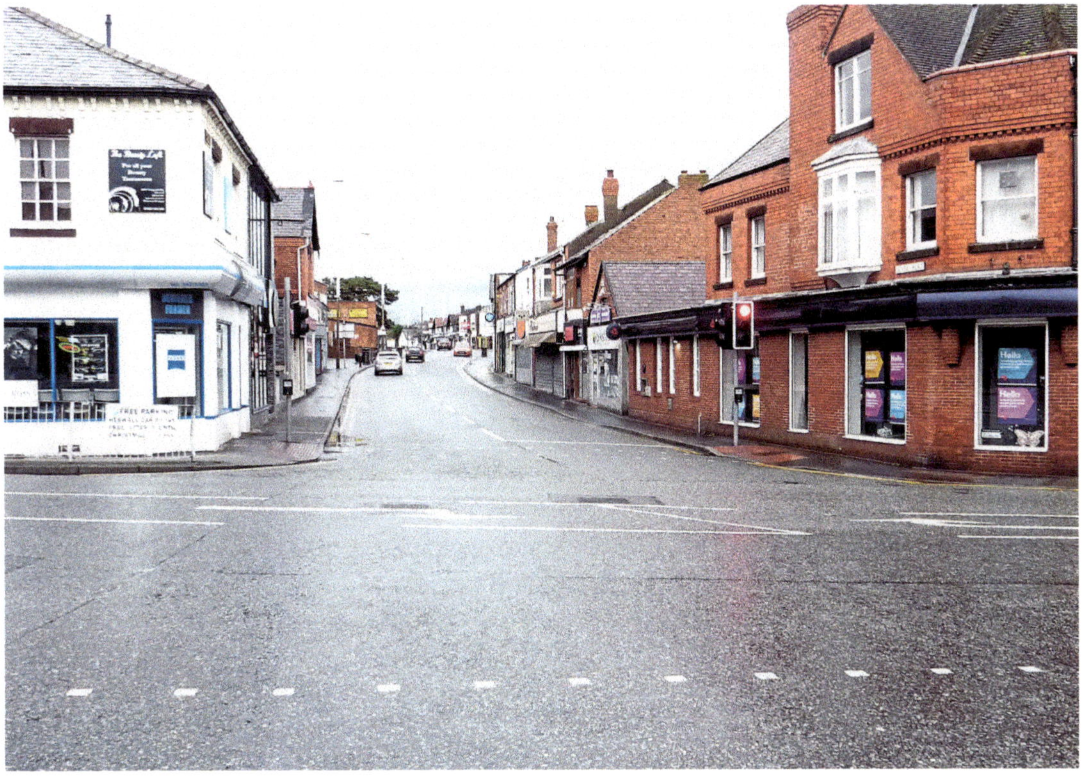

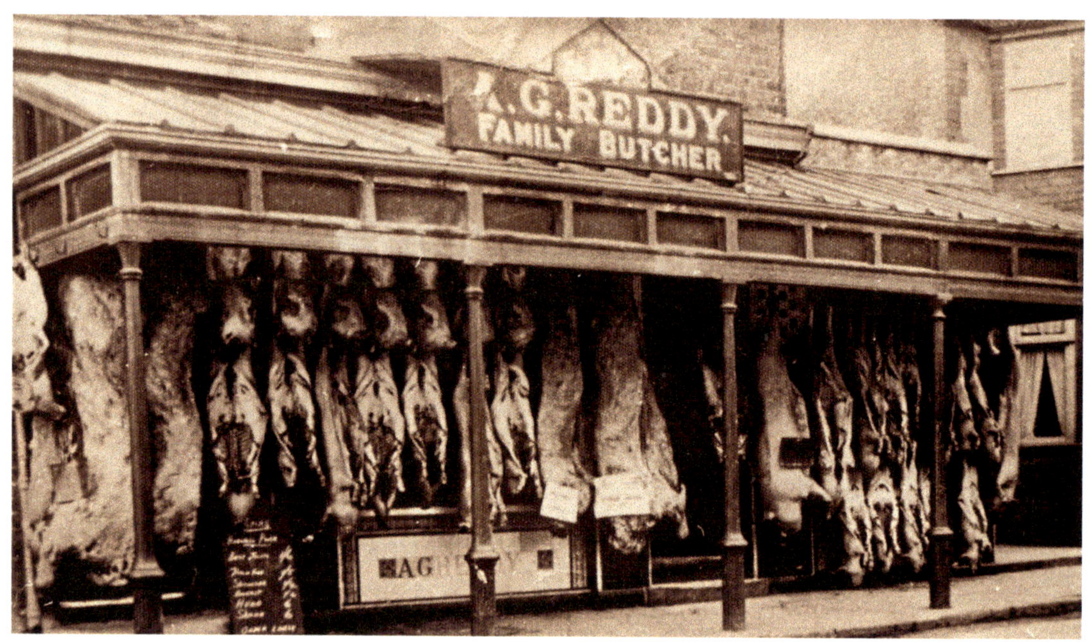

Reddy's Butchers, Pensby Road

An impressive show for A. G. Reddy's butcher's shop for Christmas 1931. With butcher's shops in both Pensby Road and the Lydiate, the Reddy family were in business for ninety-nine years in Heswall. After closure, this shop became the Stanneylands restaurant, and then a variety of other shops. Recently it has reopened as a restaurant.

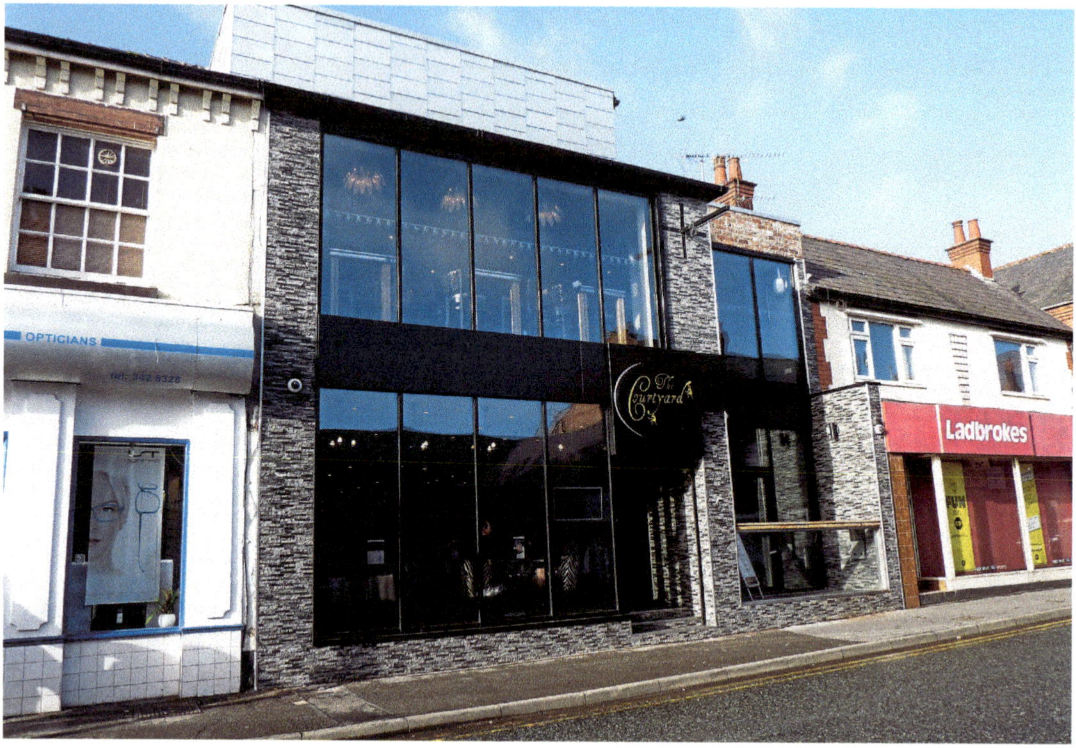

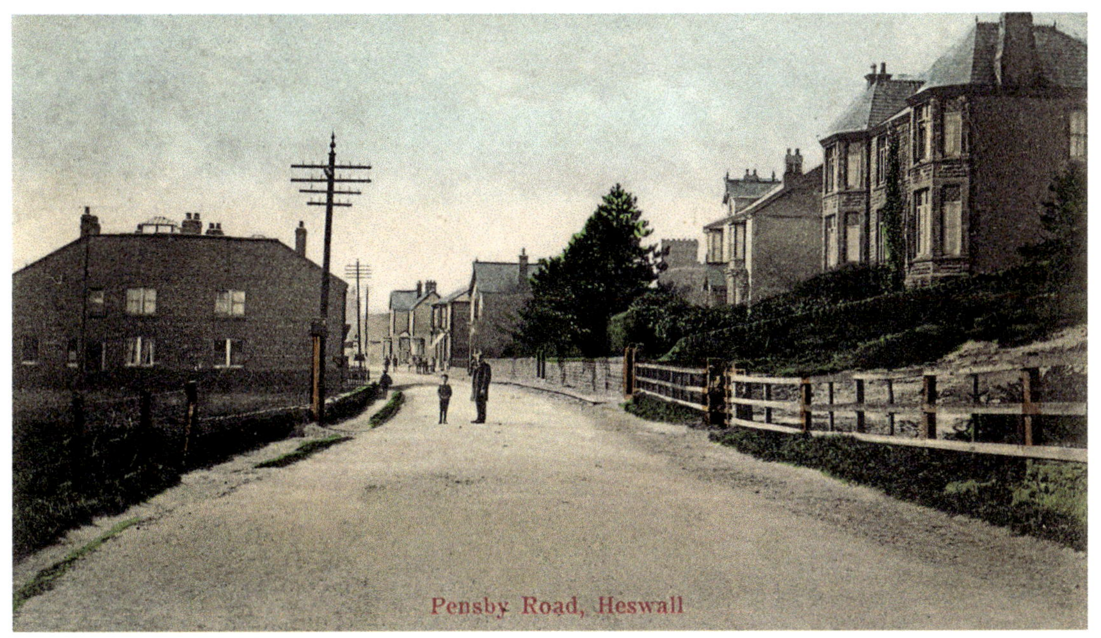

Looking Down Pensby Road

Looking down to Heswall Cross, this photograph was taken before May Road was made up. The building in the foreground is Fulwood House, which was a doctor's surgery. This house and the house beyond have now been replaced by shops. The general post office was built on the land seen behind the fence on the right in 1954.

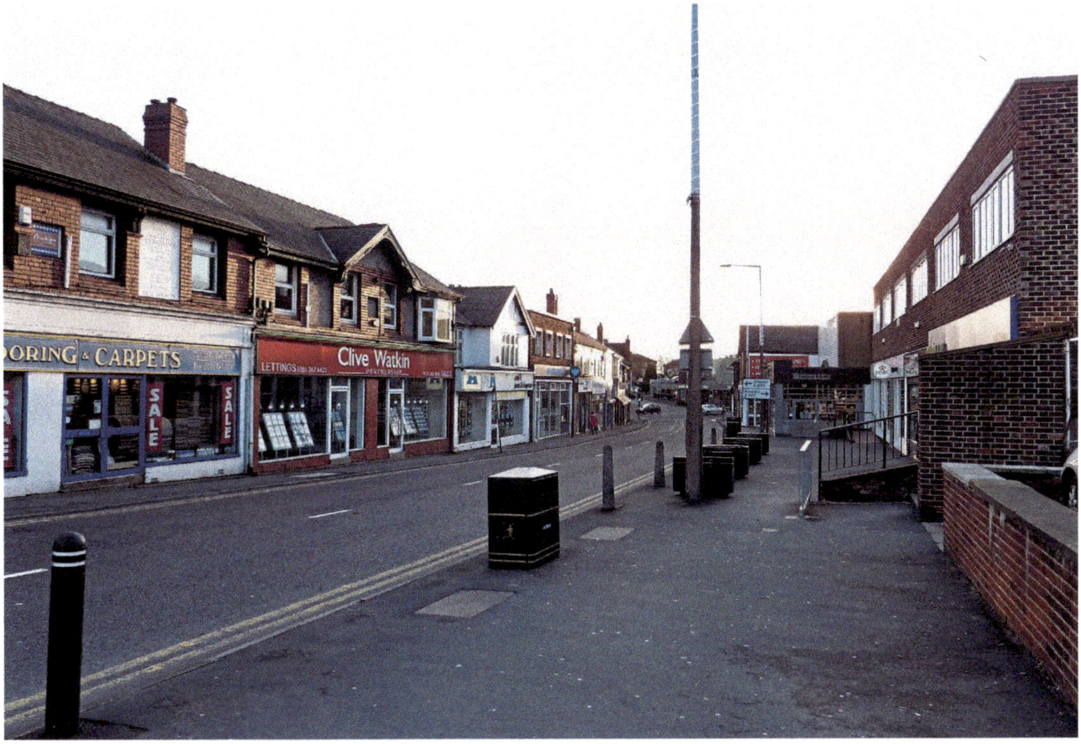

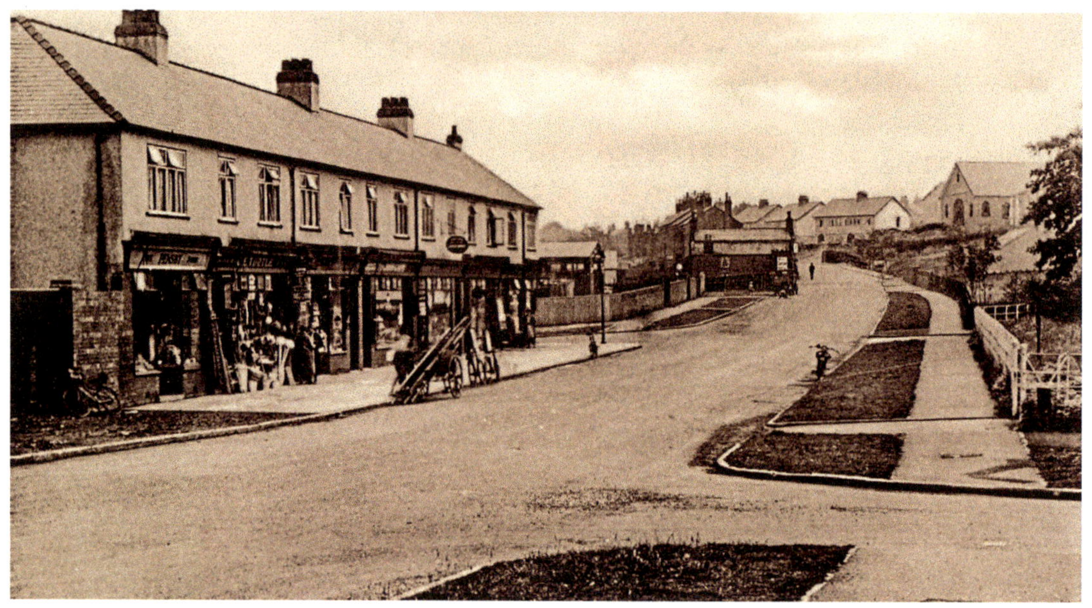

Whitfield Buildings

This group of shops at the top of Whitfield Lane is known as Whitfield Buildings. In pre-supermarket days, they contained every sort of shop, from butchers to haberdashers. Daily shopping was an essential part of post-war life and it was possible to obtain most items from these shops. The site of Roebucks Haulage Co., seen in the distance, is now the Harvest Mouse.

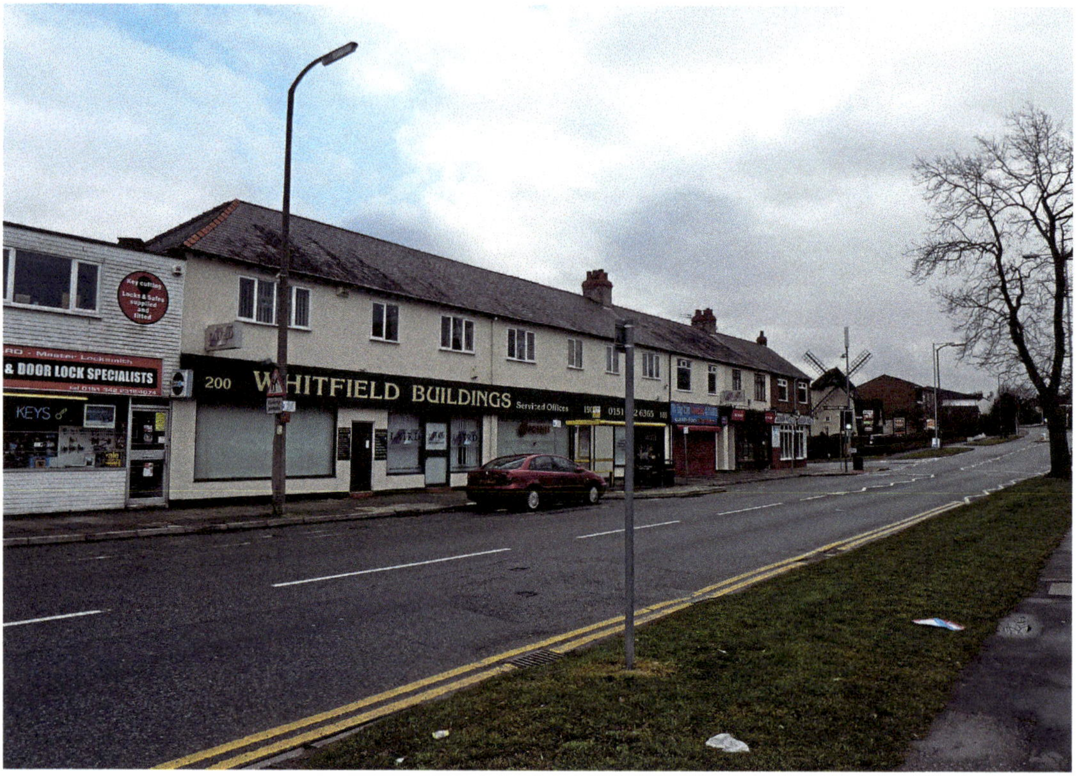

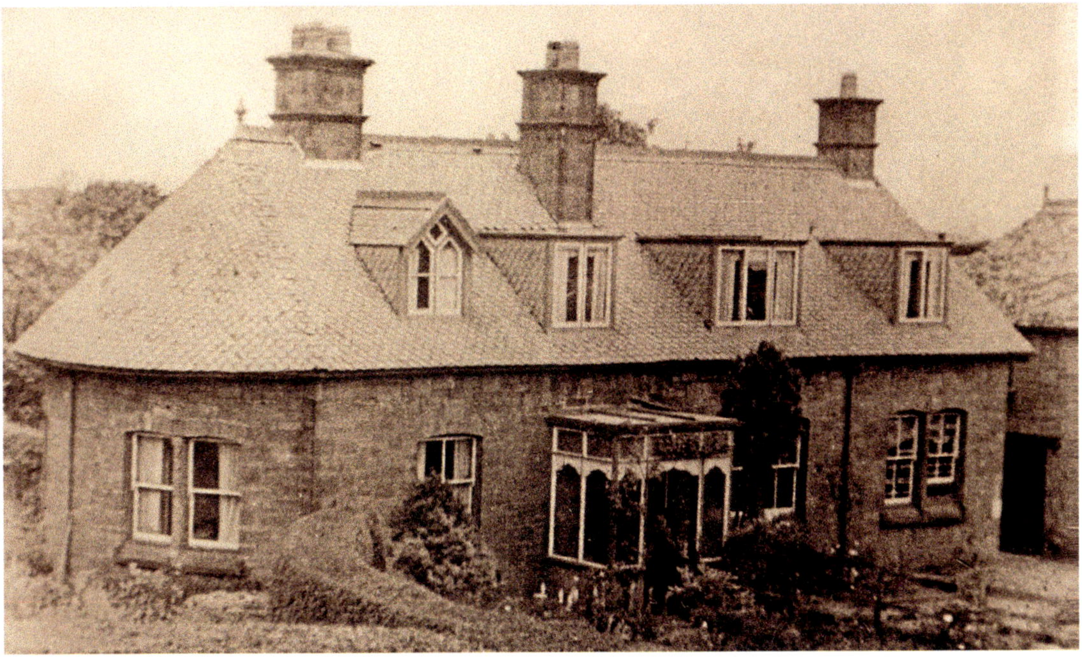

The Beehive Dairy

This dairy in Whitfield Lane, owned by the Thompson family, was so named as it was in the shape of a beehive. Heswall Primary School, which was built on its site in 1976, retains a beehive as its emblem.

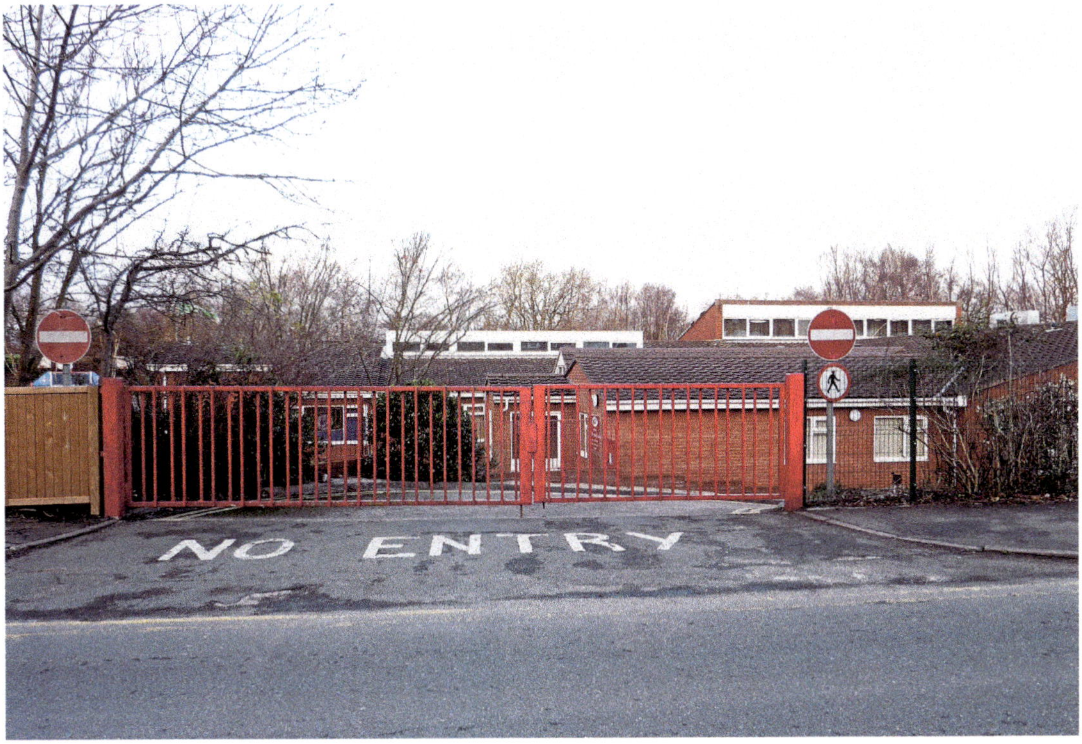

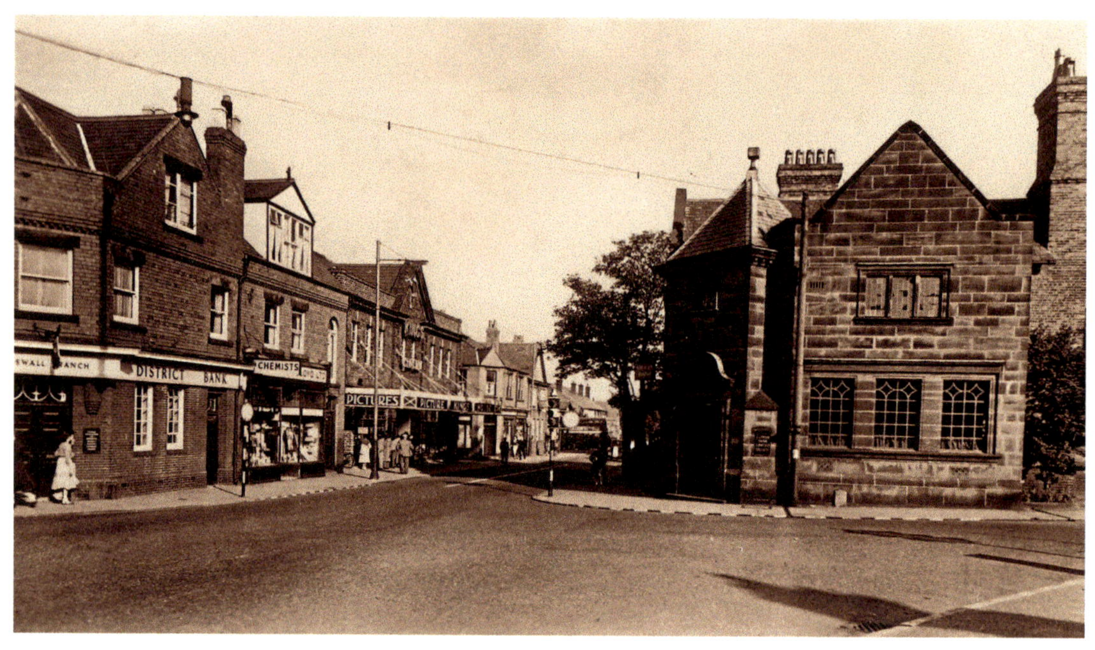

Looking Down Telegraph Road Towards Gayton

King's Cinema can be seen on the left and Lloyds Bank on the right, an attractive building which is now listed.

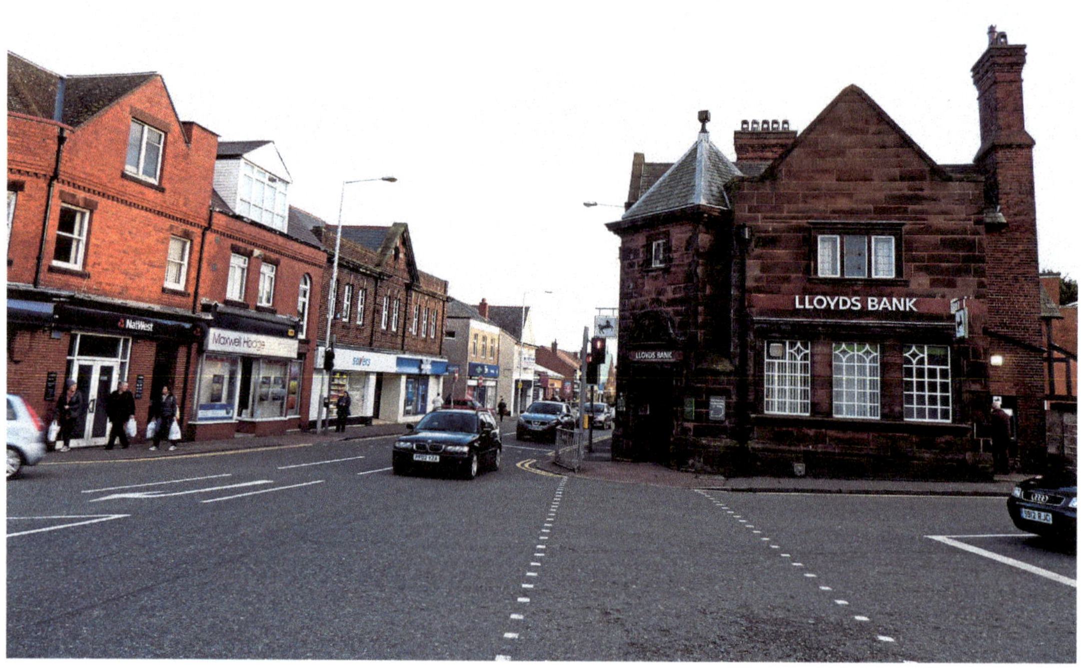

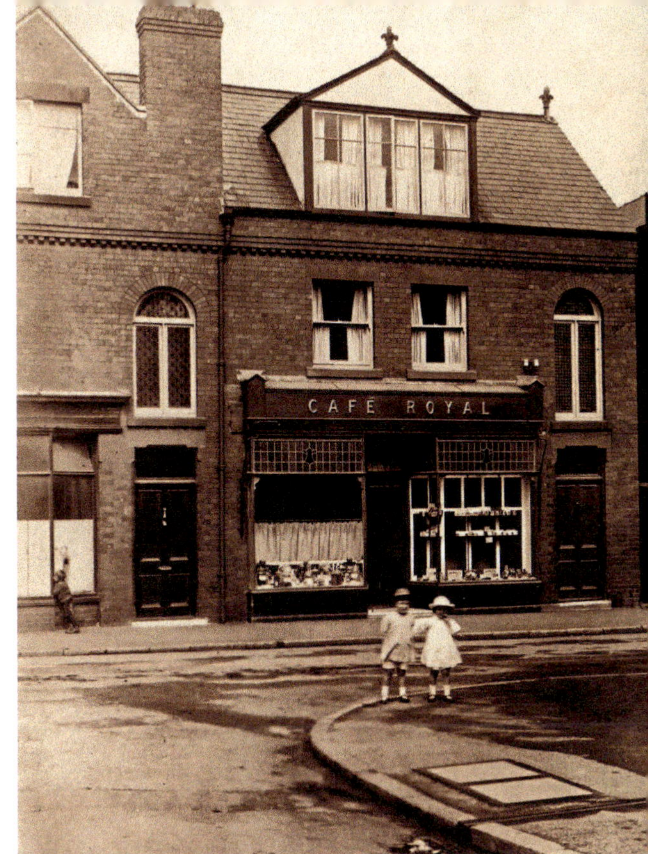

Café Royal

This café is now a solicitors' office in the centre of Heswall. Later, J. Ambrose Lloyd took over the building as a chemist, when he moved from the building next door as the District Bank took it over.

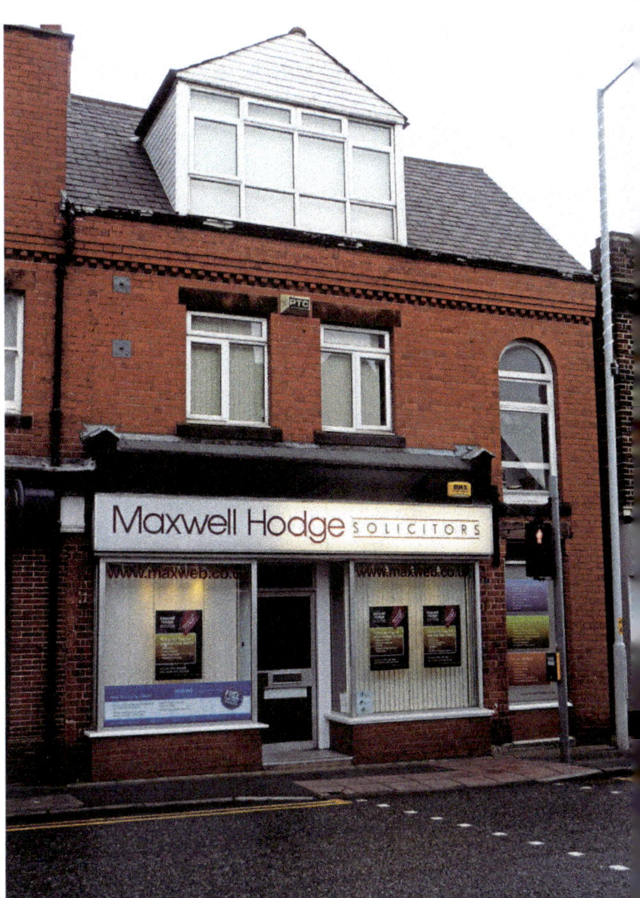

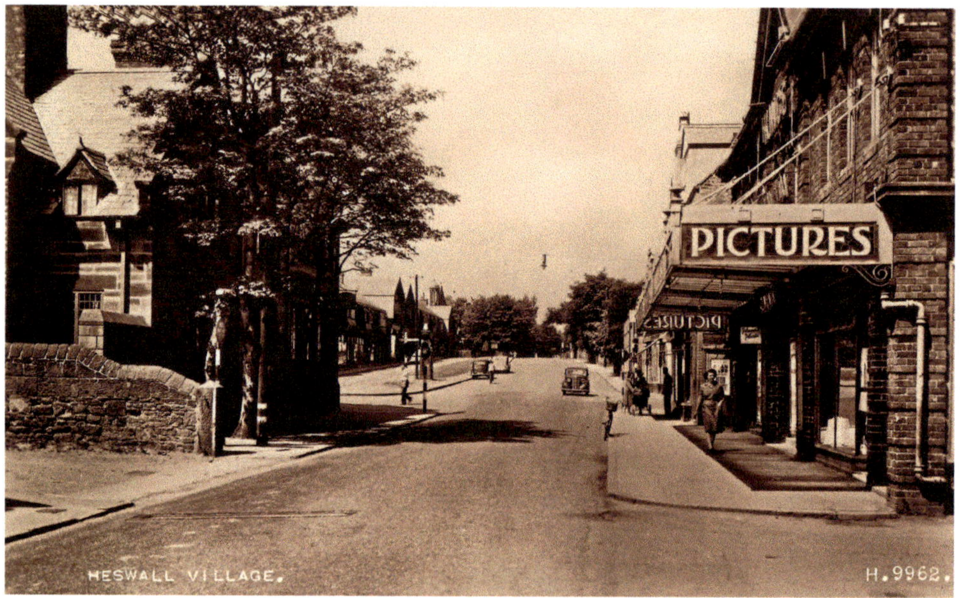

The King's Cinema

Johnny Pye was an enterprising character, who used his buses to transport the people of Heswall to Birkenhead. He stored the buses in the newly built King's Hall. He left Heswall to continue his bus service in North Wales. In 1928, King's Hall became a cinema, although films had been shown there from 1916. In 1928, it was modernised and could seat many hundreds. In 1958, the building was put up for sale and became Lennon's Supermarket, and was later divided into two shops.

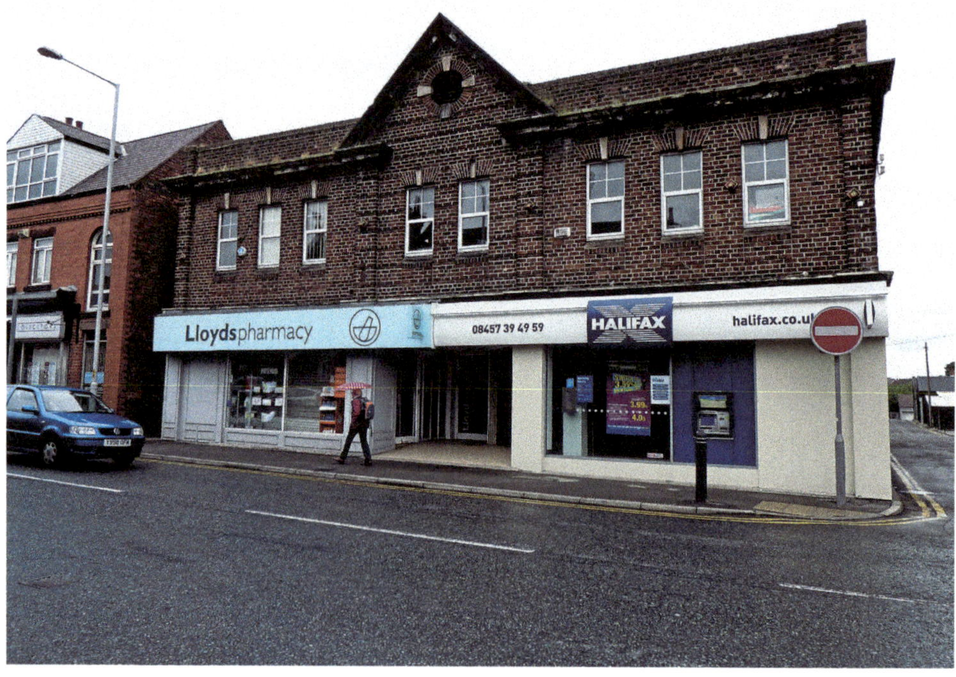

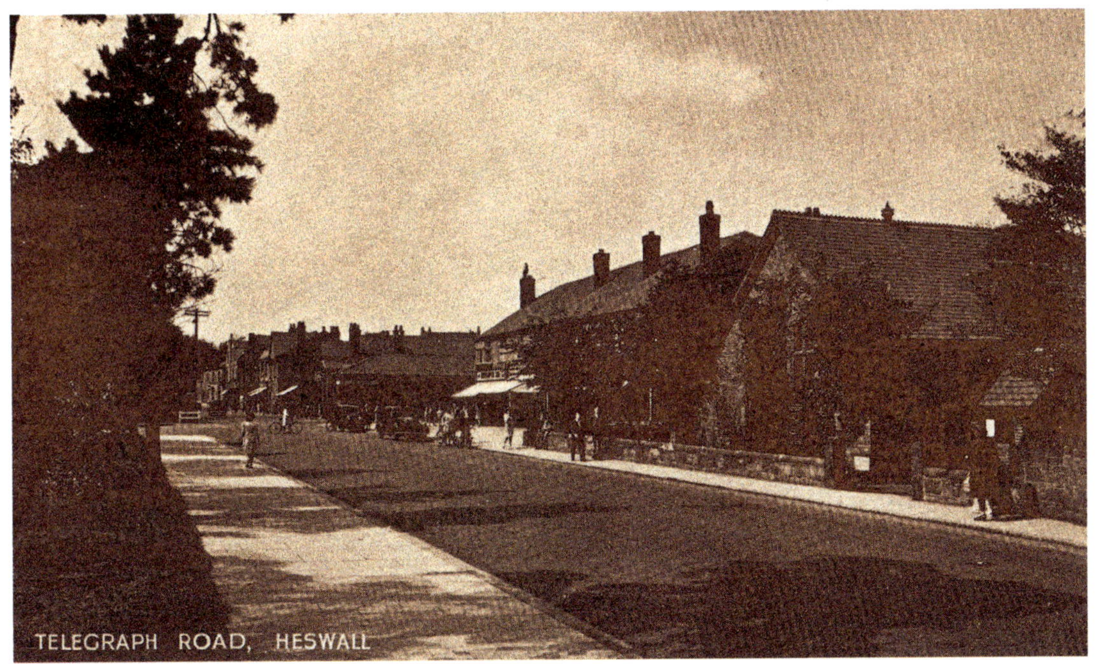

Mission Church

The Mission room was built in 1891 and cost £400 to build. It was extended in 1921 and then known as the Mission Church of the Good Shepherd. In 1925, the parish hall was added. In the 1960s, plans were made to build a new church on the site. The foundation stone of the current Church of the Good Shepherd was laid by the Bishop of Chester on 1 December 1962.

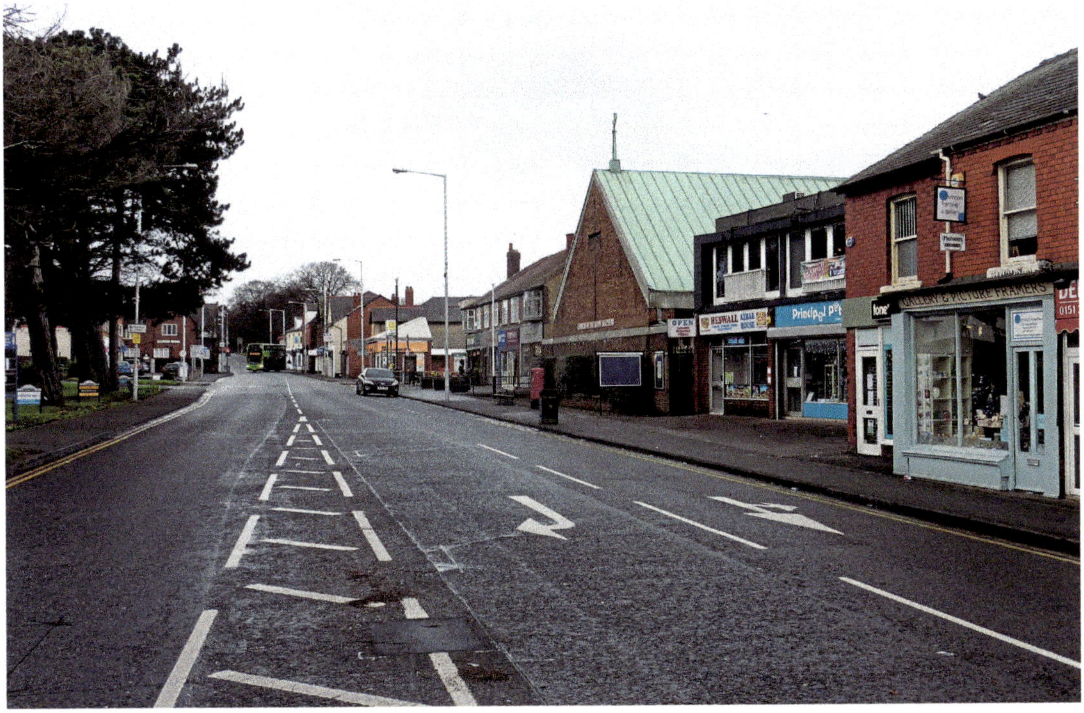

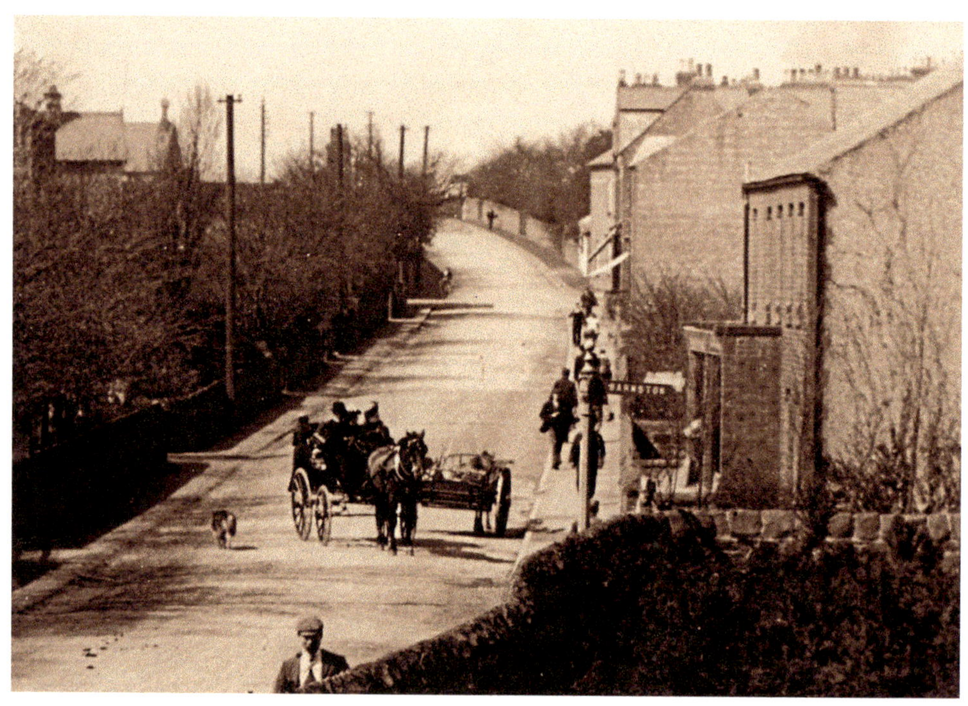

Downham Road and Telegraph Road Junction

The junction of Downham Road South, pictured here around 1900, looks very different today. The wall surrounding Hill House can be seen on the left. The house on the right was to become Fox's ironmongers for many decades.

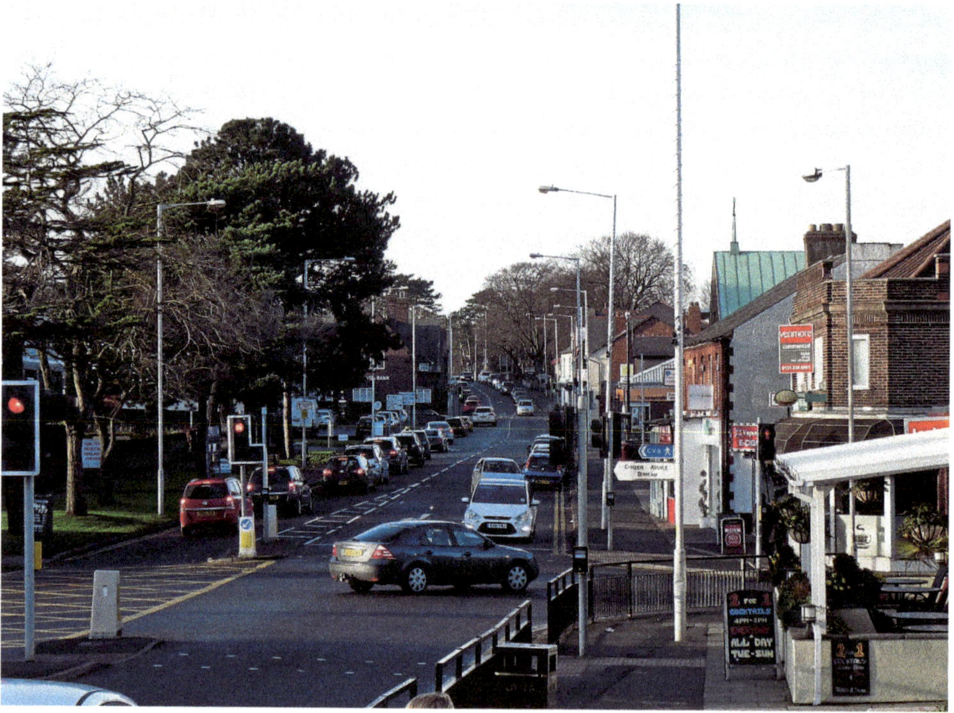

Methodist Church

Methodism in Heswall began in a farm in Downham Road South. In 1859, a hall was built in Milner Road and was known as Gayton Wesleyan chapel. In 1891, the Centenary Methodist chapel was built at a cost of £1,800, so named as John Wesley had died 100 years earlier. Over the past 100 years, this building has seen many changes and improvements.

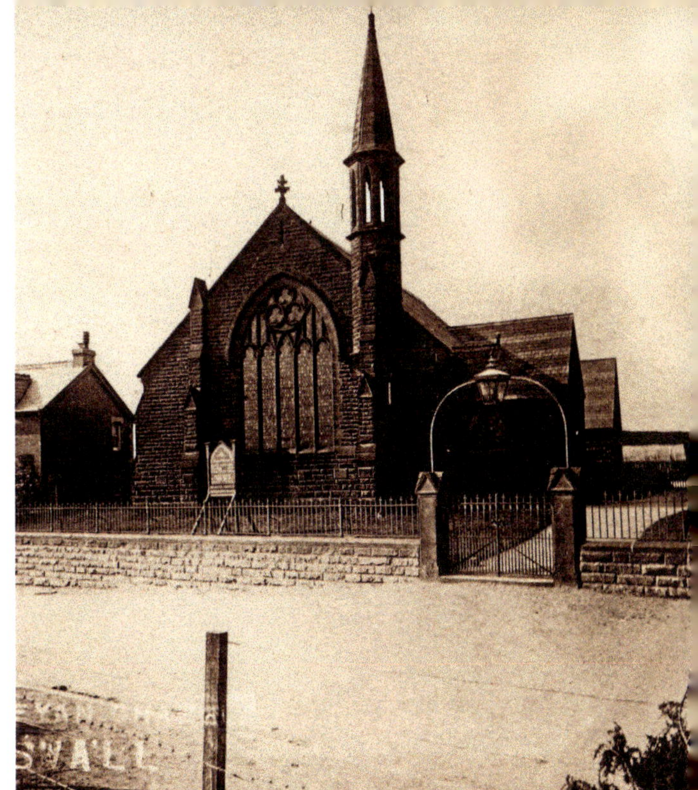

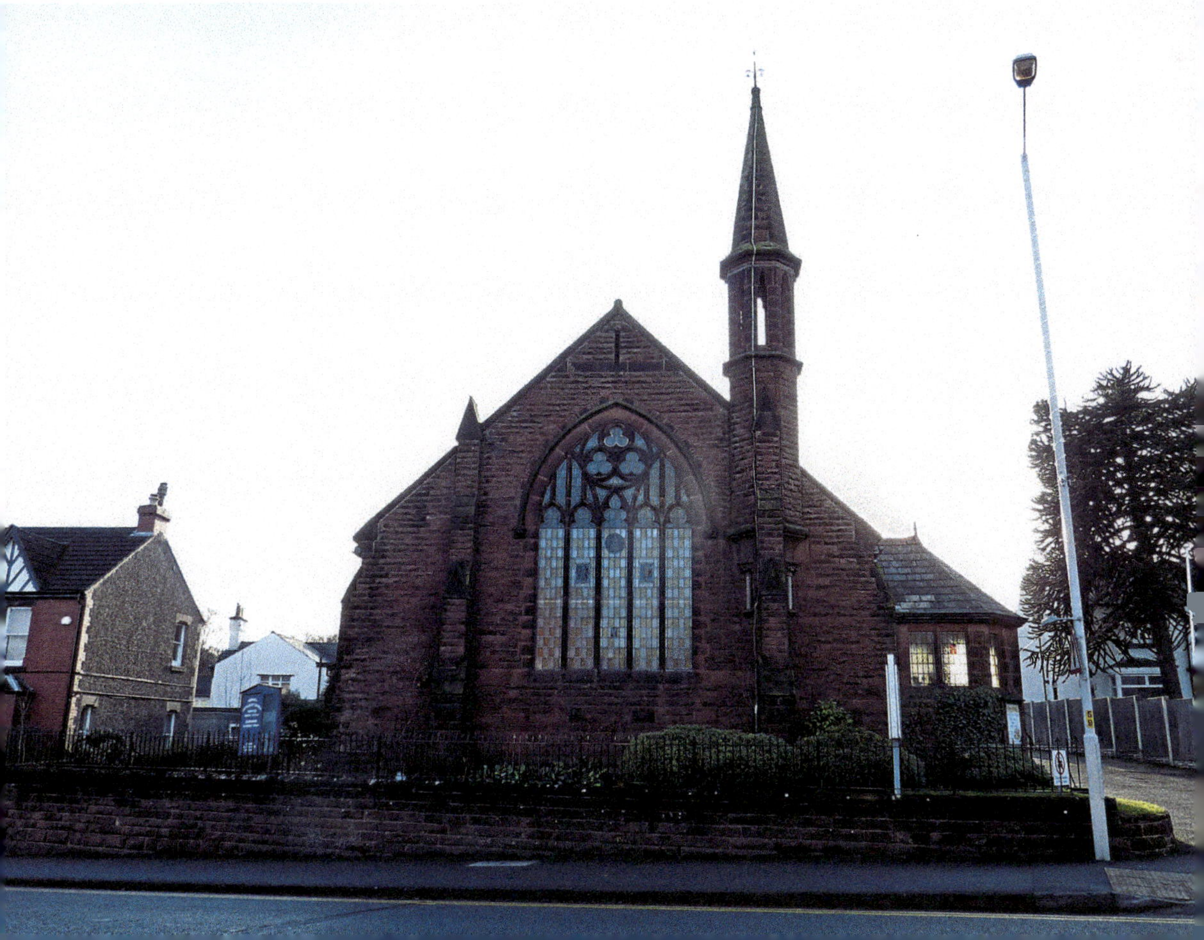

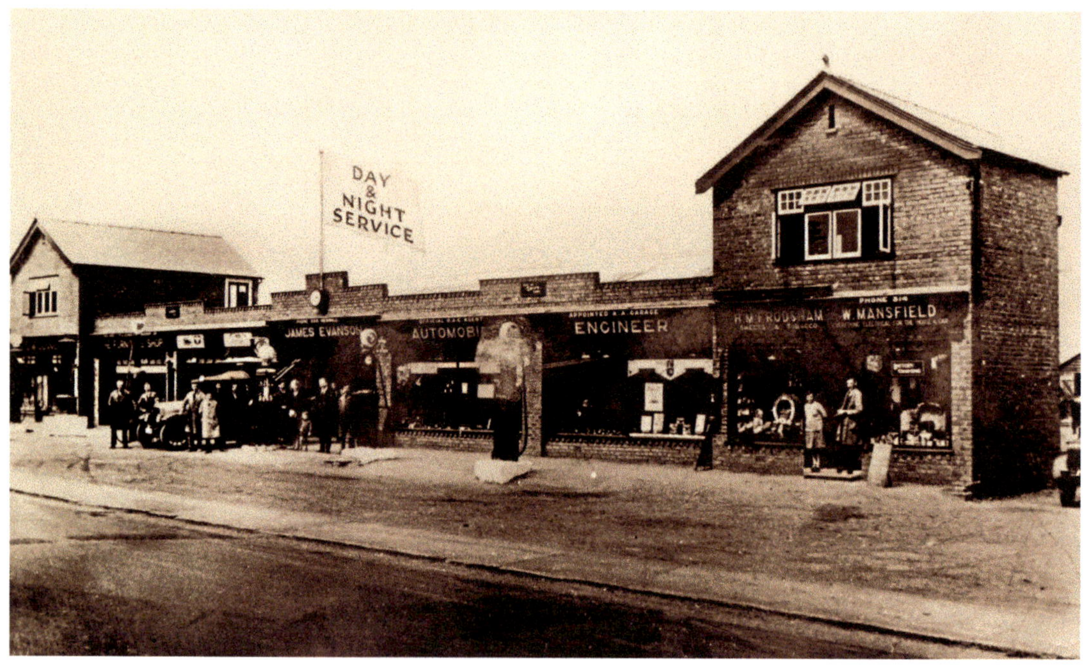

Evanson's Garage

Jim Evanson ran this garage in Telegraph Road for many years. The building also housed a couple of shops and there were rooms upstairs called the Cora Rooms named after Jim's wife. These were used by many local organisations as a meeting place. The garage was replaced by Marks & Spencer.

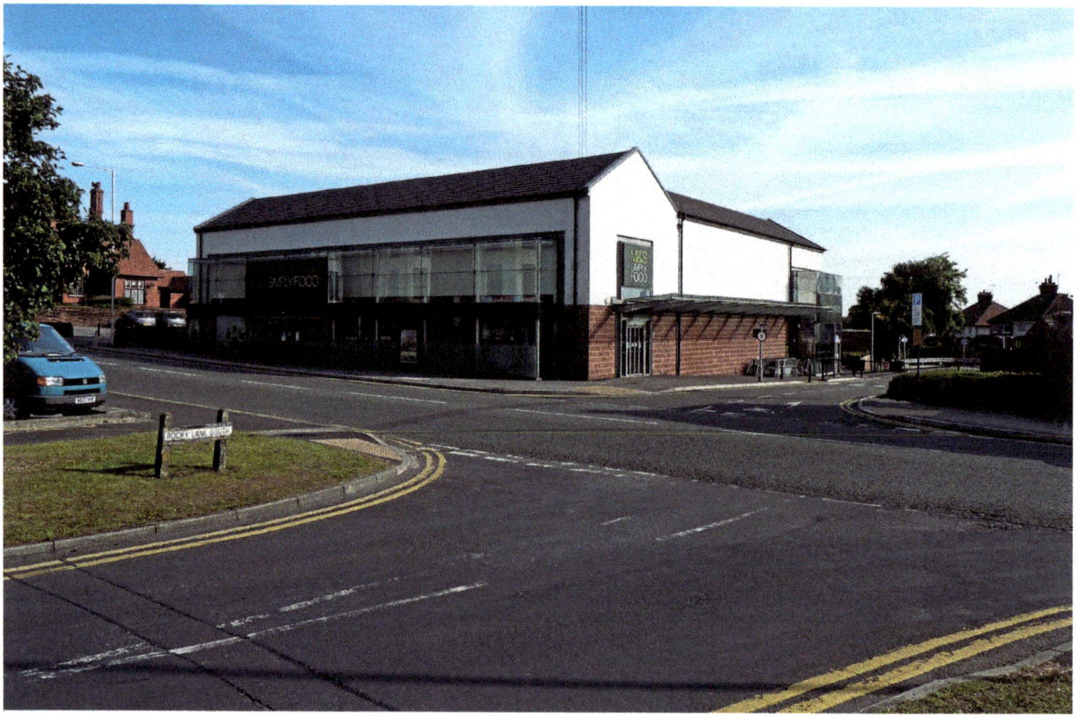

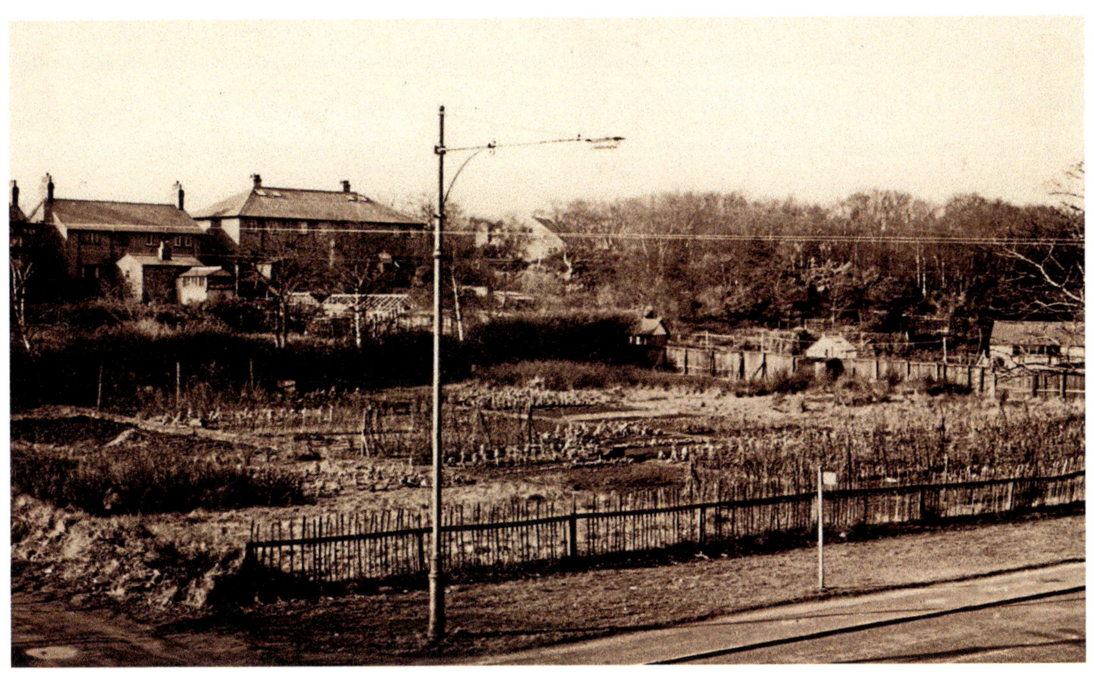

Allotments, Telegraph Road

Beacon Court now stands on the site of these allotments. The houses in the background are in Beacon Lane.

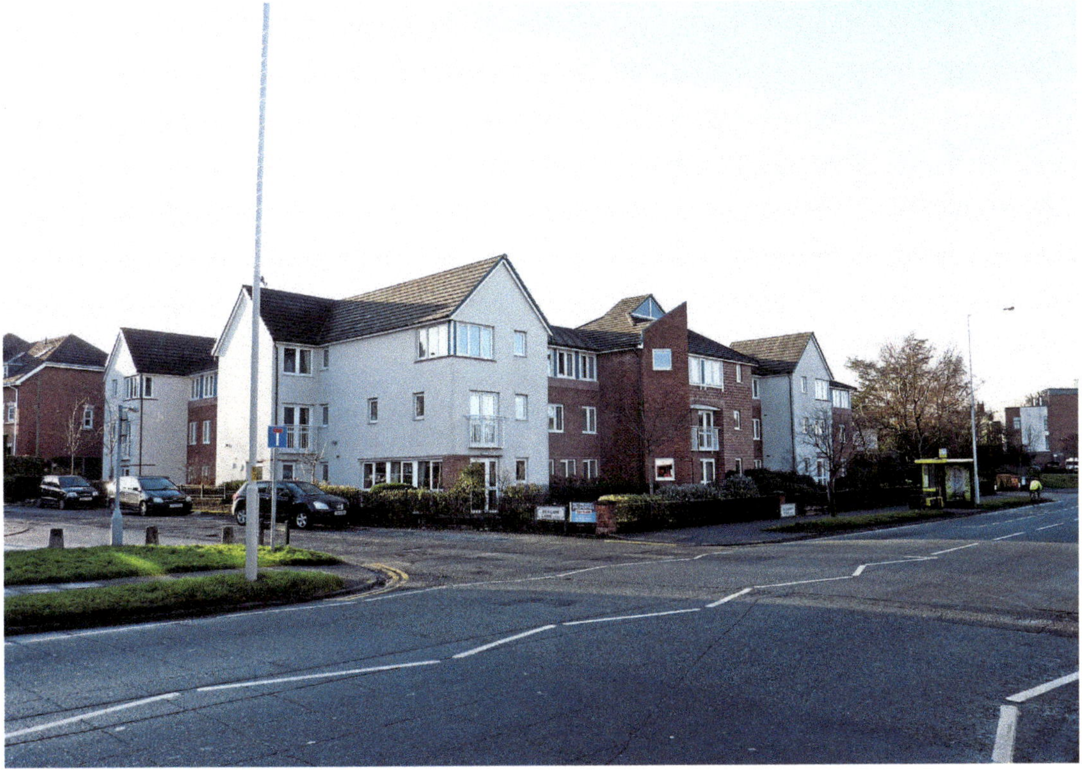

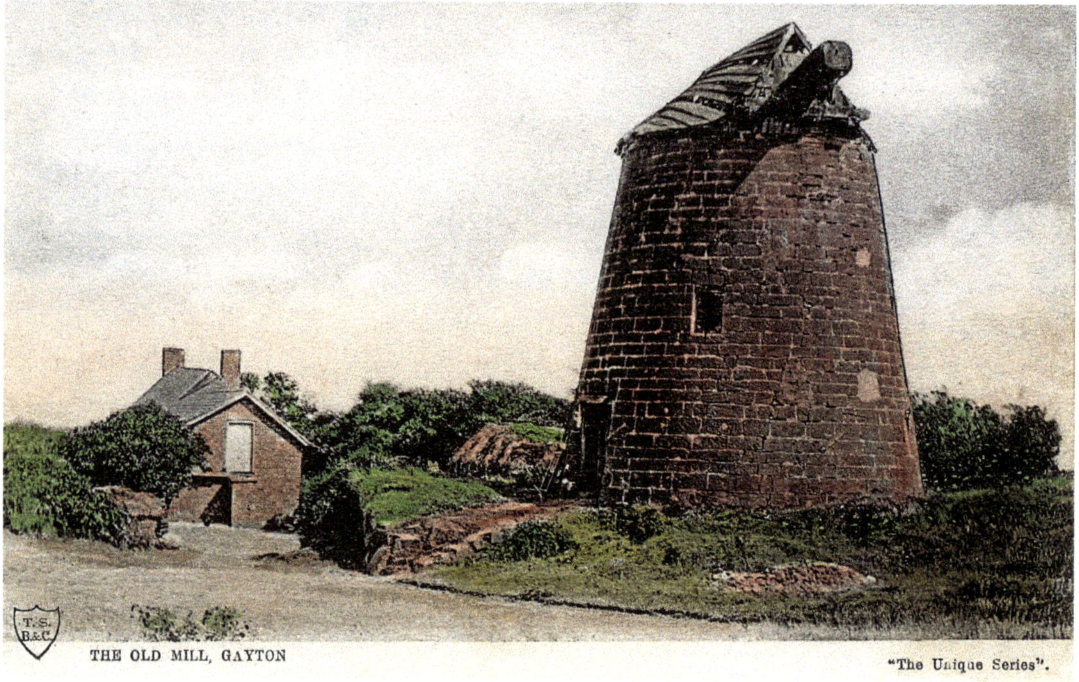

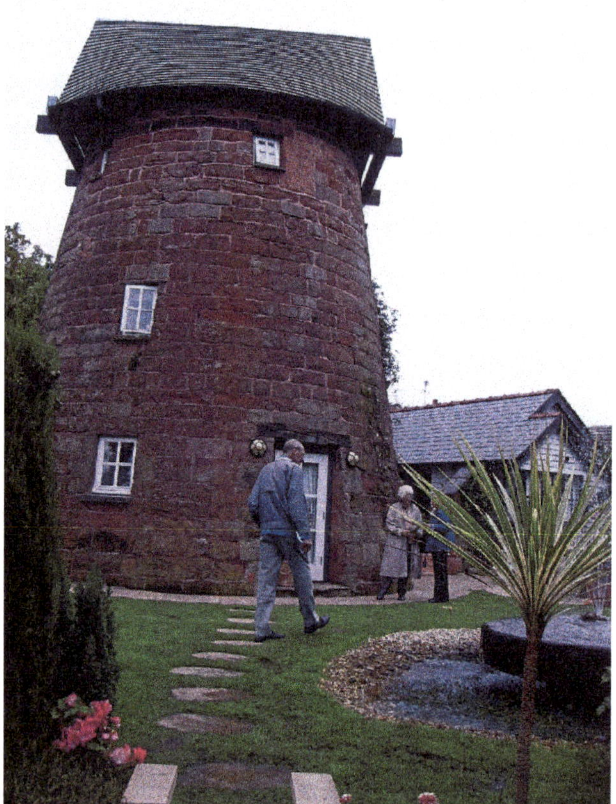

Gayton Mill

Gayton Mill, now a private house, was said to be Wirral's oldest Tower Mill, dating back to the sixteenth century. The Woodward family lived in it for many years and raised a large family there. The mill was last worked in the 1860s.

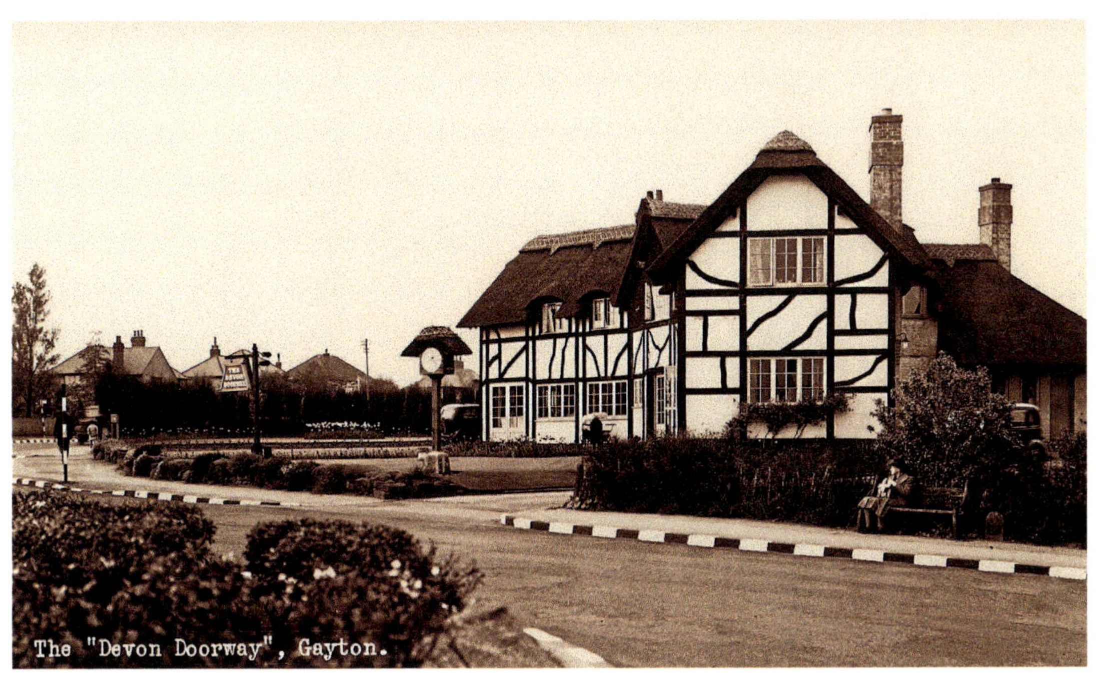

The Devon Doorway

The Devon Doorway was built in the 1930s by a Mrs Aldridge, who hailed from Devon. Now a restaurant and public house, it has been a tea room and meeting place for many organisations over the years. The original electric clock still stands in the grounds.

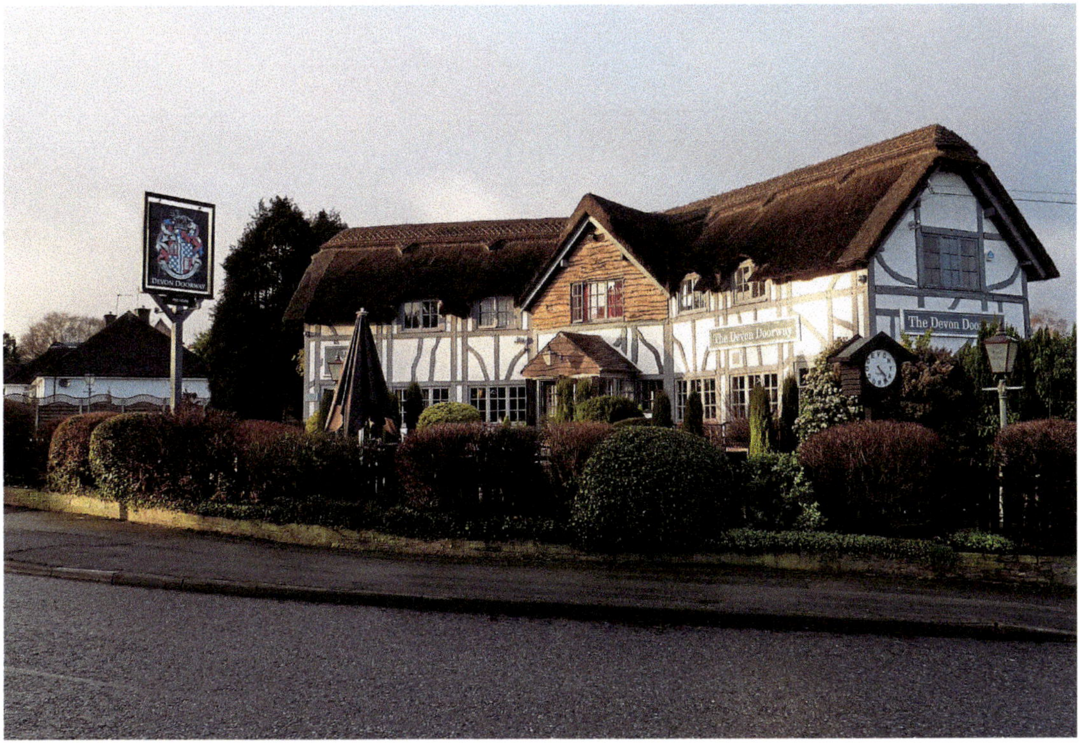

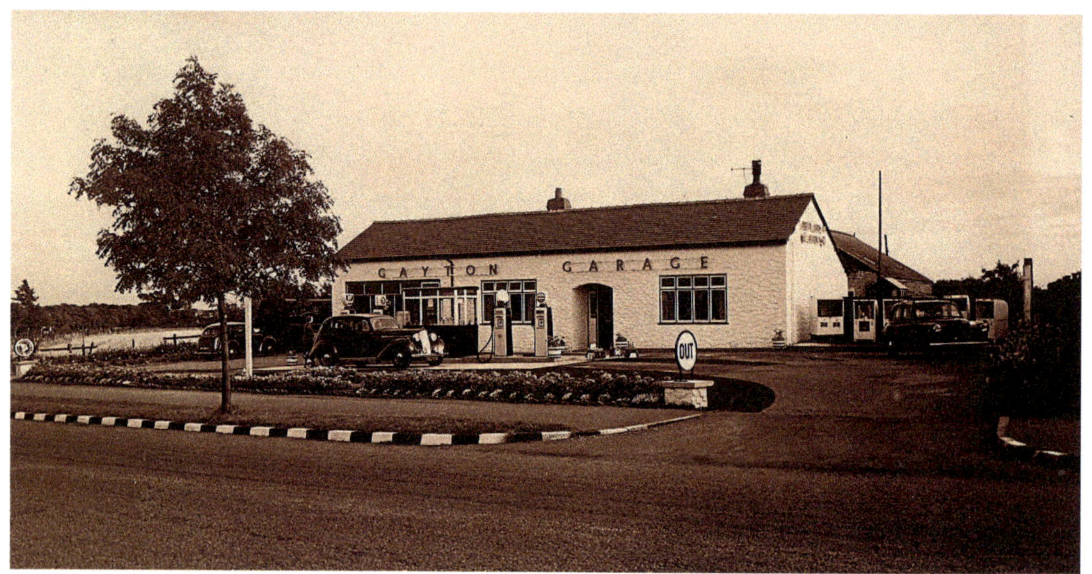

Gayton Garage

This garage was built on land once owned by the Glegg family. It is situated close to the area where the Heswall Horse Show was held for many years, an annual event that brought the whole community of Heswall together.

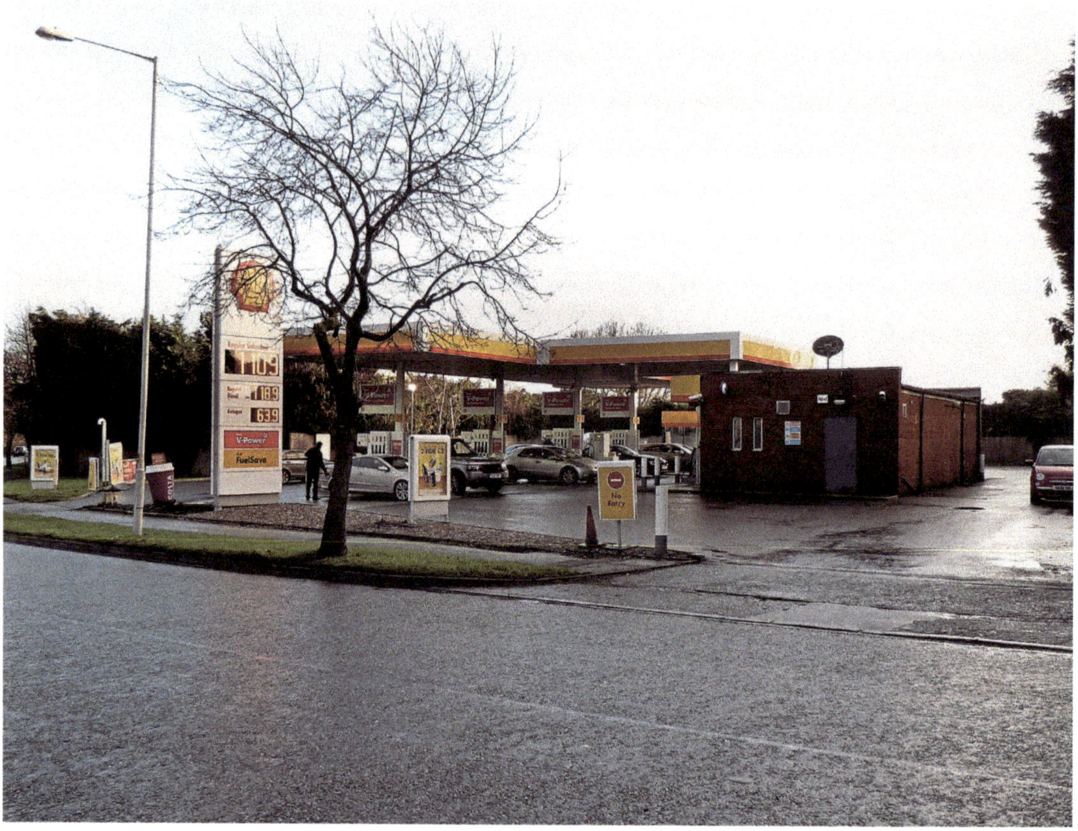

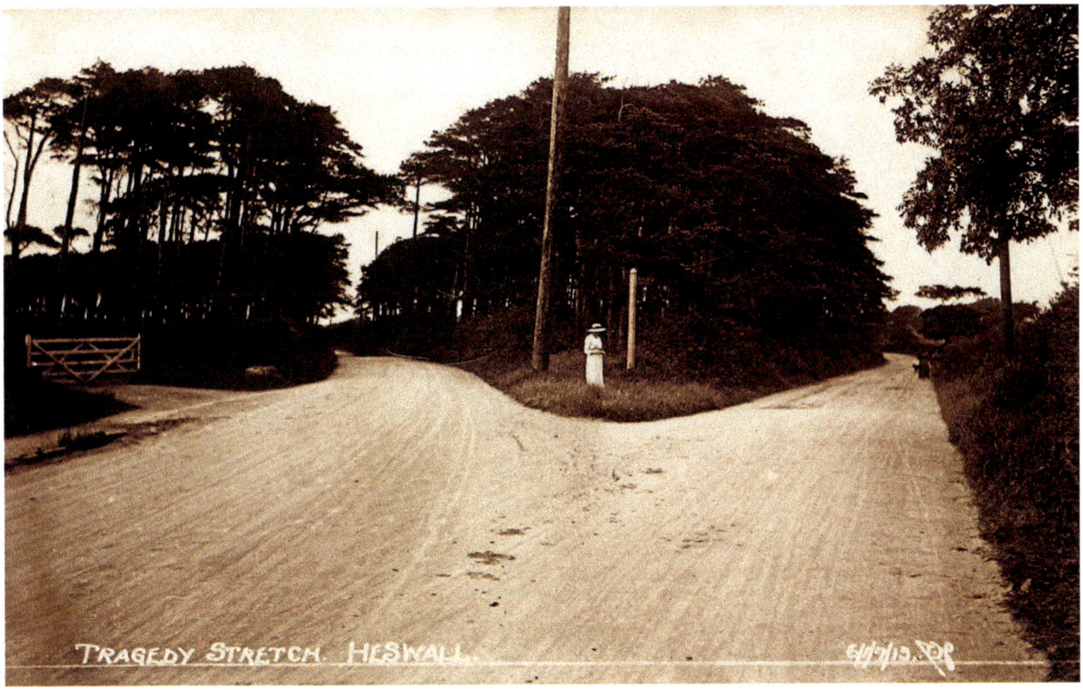

The Plantation

This wooded area between Barnston Road and Brimstage Road, donated to the public by Richard Hooper in 1930, was a place where local children would be found on the day before Oak Apple Day (or Nettling Day as it was called in Heswall!). On 29 May, all children would wear a sprig of oak taken from the Plantation. If they did not, the boys would strike them over the leg with nettles.

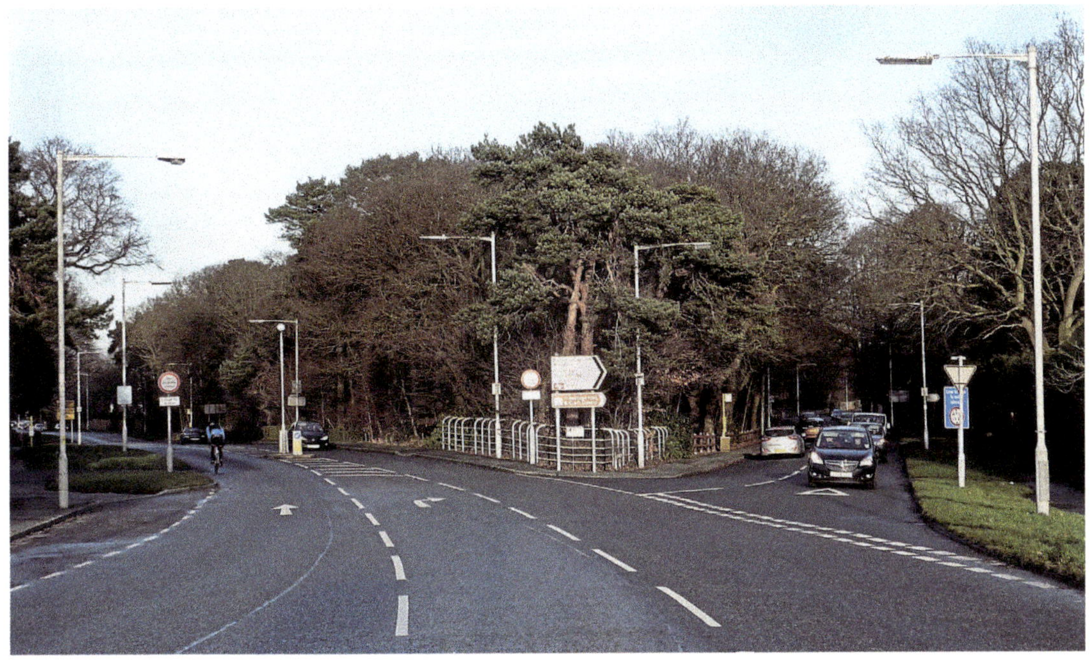

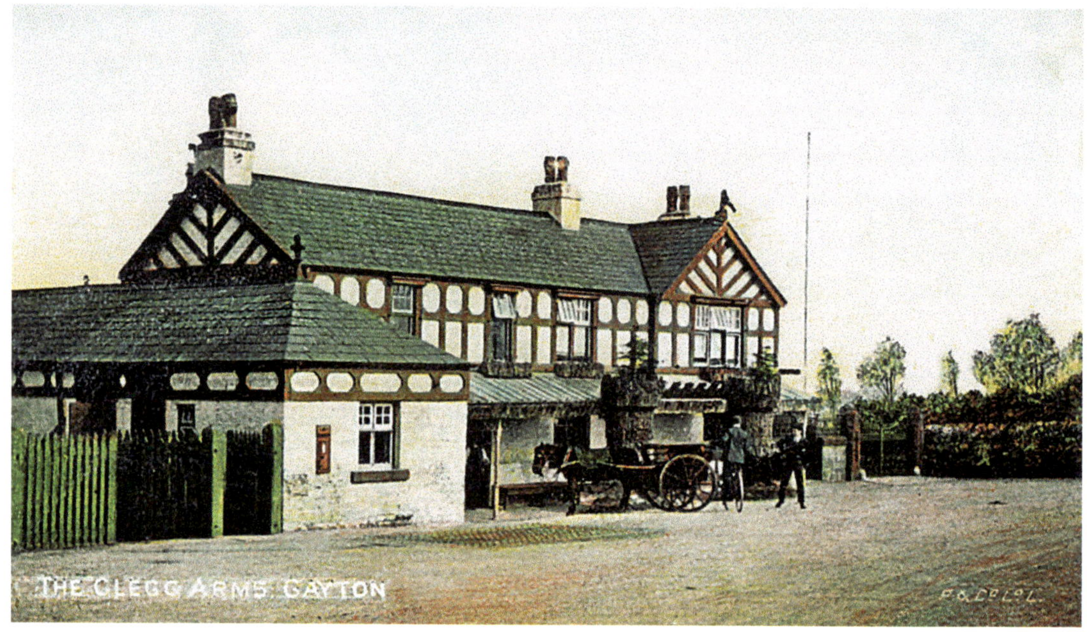

Glegg Arms

Originally called Crabbe's Inn after Edward Crabbe, who was the landlord in the 1850s, it was renamed the Glegg Arms, commemorating the Glegg family, who owned the Gayton estate from 1330 until 1921. Early maps show a smithy attached to the inn. At the front was a public weigh bridge and a veranda surrounded by castellated turrets.

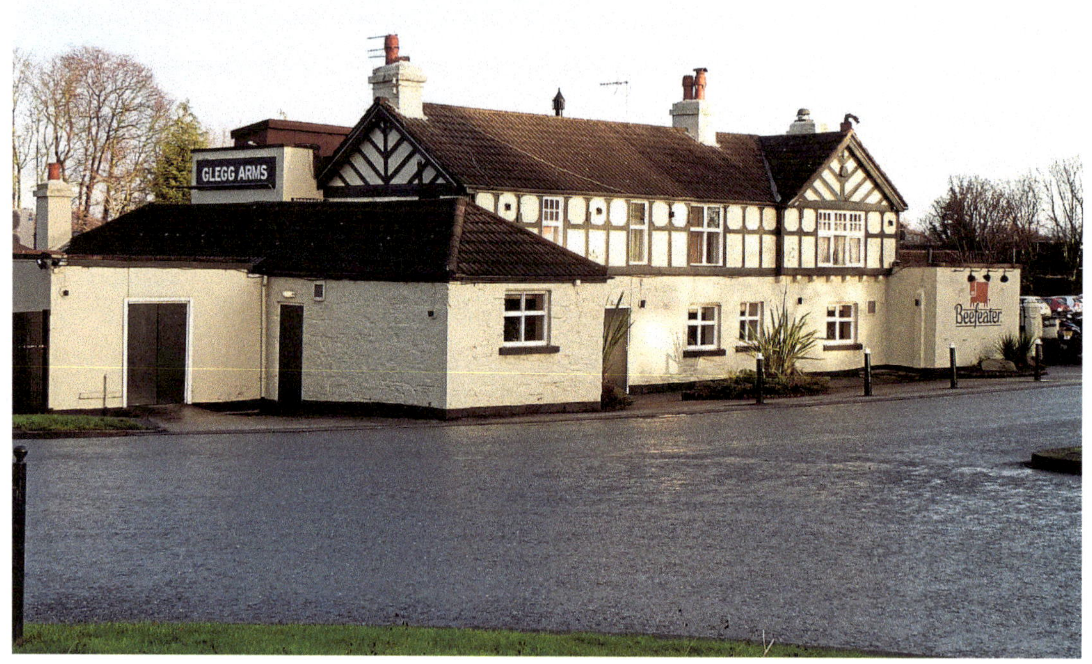

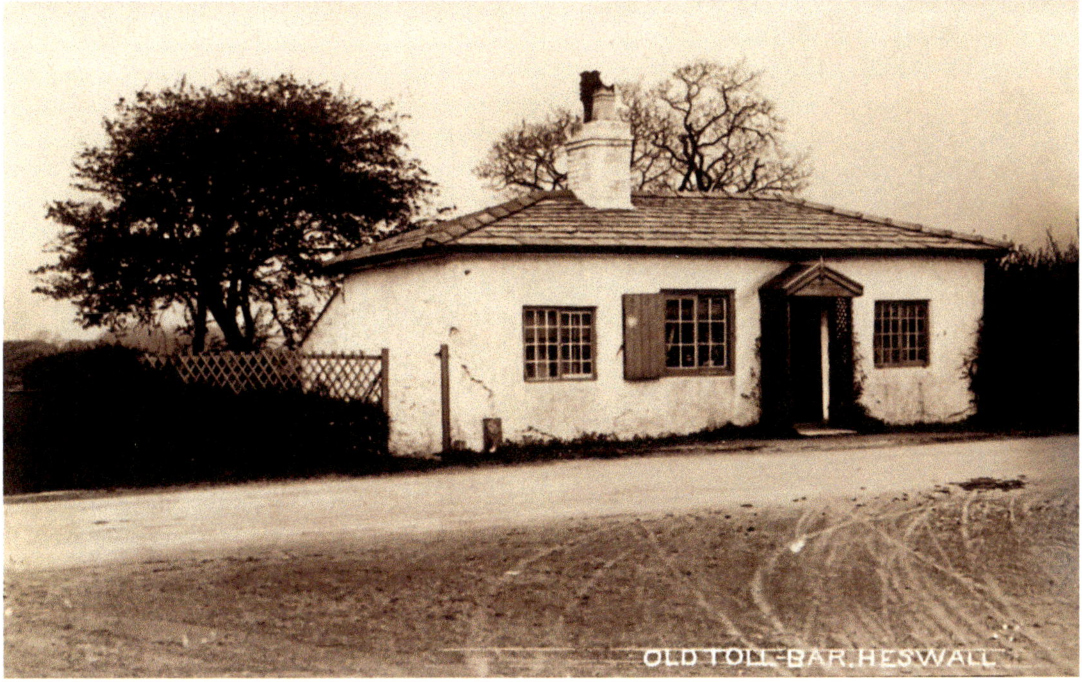

Toll Bar Cottage

Little remains of this cottage, built to collect tolls on the turnpike road from Neston, which was last inhabited in 1965. It was sold in 1979 and now only a few traces within a stable complex remain.

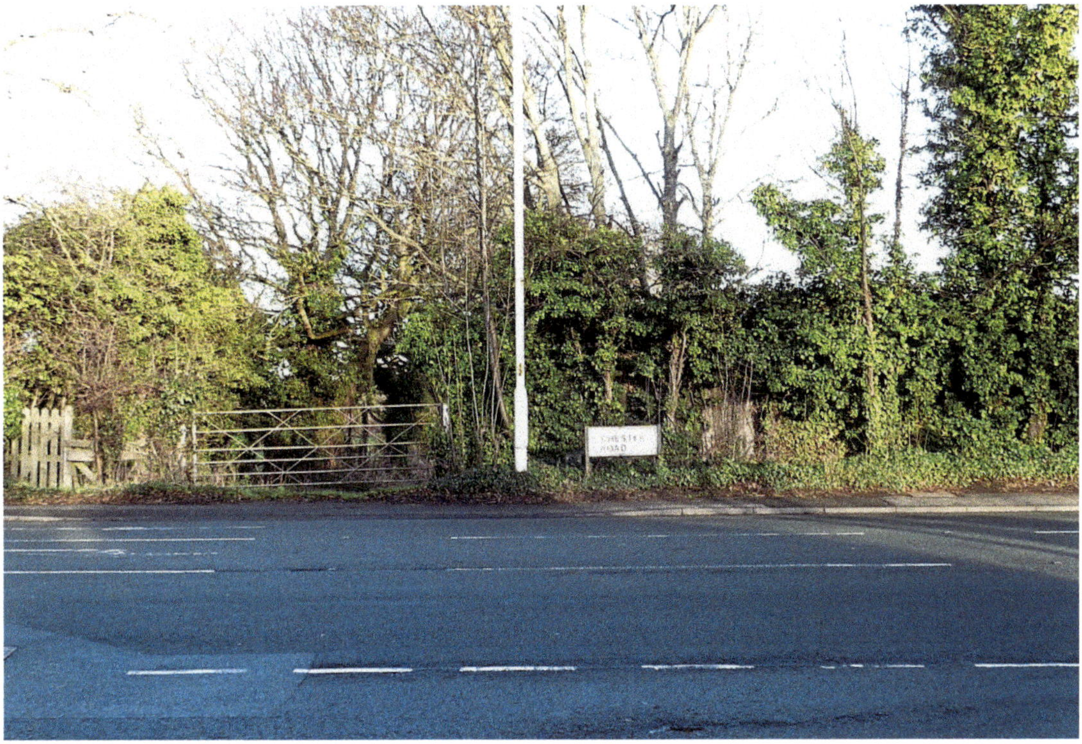

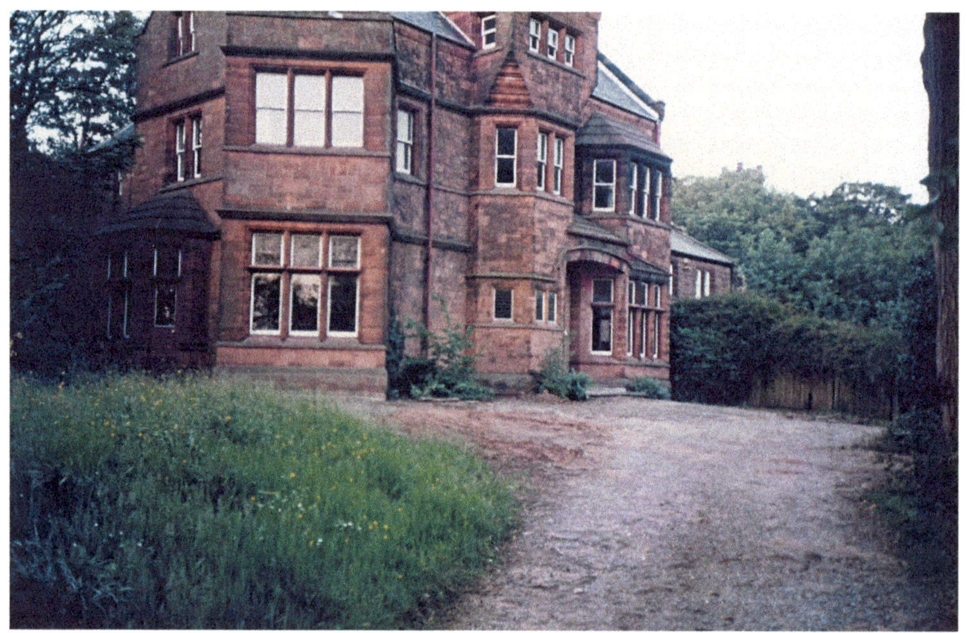

Broomlands School

The road called Broomlands off Thurstaston Road replaces this imposing house. It was originally called Bank House and the Tidswell family lived there for many years. Mrs Tidswell gave her house over in the First World War to be used for soldiers' convalescence. During the 1940s to the late 1960s, the house became Broomlands School, a private day school run by the Widdowson family. In the 1990s, the land was sold. Part of the original house was retained and is at the top of Broomlands among the modern houses built there.

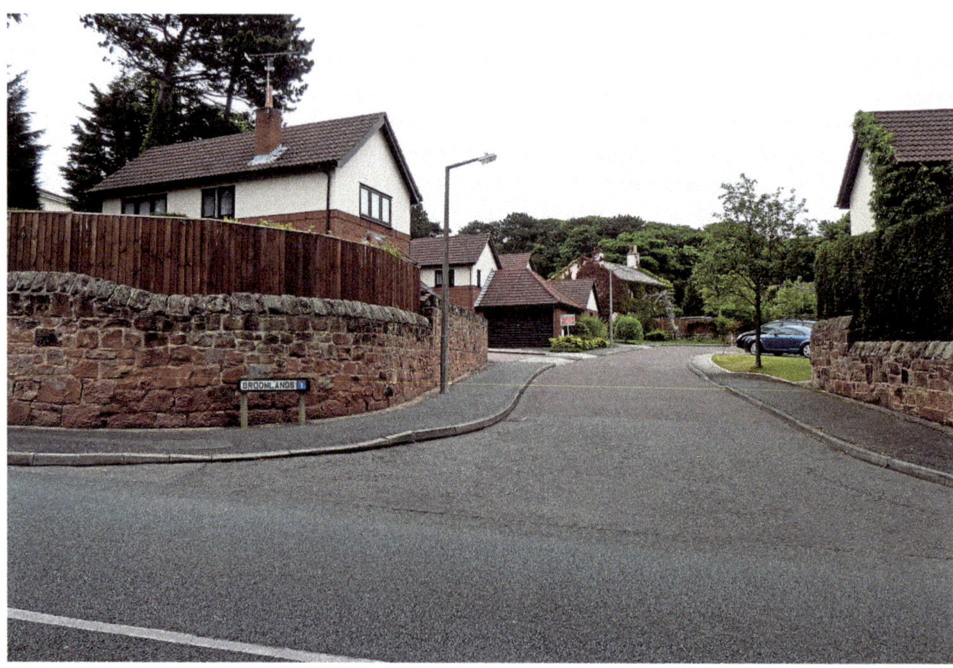

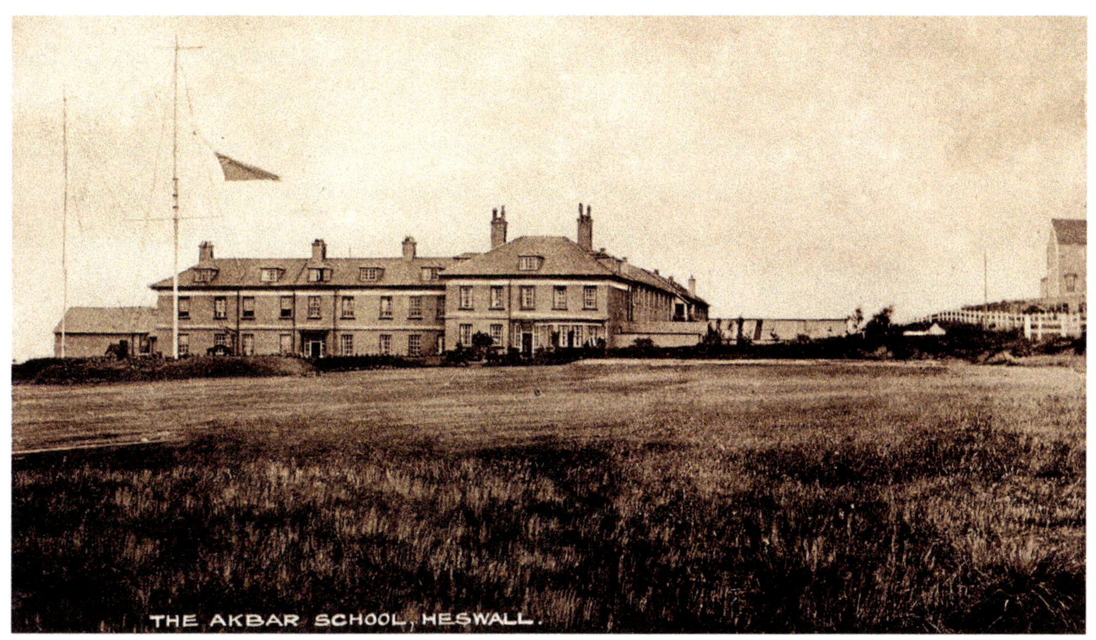

The Akbar

Originally this was the name of a reformatory ship in the River Mersey, which had to be hastily abandoned in 1907 on safety grounds. After a short time at the camp in Broad Lane, the institution was moved to a permanent building in Greenfield Lane off Oldfield Road at a cost of £17,000. It was one of six approved schools that were closed in 1956. Halyard House still remains, converted into flats.

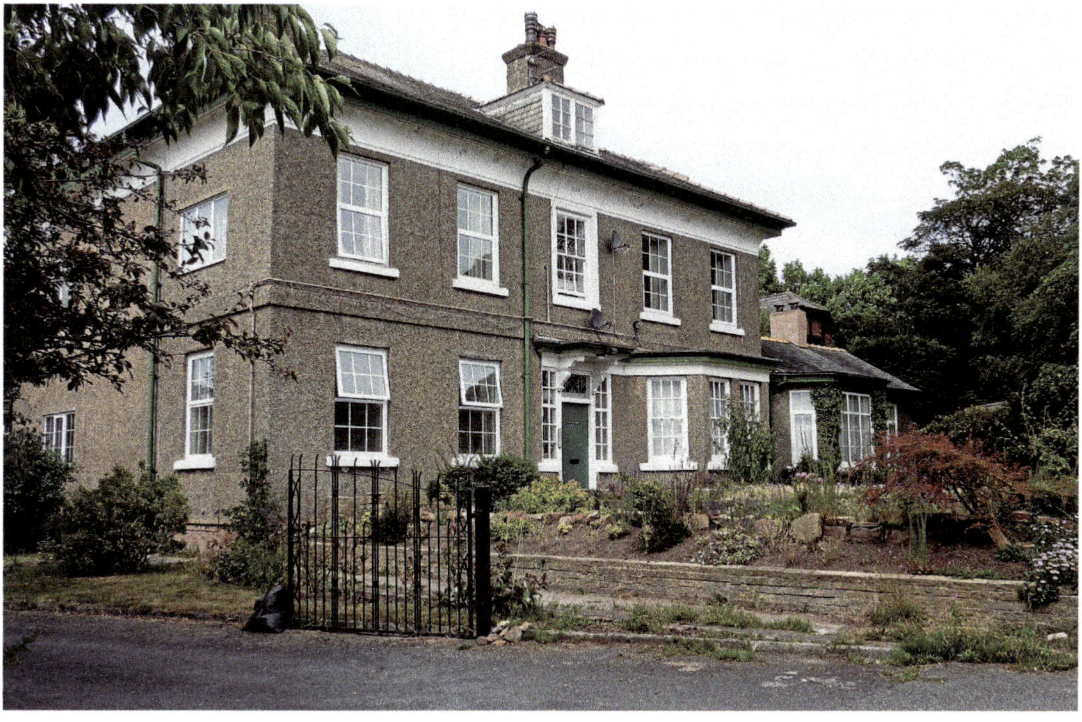

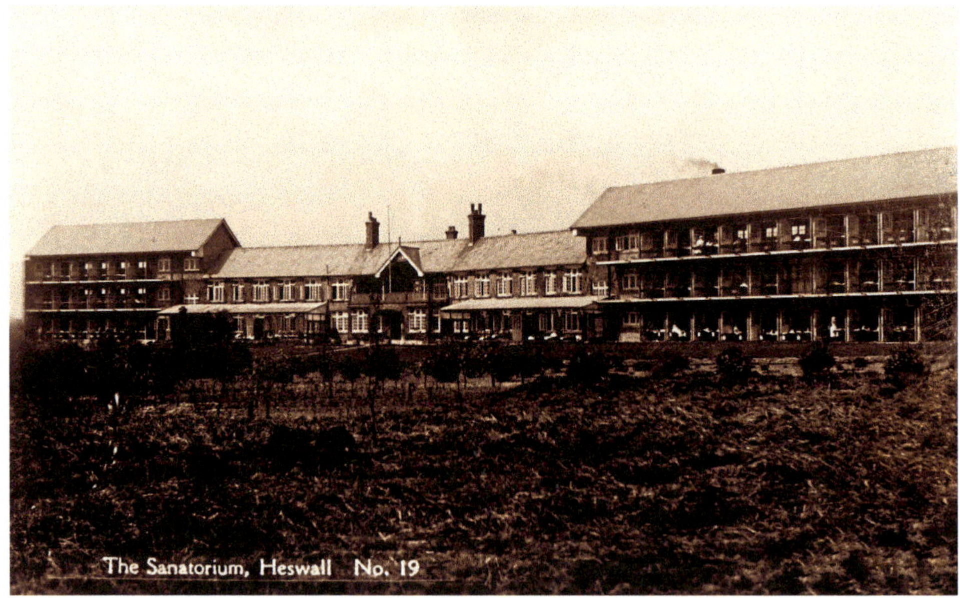

Cleaver Hospital

Oldfield and Dale Gardens now occupy the site of Cleaver Hospital. The hospital opened in 1902 as a children's tuberculosis sanatorium. During the Second World War, the children were evacuated to Rhuddlan and the hospital then admitted adults. In 1950, the name was changed from Toxteth Park Joint Hospital to Cleaver Hospital, honouring Mr H. P. Cleaver, who inspired its building. The hospital closed in 1983 and in 1988 the land was sold for £2 million. The nurses' home from the hospital still remains.

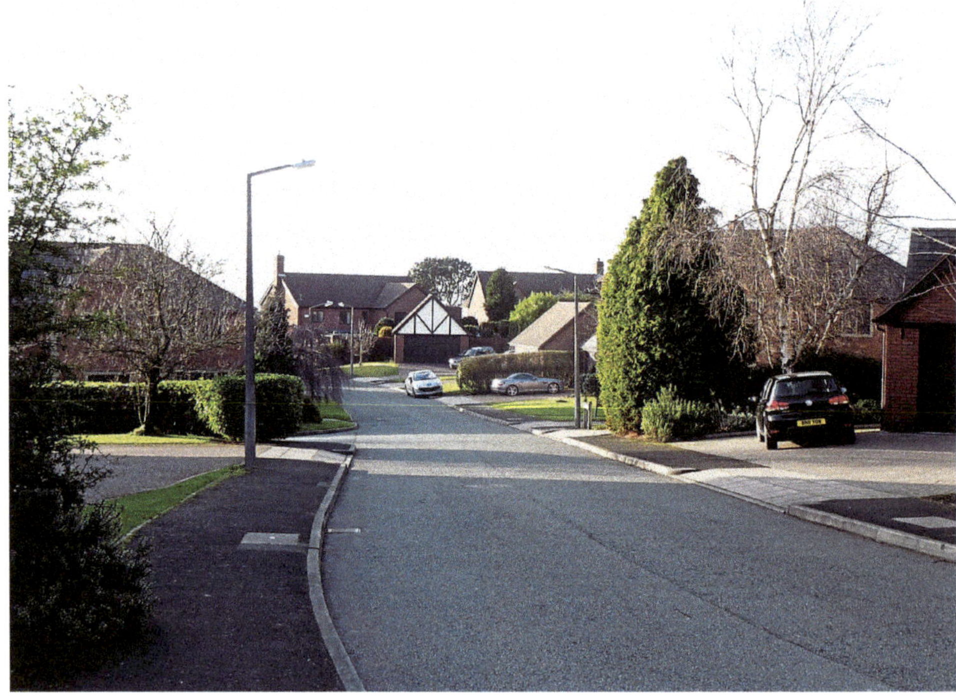

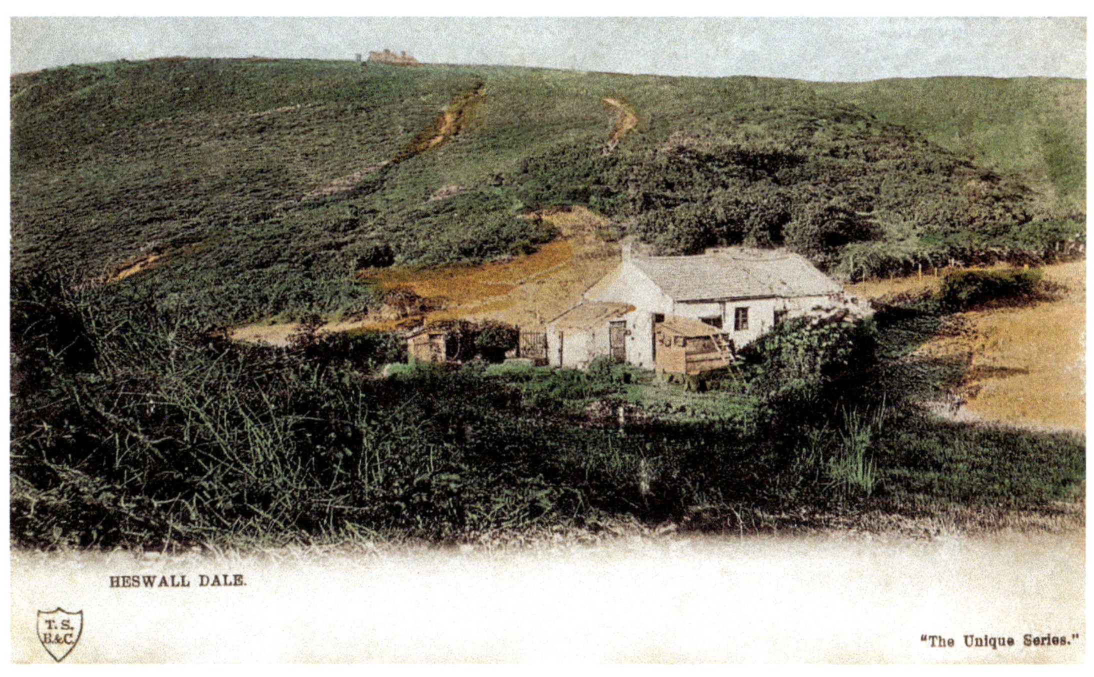

Kemp's Cottage, The Dales

This cottage was situated off Piper's Lane, at the top of Bush Way. It was named after Mr Kemp, a roadman who is reputed to have had thirteen children! The cottage was demolished in the early 1900s and no traces remain. The land has been donated to the public and forms part of the Heswall Dales.

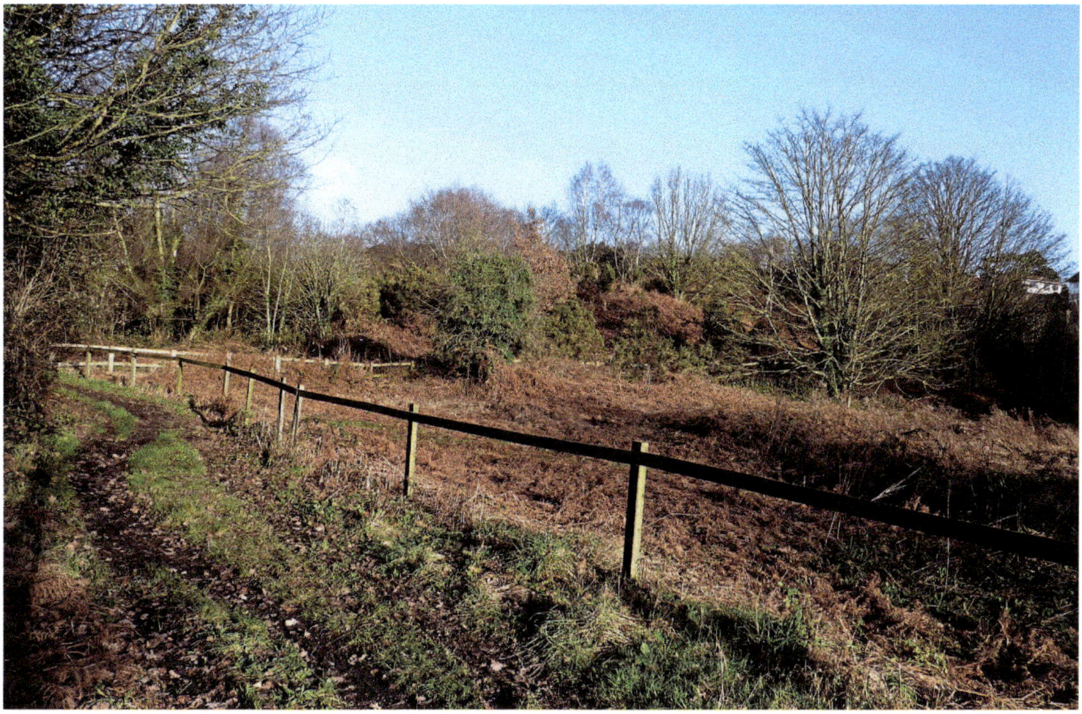

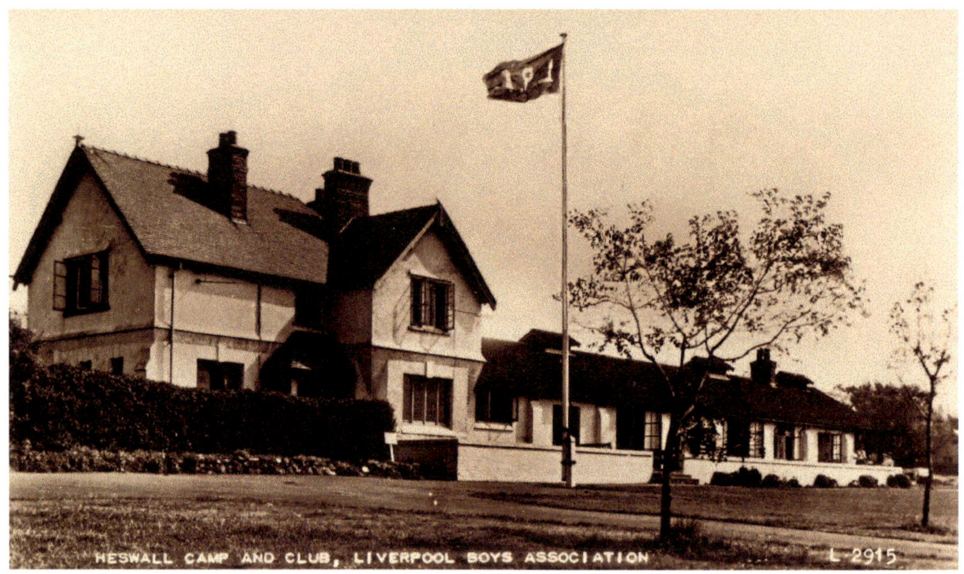

Heswall Boys' Club

In 1904, the Liverpool Juvenile Reformatory Association started to construct an onshore holiday camp on farmland in Broad Lane close to the railway line. It was subsequently sold to the Liverpool Asylum based in Myrtle Street, Liverpool. They sold it in 1936 to the Liverpool Boys' Association for £1,900. More than fifty youth clubs were affiliated to the Liverpool Boys' Association and used the camp's facilities from the 1930s to the 1960s. The camp closed in 1991 due to lack of funding, and for many years the site was derelict. It was not until 2007 that the site was finally redeveloped by Regency Hospitals to provide specialist healthcare.

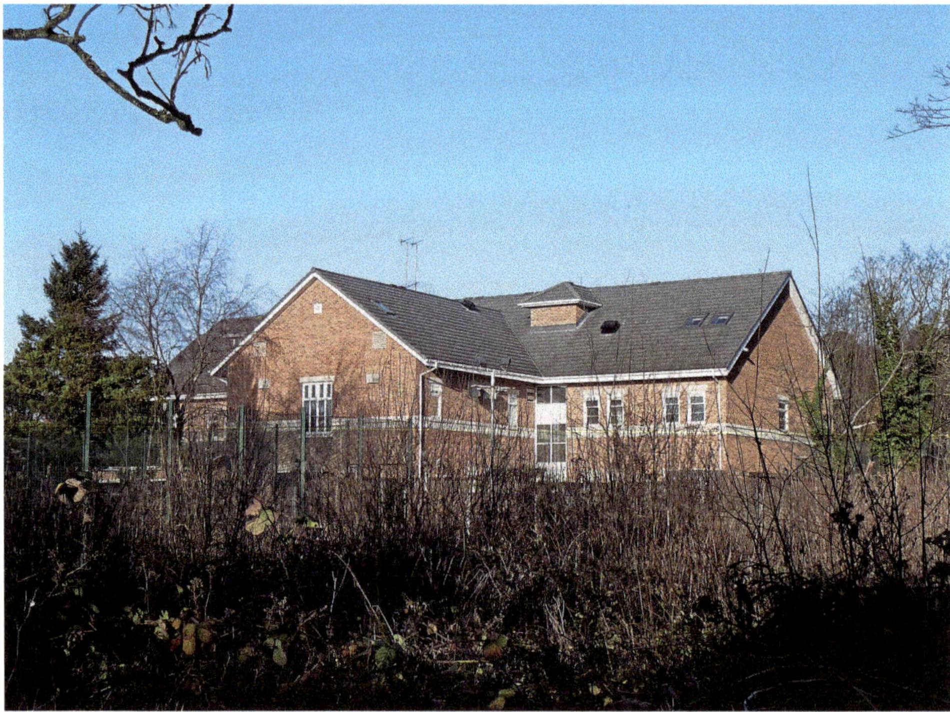

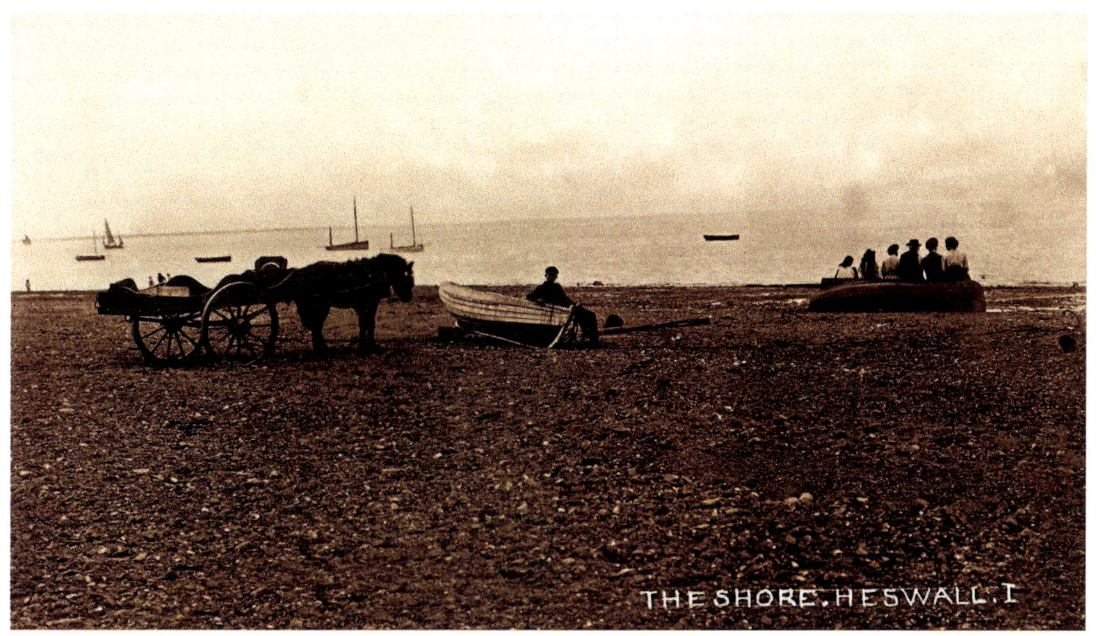

Heswall Shore

Plenty of sand, boats on the river and no spartina grass in sight – this was Heswall shore in the first half of the twentieth century. Fish were caught by the boat owners and sold to the Heswall folk the same day. Mostyn Avenue and Banks Road were home to many of the fishermen and their families.

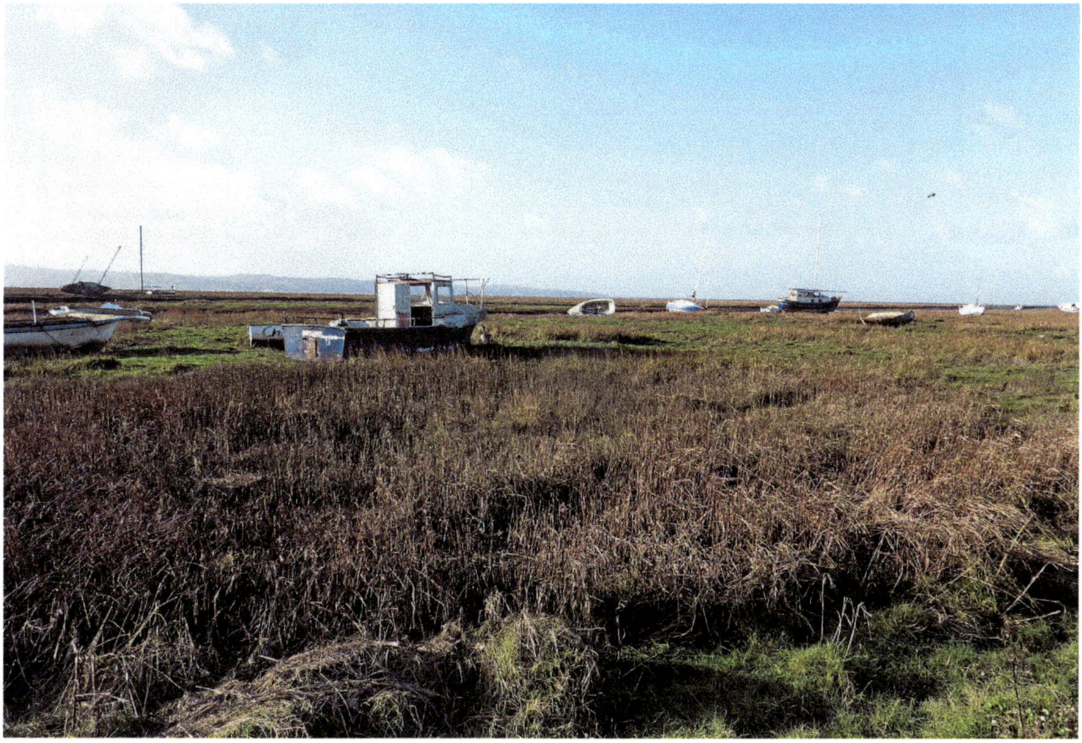

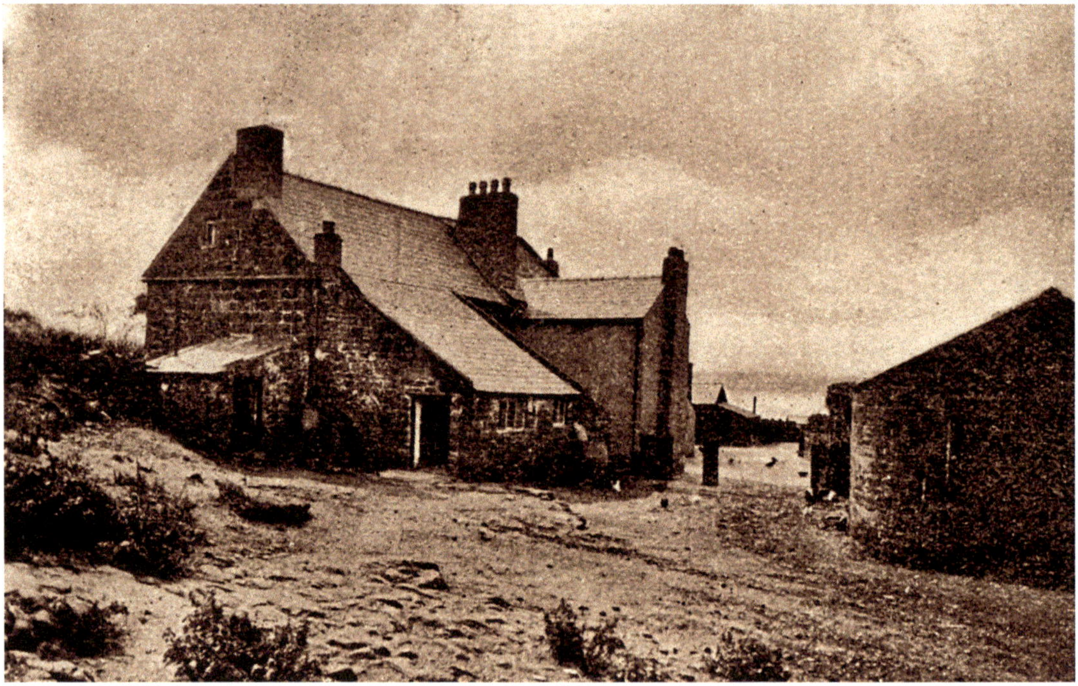

Oldfield Farm

Now divided into several dwellings, this old hall was documented on maps as far back as 1295. Sir Rowland Stanley of Hooton spent the last years of his life here with his third wife and died aged ninety-six in 1614, the oldest knight of the land.

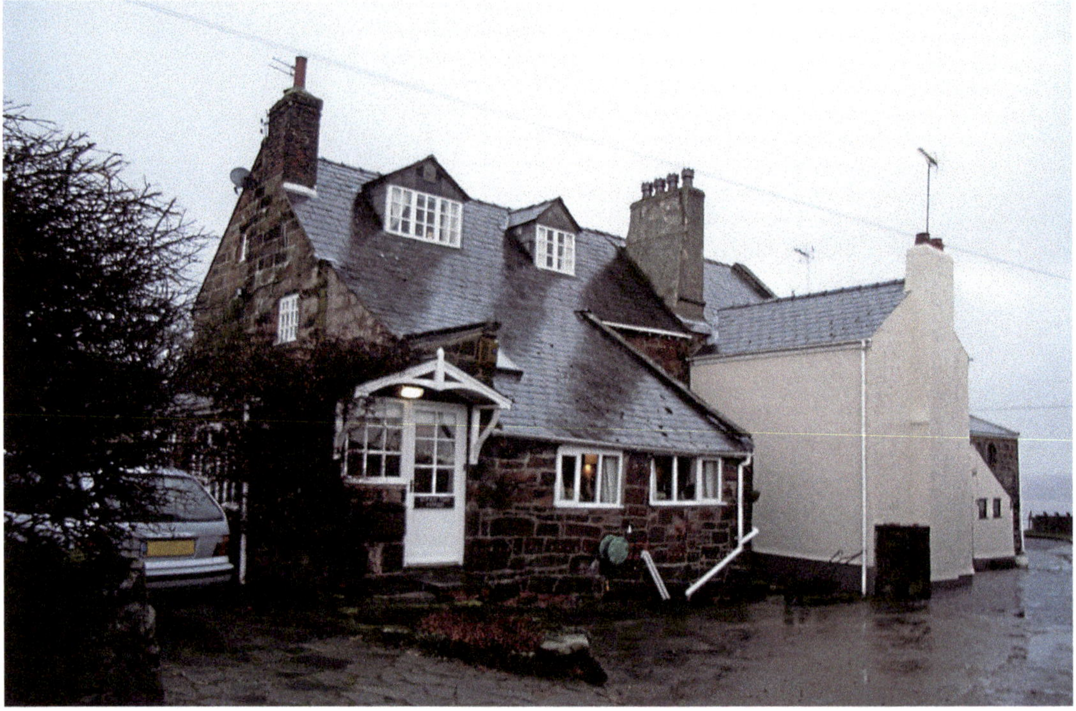

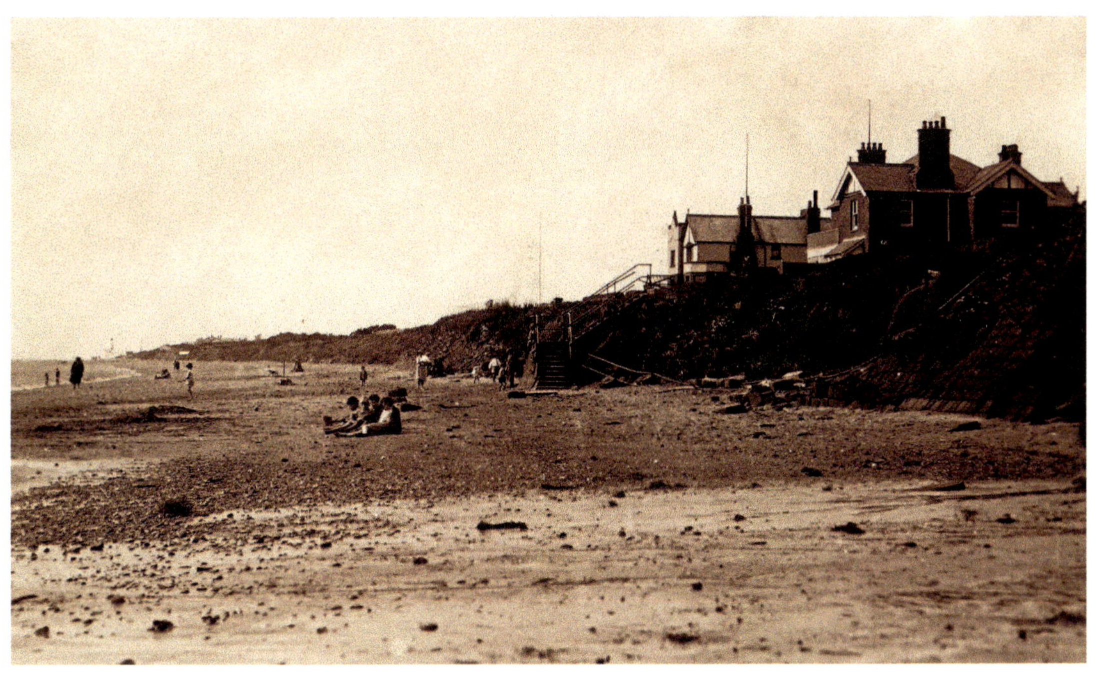

Beach at Marine Drive

The beach below Marine Drive was once a popular bathing beach, with day trippers arriving by train to enjoy the sea and sand. The continuing silting of the Dee Estuary on the Heswall side, and the encroachment of spartina grass, now renders this but a distant memory.

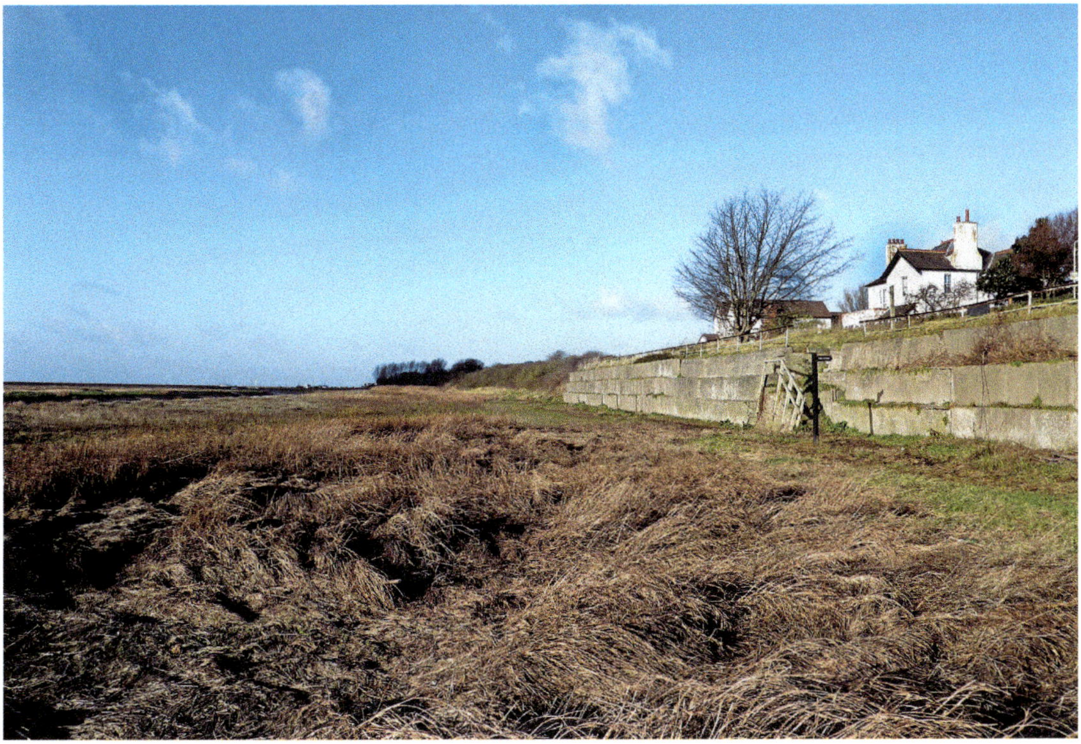

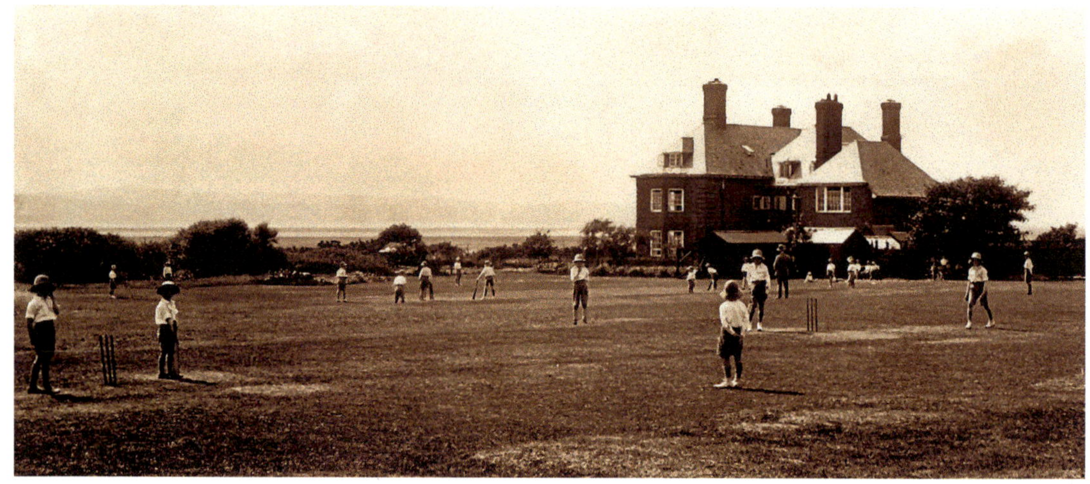

St Fillan's School

This preparatory school was situated at the end of Riverbank Road. Built in the early 1900s, Miss Gore and Miss Whittall were the first principals. Capt. Deedes was later headmaster and the boys who were mostly boarders were prepared for the Royal Navy and public schools. In the 1930s the fees were £30 per term. The building became a rest home from 1945–50, later becoming the Margaret Beavan home for convalescent children. It was also a convent and a health spa before being converted into several residences.

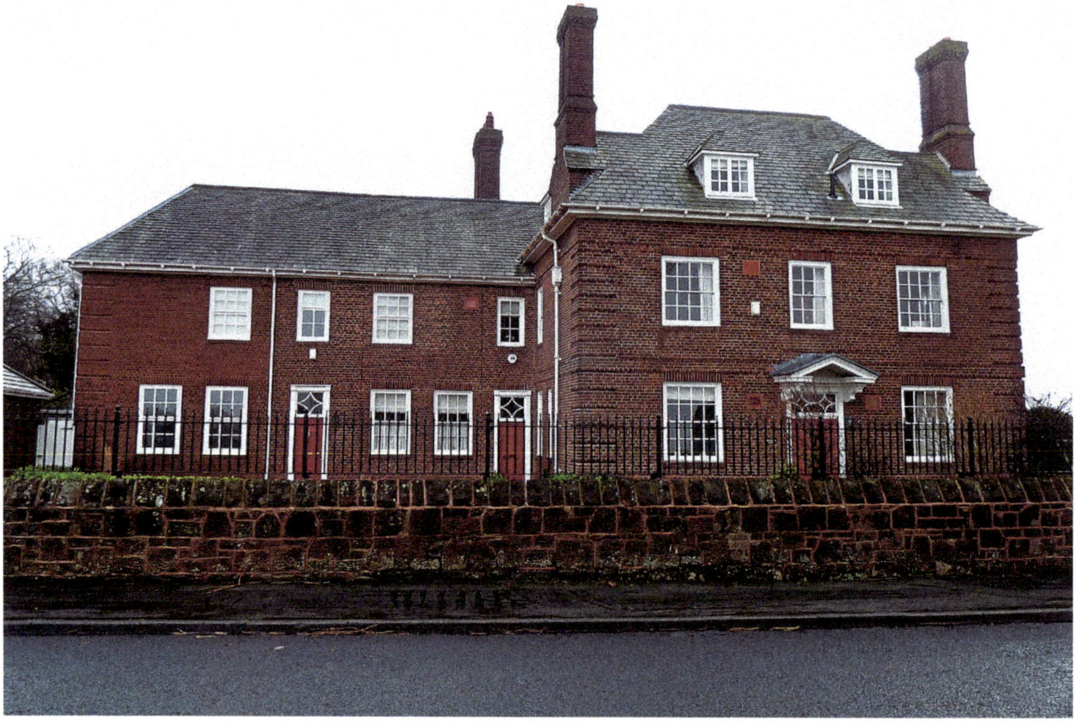

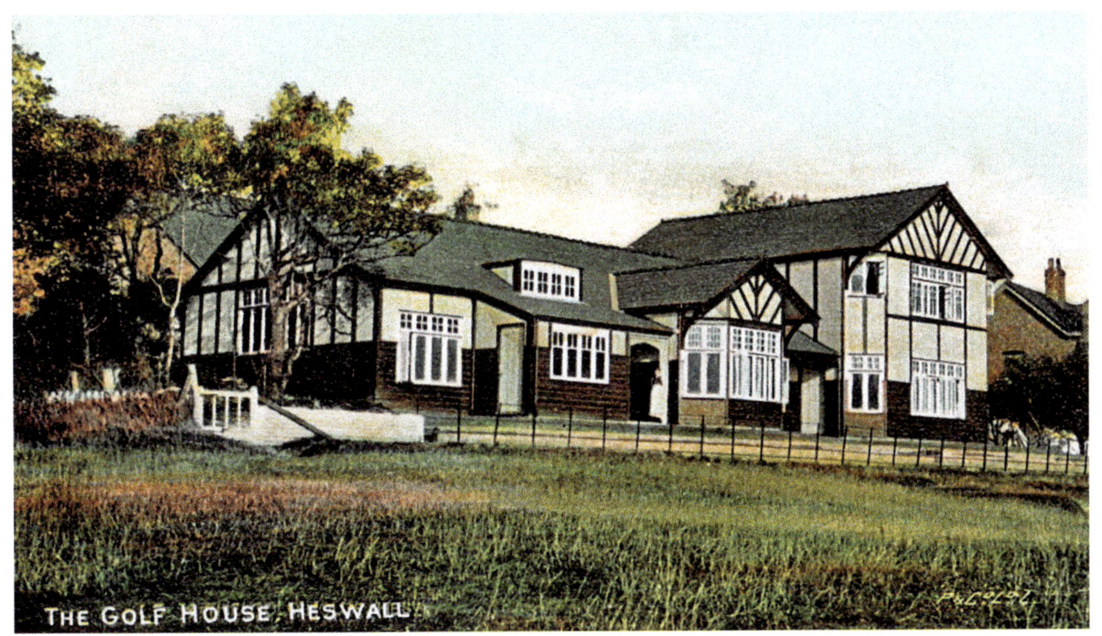

Heswall Golf Club

This was founded on land leased by John Baskervyle Glegg. The original nine-hole course was ready for opening in September 1902. This first wooden clubhouse burnt down in 1924. A new clubhouse was erected in front of the old building and was opened in June 1926 by Herbert Rouse.

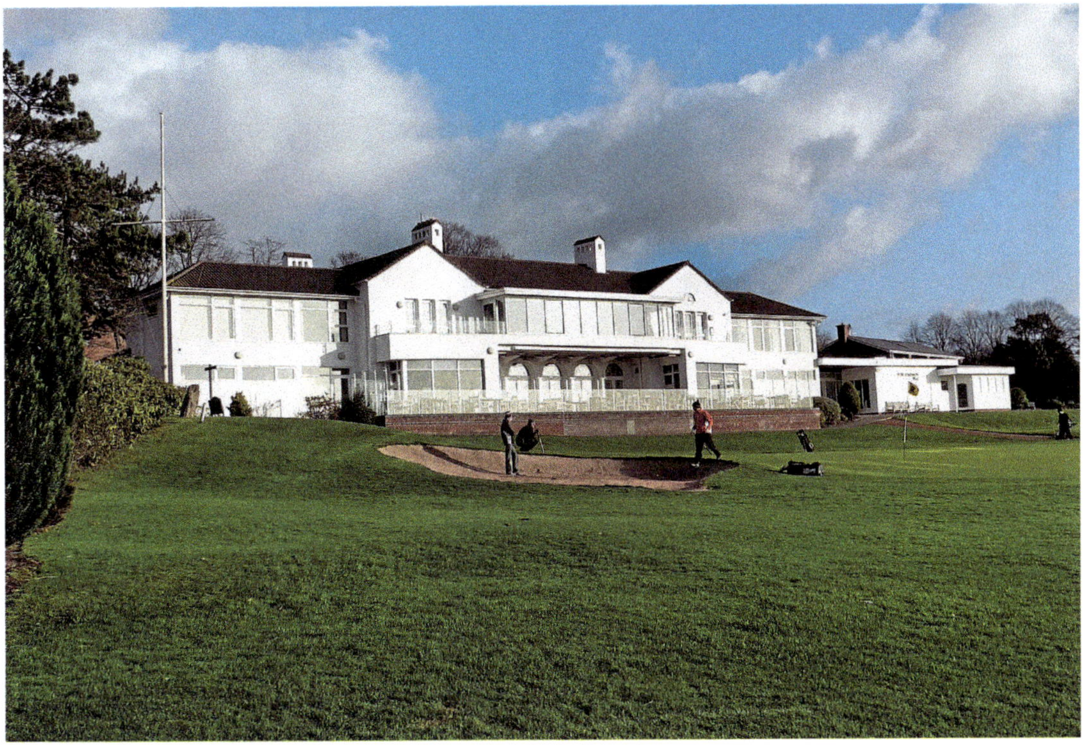

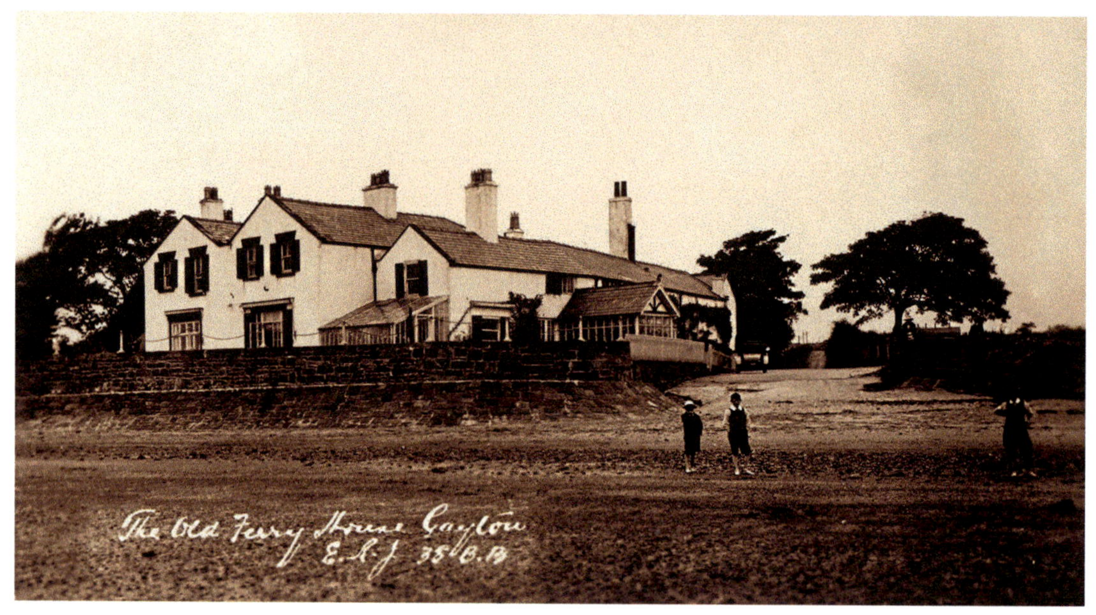

Gayton Cottage

This building situated at the bottom of Cottage Lane serviced the ferry between Heswall and North Wales, which operated until about the 1830s. It is now a private residence.

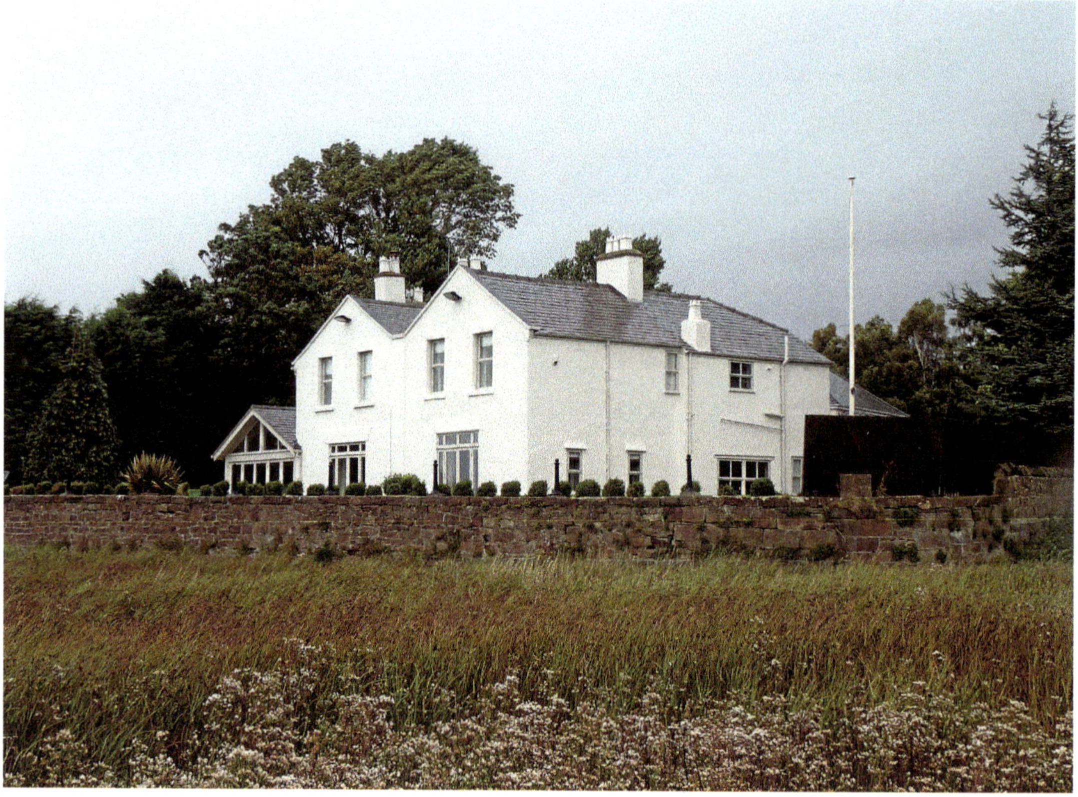